CARTE

DU

RESTAURANT FRANÇAIS

DES

FRÈRES DELMONICO,

CORNER OF

BEAVER, WILLIAM, AND SOUTH WILLIAM STREETS,

NEW YORK.

———————

T. & C. WOOD, STATIONERS, 18 WALL STREET.

1838.

CARTE

DU

RESTURANT FRANÇAIS, DES
Frères DELMONICO,

CORNER OF

Beaver, William and _____ *Streets,*

NEW-YORK.

POTAGES.	s.	d.	SOUPS.
Consommé			Broth
Potage Julienné			Vegetable Soup
" au vermicelli . . .			Vermicelli do
" au macaroni . . .			Macaroni do
" au pain			Bread do
" aux choux . . .			Cabbage do
" au riz : . . .			Rice do
" aux huîtres . . .		2	Oysters do
" à la purée . . .			Purée do
" Conti			Conti do
" de tortue		2	Turtle do
" de santé			Diet do

HORS D'ŒVRES.			SIDE DISHES.
Saucisses			Sausages
" à la Chipolata .			Chipolata sausages
Saucisson de Lyon . .		6	Lyons sausage
Boudin noir			Black Pudding
Thon mariné			Pickled tunny fish
Salade de Laitue . . .			Salad of lettuce
" de chicorée			" of endive

HORS D'ŒVRES.	s.	d.	SIDE DISHES.
Salade de céleri			Celery salad
" d'anchoix		6	Anchovies salad
" d'homard			Lobster salad
Homard au naturel			Boiled lobster
" à la maître d'hotel			Fricasseed lobster
" en mayonnaise			Mayonnaise of lobster
Sardines à l'huile			Sardins with fresh oil
Tête de veau à la vinaigrette			Calf's head with pep. and vin.
Langue de mouton marinée			Lamb's tongue pickled
Rognons à la brochette			Lamb's kidneys broiled
" au vin de Champagne		6	" " Champagne sauce
Jambon de Virginie			Virginia ham boiled
" de Bayonne			Bayonne do do
" de Mayence			Westphalia do do
" frit aux œufs		6	Fried ham and eggs
Choux-croute au petit salé	2		Sour krout with bacon
" " garnie	2		" " with sausages
Artichaux à la poivrade			Artichokes with pep. and vin.
Radis			Radishes
Beurre			Butter
Huitres fraîches	3		Raw Oysters
" frites	3		Fried do
" à la poulette	3		Stewed do
" aux fines herbes	3		Stewed with parsley do
Coquille d'huitres	3		Oysters scolloped in the shell

ENTRÉES DE BŒUF.			BEEF.
Bœuf au naturel			Boiled beef, plain
" aux choux			" " with cabbage
" aux légumes			" " with vegetables
" aux cornichons			" " with pickles
" aux tomates			" " tomata sauce
" aux haricots			" " with beans
" aux épinards			" " with spinage
" à la royale			" " royal fashion
" à la bourgeoise			" " family fashion
" à la sauce piquante			" " with sour sauce
" à l'oseille			" " with sorrel
" à l'Italienne			" " Italian fashion
" à la mode			Beef a-la-mode
Beef-steak au naturel			Beef steak
" aux pommes de terre			" with potatoes

	s.	d.	
ENTRÉES DE BŒUF.			**BEEF.**
Beef-steak aux cornichons			Beef-steak with pickles
" au beurre d'anchoix			" with anchovy sauce
" à la sauce tomate			" with tomata sauce
" à la Montigny			" Montigny fashion
" aux légumes			" with vegetables
Beef-steak Américain	1	6	American beef-steak
Filet de bœuf, sauté	1	6	Tender-loin with sauce
" " aux olives	1	6	" with olives
" " aux tomates	1	6	" with tomata sauce
" " aux champignons	2	0	" with mushrooms
" " au vin de Madère	1	6	" with Madeira sauce
Entre côte de bœuf à la sauce	1	6	
Langue de bœuf à la sauce			Beef's tongue with sauce
ENTRÉES DE VEAU.			**VEAL.**
Filet de veau	1		Fillet of veal
Poitrine de veau à la sauce			Breast of veal with sauce
" " farcie			" " stuffed
Tendon de veau aux légumes			Tendon of veal with vegetables
Veau à l'Impériale	1	6	Veal dressed Imperial fashion
" à l'Impératrice	1	6	" " Empress fashion
" à la bourgeoise	1	6	" " family fashion
Cotelette de veau panée	1		Veal cutlet, breaded
" " aux truffes	1	9	" " with truffles
" " aux champignons	1	9	" " with mushrooms
" " en papillote	1	6	" " in paper
" " à la sauce Robert	1	6	" " with Robert sauce
" " sautée dans sa glace	1	6	" " with gravy
Blanquette de veau	1	6	Veal with white sauce
" " à la Perigueux			" Perigueux fashion
Escalope de veau	1		Veal scolloped
Fricandeau au jus	1		Fricando of veal with gravy
" aux épinards	1	6	" " with spinage
" à l'oseille	1	6	" " with sorrel
Carbonade de veau	1		Carbonade of veal
" aux petits pois	1	6	" with green peas
" aux fines herbes	1	6	" with herbs
Ris de veau piqués	1	6	Veal sweetbread, larded
" " à l'oseille	1	6	" " with sorrel
" " à la financière	2	0	" " financier fashion
" " aux champagnons	2	0	" " with mushrooms
" " aux truffes	2		" " with truffles

ENTRÉES DE VEAU.	s.	d.	VEAL.
Ris de veau à la sauce tomate		6	Veal sweetbread, with tomata sauce
" " à la St. Cloud			" " St. Cloud fashion
Coquille de ris de veau	2		" " scolloped in the shell
Foie de veau sauté à l'Italienne			Calf's liver with Italian sauce
" " à la Provençale			" " with Provinçale do
" " à la bourgeoise			" " family fashion
Hatelet de foie de veau		6	Hatelet of liver
Tête de veau à la poulette		6	Calf's head fricasseed
" " aux champignons	2		" " with mushrooms
" " en tortue	2		Mock turtle
Oreille de veau frite			Calf's ear, fried
" " farcie			" stuffed
Cervelles de veau frites			Calf's brains, fried
" " en marinade			" pickled
" " à la maitre d'hôtel			" fricasseed
" " au beurre noir			" with black sauce
Vol au vent garnie			Veal pie
" " de cervelle à l'Allemande			Brain patty, German fashion
Pâté de quenelle chaud			Hot grenelle pie

ENTRÉES DE MOUTON. MUTTON AND LAMB.

	s.	d.	
Poitrine de mouton au naturel			Breast of mutton plain
" " à la St. Menéhould			" " St. Menehould fashion
" " aux légumes			" " with vegetables
Filet de mouton mariné			Tenderloin of mutton pickled
Pieds de mouton farcis			Feet of mutton, stuffed
Mouton braisé			Mutton braisé
Cotelette de mouton, nature			Mutton chops, plain
" " à la sauce		6	" " with sauce
" " sautée aux truffes			" " with truffle sauce
" " à la minute			" " broiled
" " à la Jardinière		6	" " Jardineer fashion
" " en papillotte		6	" " in paper
" " à l'Imperatrice	8		" " empress fashion
Cotelette d'agneau			Lamb chop
Poitrine d'agneau			Breast of Lamb
Escalope d'agneau	2	6	Lamb scolloped
Balotines d'agneau			Lambs meat balls, with gravy
Ris d'agneau glacé		6	Lamb sweetbread with jelly
" " aux truffes			" " with truffles
" " à la financière	2	6	" " financier fashion

ENTRÉES DE VOLAILLE.	s.	d.	POULTRY.
Poulet sauté . . .			Chicken with sauce
" sauté à la Marengo .			" with Marengo sauce
" aux truffes . .			" wite truffles
" au riz . . .			" with rice
" à la financière . .			" financier
" à la Lyonnaise . .			" Lyons fashion
" à la Tartare . .			" Tartar do
" à l'Italienne . .			" Italian do
" à la Provençale . .			" Provençal do
" à la reine au blanc .			Breast of chicken, Queen's sauce
Escalope de filet de volaille .			Fillet of chicken, scolloped
Cuisse de poulet en papillotte .			Leg of chicken in paper
Galantine de volaille .			Galantine, or boned chicken, cold
" " aux truffes			" with truffles
Suprême de volaille . .			Supreme of chicken
" " aux truffes .			" with truffles
Capilotade de volaille . .			Capilotade
Pâté de volaille . . .			Chicken pie
" " aux truffes .			" with truffles
Coquille de filet de volaille .			Fowl scolloped
" " aux truffes .			" " with truffles
" " aux champignons			" " with mushrooms
Fricassée de poulet garnie .			Fricasseed chicken
Filet de poulet à la bigarrure .			Fillet of fowl with mixed sauce
Fritot de poulet . .			Fried chicken
Croquette de poulet .			Chicken forced-meat balls
Balotines de volaille .			Chicken balls
Mayonnaise de volaille . .			Chicken moyonnaise
Salade de volaille . .			Chicken salad
Marinade de volaille . .			Pickled chicken
Vol au vent à la financière .			Chicken pie financier
" " de filet de volaille .			Pie of chicken fillet
" " de volaille aux truffes			Chicken pie with truffles
" " aux champignons .			" " with mushrooms
Petits Patés salpiquants . .			Little pies, seasoned
" " à la Bechamelle aux truffs			" " with truffles
Chapon au gros sel . .			Boiled capon
" au riz glacé . .			" " with jelly and rice
Cuisse de dindon grillée .			Leg of turkey, devilled
Canard aux olives . .			Duck with olives
" aux navets . .			" " with turnips
Petits asqics à la moderne .			Small aspicks modern fashion

2

ENTRÉES DE VOLAILLE.	s.	d.	POULTRY.

ENTRÉES DE VOLAILLE.

Pigeon aux petits pois - · · 2 6 — Pigeon with green peas

" en Macédoine · · 2 6 — " Macedonia or jumble

Compote de pigeon · · 2 6 — Stewed pigeon

Pigeon en crapaudine · · 2 6 — Crapodeen pigeon

Paté de foie gras de Strasbourg · 1 6 — Goose liver pie of Strasburg

ENTRÉES DE GIBIER.

GAME.

Faisan aux choux · · · 6 — Partridge with cabbage

" à la gelée · · 6 3 — " with jelly

" sauté · · · 3 — " with sauce

Filet de faisan sauté · · 3 — " fillet with sauce

Coquille de faisan · · 3 — " scolloped

Salmi de faisan · · · 3 — " in salmee

Croquette de faisan · · 3 — Forced-meat balls of pheasant

Faisan en crapaudine · · 3 — Crapodeen partridge

Suprême de faisan · · 3 9 — Supreme of partridge

Caille aux laitues · · · 2 6 — Quail with lettuce

" à la purée · · 2 6 — " with purée

" en crapaudine · · 2 6 — Crapodeen quail

Pâté de gibier aux truffes · 3 9 — Game pie with truffles

Salmi de becasse · · · 3 — Woodcock salmee

Canard sauvage en salmi · · — Wild duck salmee

Fromage de gibier · · · — Welsh rabbit

Cotelette de chevreuil · · — Venison chop

Filet de chevreuil · · · 1 6 — " tenderloin

Beefsteak de chevreuil · · 1 6 — " steak

Coquille de chevreuil · · 1 6 — " scolloped

Civet de lièvre · · · 1 6 — Hare stewed

Lapreau sauté · · · 1 6 — Young Rabbit with sauce

RÔTS.

ROASTS.

Rosbif · · · · · — Roast beef

Filet de bœuf piqué · rôti 1 6 — Tenderloin of beef roasted

Aloyau de bœuf · · " — Short rib of beef roasted

Veau · · · · " — Roast veal

Poitrine de veau : · " — Breast of veal roasted

Gigot de mouton , · " — Roast leg of mutton

Agneau · · · " — " lamb

Chevreuil · · · " — " venison

Poulet · · · " · 2 6 — " chicken

Dindon · · · " · 2 6 — Roast turkey

RÔTS.	s.	d.	ROASTS.
Canard . . . . . rôti .			Roast duck
Canard au dos de canevas " .	1	3	" canvass-back duck
Pigeon de volière . " .			" pigeon
" sauvage . " .	2		" wild pigeon
Caille . . . " .	2	6	" quail
Faisan . . . " .			" pheasant or partridge
Pintarde . . . " .			" Guinea fowl
Becasse : . . " .	3		" woodcock
Becassine . . " .			" snipe
Pluvier doré . . " .			" plover

ENTRÉES DE POISSON.   FISH.

	s.	d.	
Sheepshead à la sauce . . .			Sheepshead boiled, with sauce
Poisson noir à la sauce . . .			Blackfish boiled with sauce
" " en matelotte . .	1	6	" stewed
Turbot à la sauce			Turbot with sauce
Vol au vent de turbot . . .		6	" pie
Rissole			Rissole
Saumon au bleu à l'huile . .			Salmon boiled, with oil
" sauce aux câpres . .			" with caper sauce
" à la Genoise . .			" Genoese fashion
" en marinade . . .			" pickled
Vol au vent de saumon . . .			Salmon pie
Raye à la sauce			Ray with sauce
" au beurre noir . . .	1		" with black sauce
Basse rayée à la sauce . . .			Streaked bass with sauce
Morue à la Provençale . . .	1	6	Codfish, Provençal fashion
" à la Flamande . .		6	" Flemish fashion
" au beurre noir . . .			" with black sauce
" sauce aux câpres . .			" with caper sauce
Alôse à l'oseille			Shad, with sorrel
" frite			Fried shad
" au gratin			Toasted shad
" sauce au beurre . .			Shad with butter sauce
Maquereau à la maître d'hôtel .			Mackerel fricasseed
" au beurre noir . .			" with black sauce
Merlan frit			Fried whiting
" au gratin . . .			Toasted whiting
Sole frite . . . :			Fried sole
" sauce aux câpres . :			Sole with caper sauce
" sur le plat aux fines herbes .		6	" with parsley sauce

ENTRÉES DE POISSON.	s.	d.	FISH.
Filet de sole sauté		6	Filet of sole, with sauce
" " en mayonnaise			" " mayonnaise
" " à la maître d'hôtel			" " fricasseed
" " en marinade			" " pickled
" " à la harly			" " harly fashion
" " en turban			" " in mould
Brochet au beurre		6	Pike, with butter sauce
" à la Genoise		6	" Genoese fashion
Truite au bleu	2		Boiled trout
" à la Genoise	2		Trout, Genoese fashion
" frite	2		Fried trout
Anguille à la Tartare		6	Eels, Tartar fashion
" à la poulette		6	" stewed
" en matelotte		6	" black stewed
Moules à la poulette			Muscles stewed
" aux fines herbes			" fricasseed
Eperlan frit			Fried smelt
Beefsteak de tortue			Turtle steak
Filet de tortue mignon piqué			" filet, larded

ENTREMETS.			VEGETABLES, EGGS, &c.
Pommes de terre au naturel		6	Boiled potatoes
" " frites			Fried do
Pommes de terre à la maître d'hôtel			Fricasseed potatoes
" " à la Lyonnaise			Potatoes, Lyons fashion
" " à la Provençale			" Provençal fashion
Epinards au jus			Spinage with gravy
" à la crème			" with cream
Chicorée au jus			Endive with sauce
" à la crème			" with cream
Macédoine de légumes			Jumble of vegetables
Petits pois au naturel	2		Green peas, boiled
" " au lard	2		" " with bacon
" " au sauce	2		" " with sugar
Haricots nouveaux à la maître d'hôtel			Fresh beans with butter sauce
" blancs à la maître d'hôtel			White beans, fricasseed
" " à la Bretonne			" " Breton fashion
" " à l'Espagnole			" " Spanish do
" " à l'Italienne			" " Italian do
" " à l'Anglaise			" " English do

ENTREMETS.

	s.	d.	VEGETABLES, EGGS, &c.
Choux-fleurs à la sauce blanche			Cauliflowers with white sauce
" " à l'huile			" with oil
" " au jus			" with gravy
Salsifis frits			Fried salsifi
" à la sauce			Salsifi with sauce
" au jus			" with gravy
Artichaux à la sauce			Artichokes with sauce
" à la Barigoule			" Barigoule fashion
Champignons à la Provençale	3		Mushrooms, Provençal do
Croute au champignons	3		Crusts of mushrooms
Aubergine à la sauce			Egg-plant with sauce
" farcie			" stuffed and baked
Asperges à la sauce	2		Asparagus with sauce
" à l'huile	2		" with oil
" au jus	2		" with gravy
Truffes sautées au Champagne			Truffles with Champaign sauce
Croute aux truffes			Crusts of truffles
Fromage au gratin			Welch rabbit
Macaroni à l'Italienne			Macaroni with gravy
" au gratin			" browned
Œuf à la coque		6	Eggs, boiled in the shell
" frits au jambon		6	" fried with ham
" pochés au jus			" poached
" brouillés au jus			" scrambled
" " aux truffes			" " with truffles
" " aux champignons			" " with mushrooms
Omelette aux fines herbes		6	Omelet with parsley
" au lard			" with bacon
" à la Célestine	2		" Celestine fashion
" aux rognons	2		" with kidneys
" au fromage		6	" with cheese
" aux truffes			" with truffles

ENTREMETS SUCRÉS.

	s.	d.	PASTRY, CAKES.
Beignets de pomme			Apple fritters
" à la reine			Queens do
Tourte de pommes		6	Apple tart
" aux confitures		6	Tart with preserves
Charlotte de pommes		3	Apple charlotte
" Russe			Russian do
Petit pôt de crème		6	Custards

3

ENTREMETS SUCRÉS.	s.	d.	PASTRY, CAKES.
Crême au bain marie			
" frite			Fried cream
Gelée de groseilles		6	Currant jelly
" au rhum			Rum do
Soufflé au riz			Rice soufflay
Omelette soufflée			Omelet do
" aux confitures			" with preserves
" au sucre		6	" with sugar
Puddin au riz			Rice pudding
Croquette de riz			Rice Balls
" de pommes			Potato do
Gateau au riz			Rice Cake

DESSERT.   DESSERT.

Orange et sucre			Orange and sugar
Salade d'oranges			" salad
Fraises et sucre			Strawberries and sugar
Framboises et sucre			Raspberries and sugar
Gâteau de pommes			Apple cake
" à la crème			Cream cake
Compote de pommes		6	Stewed apples
" à la Polonnaise			" " Polish fashion
" de poires			" pears
" de pruneaux			" prunes
" de pêches			" peaches
Pêche			Peach
" à l'eau de vie			Brandy peach
Meringues à la crème			French kisses
" aux confitures			" " with preserves
Macarons		6	Macaroons
Biscuits au moule			Sponge Cakes
Fromage de Chester			Chester cheese
" Parmésan			Parmesan do
" de Gruyère		6	Gruyere do
tête de mort		6	Dutch do
La demi-tasse de café			Cup of coffee
Punch au rhum			Rum punch
" à l'eau de vie			Brandy do
" au whiskey			Whiskey do
" à la Romaine		6	Roman do

LIQUEURS.

Extrait d'absinthe	0 6	Crème de chocolat	0 6
Eau de vie de Cognac	0 6	Vanille	0 6
" " d'Andaye	1 0	Huile de rose	0 6
" " de Dantzig	1 0	" de Vénus	0 6
Kirschenwasser	0 6	Crème de Moka	0 6
		Parfait amour	0 6
Rhum vieux	0 6		
Anisette de Bordeaux	0 6	Anisao de Majorca	0 6
Noyeau	0 6	Angelique	
Canelle	0 6	Al kermes	1 0
Crême de menthe	0 6	Elixir	1 0
" d'absinthe	0 6	Ratafia de Grenoble	0 6
Cuiraçao de Hollande	0 6	Scubac	1 0

VINS—WINES

Red Bordeaux—Bordeaux Rouge.

Lafitte,	1825	20
Chateau Margaux,	1825	20
Latour,	1825	20
Haut Brion,	1825	16
Léoville,	1825	12 & 16
Larose,	1825	16
Mouton,	1825	16
Rawzan,	1825	16
Chateau Langoa,	1825	12
Pichon,	1825	12
Ducru, 1825		12
Callon, 1825		12
Chateau Beycheville		12
Batailley		12
St. Pierre		12
D'Aux		12
St. Julien		4 & 8
St. Estephe		8
Vieu Claret		8
Ordinair		

Bordeaux Blanc—White Bordeaux.

Barsac	16
Sauterne	4 12 & 16
Grave	8
Blanc ordinair	3

Rhône Rouge—Red Rhone.

Hermitage	12
Côtes roties	12
St. Joseph	8
Roussillon	8
La Nerthe	4
St. George	8

Rhône Blanc—White Rhone.

Hermitage	12
Cotillon	8
Condrieux	8
St. Peray	8

Bourgogne—Burgundy.

Clos Vougeot	20 & 24
Chambertin	16
Nuit-Richebourg	16
Beaune 1ere.	16
Volney	16
Chabli	8

Blanc du Rhin—White Rhine.

Laubensheimer	~~16~~ 12
Rudesheimer	~~16~~ 12
Hochheimer	~~16~~ 12
Stein-wein	~~48~~ 12
Johannisberger, 1822	~~24~~ 16

Champagne.

Delmonico Brand	~~16~~ 12
Sillery	~~16~~ 12
Anchor	~~16~~ 12
Montebello	~~16~~ 12
Key brand	~~16~~ 12
Oeil de perdrix *Heichick*	~~16~~ 12

Madère.

Faquàrt	48
Old Reserve, 1822	40
Old Madeira	12 & ~~20~~ 16
Romanée—Sherry	32
Sherry	12 & ~~20~~ 16
Porto	12 & ~~20~~ 16

Brown Stout - - - 4

Sherry   Sherry

Pale Pesmaster 48   Amontillado 40
... Gordon 40   Malmsey 40
Gold ... 40   Bread ... 40

And now, GRANDCHILDREN,
Be good,
    Be better,
        Be best,
And never neglect your stomachs

DELMONICO'S

A Century of Splendor

"For my part, I mind my belly very studiously and very carefully, for I look upon it, that he who does not mind his belly, will hardly mind anything else."

—*Samuel Johnson*

DELMONICO'S

A Century of Splendor

BY

LATELY THOMAS

Illustrated with Photographs

HOUGHTON MIFFLIN COMPANY BOSTON
1967

FIRST PRINTING W

CONTENTS

PART I

Water and Wine, and Wine and Water

PART II

Lorenzo the Great

Contents

PART III

Changes and Portents of Change

PART IV

"Del's" in the Nineties

PART V

"Sunset and Evening Star"

ILLUSTRATIONS

WATER AND WINE,
AND WINE AND WATER

CHAPTER I

A LITTLE SPLASH
IN A SMALL POND

ACCORDING to New York's preeminent historian, Mrs. Martha J. Lamb, the modern city may be dated from a ceremony that took place on November 4, 1825. On that day, a festooned, garlanded barge, the *Seneca Chief*, nosed into lower New York Bay, towed by the churning paddlewheels of a Hudson River steamboat. On board the barge, in view of thousands of spectators on a fleet of escorting craft (the parasols of the ladies giving a flowery aspect to the aquatic scene), Governor DeWitt Clinton held high a keg painted green with gilded hoops, and ceremoniously poured its contents into the bay. The keg contained Lake Erie water, brought there on the *Seneca Chief* to signalize the inauguration of the Erie Canal. At this symbolic consummation of the marriage of America's inland seas with the oceans of the world, cannon boomed and the throngs cheered. They had good reason to rejoice, for that final ritual started New York City upon a century of expansion in population and wealth that has no counterpart. It was the Erie Canal that converted a straggling overgrown town into a vast metropolis.

Water had played a dominant role in the city's affairs from its beginning. Situated at the confluence of many streams, upon a harbor connecting it with the remotest ports, New York had always been a trading center. The first Dutch had settled at the tip of Manhattan Island because it was convenient for carrying on the business of barter — beads for beaver pelts brought down the Hudson by Indians. As commerce grew, the town grew with it.

The "better class" of Manhattan had always been its wealthy merchants, who as they attained to riches did not disdain luxury, and whose toleration was remarkable in an age of bigotry. The Hudson River and its tributaries were highways that led into the interior, over which the goods of Europe were freighted to dwellers inland, and the back country's produce was borne down to the city for transshipment overseas. These waterways had enabled New York to forge ahead of its rival ports, Philadelphia and Boston; and with the opening of the Erie Canal in 1825 a thousand miles were added to New York's trade routes, linking the city with the heart of the continent. Already immigrants were swarming into the territories west of the mountains, and the wealth they produced would soon be channeled into New York Harbor. No wonder forward-looking New Yorkers were dazzled by so rich a prospect; no wonder they would celebrate the union of the fresh and the salt, the marriage of the seas.

2.

Among the crowds that viewed the Erie Canal pageant from lower Manhattan might have been descried a man below average height, of swarthy complexion, remarkable for little except his air of competence and his quiet reserve. His face was roughened by exposure to weather; his age might be somewhere in the late thirties; and had he been asked, he would have given his name as Giovanni, or Jean, or John Del-Monico, depending upon the language in which he was addressed. Interchangeability of language was his birthright, for he hailed from that land of many tongues, Switzerland.

After watching the procession of harbor craft enter the Narrows and disappear in the lower bay, this onlooker probably walked to a shop not far off, above whose door hung the sign, "Wine Merchant." Like other shops in the neighborhood, this store would have been closed during the passage of the harbor parade; but it is likely that Giovanni Del-Monico, after taking in the spectacle, took down the shutters of his shop and made his wares available to customers, of whom, on that day of rejoicing, he probably had many, for the celebrating lasted well into the night.

The location of this wine shop is not known, except that it stood near the Battery; but in those days practically all New York lay within a mile of the Battery. How this Swiss had come to be the proprietor of such a shop, at such a time, and in that place, is a curious story.

Giovanni Del-Monico (as the family name was then spelled) was the youngest of three sons of a farmer living at the eastern foot of Mount St. Gotthard, in the village of Mairengo and canton of Ticino, or Tessein. Ticino is Switzerland's most southerly canton, on the border of Italy, and its people are Italianate in speech and character, and Catholic in religion.

Giovanni's father, Siro Del-Monico, had been born in 1742; he married a woman named Giuseppa Beltrami, farmed in a small way, and reared a family in Mairengo. That is about all that is known about him. A tradition preserved in the family might indicate that Siro had come from Monaco, and was related in some way to the Grimaldi family ruling that principality; because of the disturbances created by the French Revolution, or as the result of a family quarrel, the tradition said, he had been forced to flee to Switzerland. This tradition may or may not find support in the family name, Del-Monico, or in the singularity that although Italian is the language of Ticino, the Delmonico family, in America at least, continued to speak French among themselves as late as 1900; and legal papers executed by members of the family in the United States uniformly listed their Christian names in the French manner, although in the cantonal archives they appear in Italian, the official language.

Siro Del-Monico's three sons were born in Mairengo and were reared there. Francesco, the eldest, was born in 1777, Pietro Antonio in 1783, and Giovanni in 1788. Upon Francesco devolved the family farm. Pietro was apprenticed to a pastry cook in Berne. Giovanni went to sea. Why, is a mystery. Perhaps some youthful adventure on Ticino's Lakes Maggiore and Lugano, that jut into Italy, gave him a hankering after boats, or perhaps it was an urge to see the world. More likely it was the hope of commercial gain that led this son of the Alps to become a sailor. In any event, by the time he was thirty, in 1818, Giovanni Del-Monico commanded a three-masted schooner named *Fidelity*, and was engaged in a triangular trade among Cuba, Spain, and the United States. A steady routine was followed: tobacco was shipped at Havana for Cadiz; there wines were picked up for New York, where lumber and other Yankee products were taken aboard to exchange for tobacco in Cuba. Occasionally the *Fidelity* poked its bowsprit into other Caribbean ports; Captain Del-Monico had been encountered by Yankee skippers and traders at Chagres and elsewhere.

By his energy, industry, and frugality, Giovanni accumulated some capital. Tiring of the sea, he looked about for a profitable occupation on land, and chose New York City, with which he was familiar, as a suitable location. Disposing of the *Fidelity*, he set up shop near the Battery as an importer of French and Spanish wines, which he bought cheaply in bulk, and bottled himself. This was about 1824. Adaptability is a heritage of the Swiss, and conforming to the prevalent language, Giovanni made himself John. So he would be styled for the rest of his days, although in legal documents he would use the form Jean.

The significance of the Erie Canal for New York's future was clear to this thrifty wine merchant. In many ways the city was little better than primitive, and it was almost totally deficient in amenities which were commonplace in Europe. As the town acquired wealth, there would be an increasing demand for the luxuries that wealth can provide, and John Del-Monico surmised that by supplying some of the things lacking in the city he might be more profitably engaged than in selling wines at retail. But prudently he decided to seek family counsel and perhaps family assistance. With this in mind, in 1826 he closed his modest shop and sailed for home.

3.

John found his brother Pietro Antonio established as a confectioner in Berne. Pietro, older than John, was of a different temperament, more phlegmatic and slow-moving, but sound in judgment and not averse to making money. He listened, sympathetically, but with an impartial mind, to his brother's account of the wonderful opportunities awaiting enterprising men in New York. Pietro was prospering where he was. He had a family, having married a Mairengo girl named Catherine Giannini, a year younger than himself. Daughters and a son had been born to them in Berne. The first child, a girl, was named Anna Maria Catherine, and the son, born in 1824 just about the time his uncle John was quitting the sea, was named Honoré.

Neither John nor Pietro Del-Monico was handicapped by the impetuosity of youth; both had succeeded in trade, both had been tempered by experience. Pietro was forty-three and John thirty-eight. John, who had traveled and seen many cities, was a sound judge of towns and men. His imagination was vigorous along practical lines, and he was endowed with foresight — a trait which the family would display consistently for years to come. Pietro was cautious but not afraid to risk capital in a sound venture. The upshot of the discussions was that Pietro agreed to join his brother in trying their hands in the New World, and towards the close of 1826 the pastry cook sold his business, gathered his family, and with John sailed for America.

The brothers were not embarking upon a new career empty-handed. Both had saved money, and the wealth they brought with them was in the form of cash — gold pieces stowed in chests which they personally carried off the ship at New York. In later years, their nephew, Lorenzo Delmonico, would estimate that his uncles arrived at New York with a capital of not less than one hundred thousand francs, or twenty thousand dollars. This was an impressive sum in 1827, when the purchasing power of the dollar was easily four or five times that of a century and a half later. A legend took root that the Delmonicos had landed without a sou, and got their start by selling peanuts in the street. This was wide of the mark. In 1827 there did appear on the sidewalks of New York a vendor of roasted chestnuts (not peanuts), a Frenchman, who made his station at Broadway and Duane Streets. He remained a well known figure for a generation, but he was not a Delmonico.

Pietro followed John's example of adapting his name to American usage; for business and social purposes he became and remained Peter. However, he, too, would adhere to the French style, Pierre Antoine, when signing documents.

4.

⸱ The brothers lost no time in getting down to business. Peter was a thorough pastry cook, and John knew the wine trade. John's advance scouting had established that there was no place in New York where fine French pastries and related delicacies could be obtained. To fill this lack, the brothers opened a cafe and pastry shop on William Street early in 1827. Whether it was by their direction, or was the sign-painter's mistake, the signboard that went up over the door of number 23 William Street read "Delmonico," and this spelling the family used from then on.

A crumbling receipt book preserved by descendants of Peter Delmonico shows an entry under date of February 2, 1827: "Recd. from Mr. J. Delmonico and Brother $312.50 in full for one-quarter rent of house at No. 23 Wm. St." The location was on the west side of William Street, between Exchange Place and Beaver Street (then called Garden Street and Beaver Lane), and the two-story, peaked-roof brick house was one of a row that lined the street. The shop lay within four or five blocks of most of the business district of the city, and just beyond that radius were the dwellings of most New Yorkers.

John was the active partner, since he had the ideas and had already dealt with New York tradesmen. Samuel Ward, a man who knew both brothers intimately and who came to consider himself practically a founding father of Delmonico's, described John as "of the meridional type, brief of speech, courteous in manner, and with that dignified mien which is acquired on the quarterdeck, whether of a frigate or a coaster. It needs no photograph to recall to my memory his bronzed cheek, coal black hair and side whiskers, clean-cut chin and luminous dark eyes." Peter was taller and broader, and as deliberate in his movements as he was placid in temperament. He yielded to his younger brother's initiative, preferring to look after the operations of the kitchen. It is significant that in that small city, where merchants quickly became known to each other, the Delmonico business in the early years was conducted under the name "Delmonico & Brother," and that reference was commonly made to John as its head.

Like prudent investors, the brothers did not go "whole hog" (an Americanism that amused foreigners of the time) but risked little upon their venture. Half a dozen pine tables, with chairs to match, comprised the furniture of the cafe. Along one side of the room was a counter spread with white napkins, upon which the day's stock of cakes and pastries was arranged neatly. John, in white apron and cap, was the counterman. Aside from the pastries that Peter confected, the shop dispensed coffee, chocolate, bonbons, orgeats, bavaroises, wines, liquors, and fancy ices. The prices were on the same scale as the setting: coffee six cents, a cup of creamy chocolate or a *petit verre* of cognac the same. There were cakes at a penny, and a prime Havana cigar was available at six cents, perfectos retailing at two for a shilling.

The first customers the little cafe attracted were European residents in the city. There was a considerable colony of these, mostly agents of export houses. Marooned in a strange country, among people with barbarous eating habits, the exiles were quick to discover the William Street oasis. They had no objection to two-tined forks and horn-handled spoons, or to cups of common earthenware. The coffee was hot and fragrant, the chocolate unlike anything served elsewhere in New York — rich, thick, and foaming — and the sight of Peter's wife presiding domestically at the cash drawer, busied between customers with keeping the house's accounts, was reassuring to Europeans.

Not all these first patrons were undistinguished or anonymous. Albert Gallatin, a prominent banker who had been in President Jefferson's cabinet as Secretary of the Treasury, frequented the Delmonicos from the start, attracted both as a fellow Swiss and as a connoisseur of food.

The novelty of a woman restaurant employee excited curiosity among the Americans; it had never been seen in the city before and they investigated the Williams Street place where the innovation was on display. Word got around swiftly in the town that comprised only 160,000 inhabitants of all ages and degrees, compressed between the Battery and the Park (City Hall Park). The tempo of the city was set by its commercial activity. Merchants, bankers, and shipping men congregated around Wall and Broad Streets, where, as now, money-making preempted their attention, and the necessity of pausing to ingest food could become a nuisance. The custom was to go home for a hot midday dinner, or to carry a lunch in one's pocket. Eating houses were few and unattractive; Niblo's Bank Coffee House, at William Street and Pine, was about the best, and the few hotels did serve in their dining rooms a passable "ordinary," a set meal served at a given hour at a fixed price. But in the business community time usually was more pressing than appetite, and no prototype of the modern snack bar had yet appeared. In this dearth of places where a bite could be obtained more or less at any hour, Delmonico's cake shop found its opportunity. Little by little it became known that delicious coffee, and cakes that melted in the mouth, could be procured at the "Frenchmen's" on William Street. Once a customer tried the fare, he usually came again, for the pastries were airy light, made with the finest butter, cream, and flavorings, the coffee strong and aromatic, and the chocolate utterly foreign to the muddy mixtures New Yorkers had been downing.

Even at the prices they charged, the Delmonicos made money, and saved it. Trade picked up so rapidly that before the year was out they sent for another member of the family to help with the work. Francesco (or François, as he was known in New York) was the eldest son of John's and Peter's brother Francesco Delmonico. An eager youth of twenty-four, he arrived in the autumn of 1827 and was put to work at once in the cafe. François proved of great value to the concern, for he was apt and willing, and the business appealed to him.

In December 1827 the brothers issued their first known advertisement. This was a simple handbill announcing that "Delmonico & Brother," at 23 William Street, were prepared to supply households with refreshments, fancy cakes, bonbons, and ices for the holidays.

In the meantime, they were encountering competition from a Frenchman named François Guerin, who had opened a pastry shop and cafe on Broadway, between Pine and Cedar Streets, opposite the City Hotel. This was the busiest spot in town, and Guerin did a lively trade, serving sandwiches, sardines, and cakes. A back room meagerly furnished with tables was available for customers who preferred to munch sitting down; but the premises at best were cramped and dingy, in contrast to the neat, spotless surroundings at Delmonico's. Guerin's prices were higher, too, his bonbons fetching fifty cents a pound, an outrageous extravagance in New York of that time; nevertheless, they sold, and both cafes prospered, sharing between them fairly evenly the patronage of people who had a Continental sweet tooth.

But Guerin was parsimonious, as the Delmonicos were not; like the majority of his compatriots, he lived for the day when he should have money enough to retire and go home to France. Having that goal in view, he was indifferent to his surroundings, laid out as little cash as possible for repairs and refurbishing, and invested nothing in expansion. Consequently his cafe became less and less inviting, although his trade held good.

The Delmonicos pursued an opposite policy: where they

made their money, they reinvested it. Evidence of this was given at the end of three years, and their successive listings in the city directory tell the story. In the editions of 1828, 1829, and 1830, the business was listed as "Delmonico & Brother, confectioners, 23 William Street"; but the next year they appeared with a double address: "Delmonico & Brother, confectioners and Restaurant Français, 23 and 25 William Street."

Thus was announced the first Delmonico restaurant, the progenitor of the many famous ones to come.

5.

It had not been easy to accomplish this expansion, fraught with risks for so recently established a concern. John, the more restless and foresighted of the brothers, probably nudged Peter into it, and the caution with which they moved is shown in John's receipt book. Rather than venture all their capital, they borrowed, in this way working with another man's money, and reserving their own nest egg for a crisis.

John's business receipts contain the entry, on May 6, 1829: "Recd. from John Delmonico $1,000.00 on account of principal due me on Bond. Nicholas N. Wyckoff." The next day, over the same signature: "Recd., New York from John Delmonico the sum of $2,412.50 on account of interest due me on my Bond, and also the interest due Samuel Harris on his Bond." If proof were needed that the Delmonicos were thriving, this would furnish it. Nicholas Wyckoff was an odd character, a descendant of a Dutch family that had settled in Williamsburg on Long Island in the time of Peter Stuyvesant. Although active as a merchant and money-lender, he preferred to call himself a simple farmer. But he was not simple-minded, and nobody could imagine Nicholas Wyckoff lending money on anything except the soundest security. Obviously the Delmonicos — in the form of their savings, current business, prospects, and themselves — provided that kind of security.

During that month of May, 1829, an entry in the receipt book shows that the expansion was in preparation: on the day when John Delmonico paid the regular quarterly rental of $312.50 for 23 William Street, he also paid $50 "for rent to this date of the room at number 25 William St." Between May, when a single room had been rented in the house adjoining the cafe, and February of the next year, the entire building was taken over, and receipts for the latter time show John Delmonico paying not only $312.50 rent for number 23 William Street, but also $225 for a quarter's rent of number 25.

Although restaurant management was new to them, and neither was a chef, the brothers seemed to grasp the essentials of the business readily. And competent technical help was procurable, for among the immigrants landing in a steady stream in quest of American dollars were French cooks of ability, who were glad to work for the Delmonicos' high wages. So a superior kitchen staff was assembled.

The novelty of the restaurant which they opened at 25 William Street, while retaining the original cafe next door, was twofold: first, in its introduction of carefully economized French cuisine that made unexpected use of a profusion of foodstuffs normally overlooked by Americans, though ready to hand; and second, in the courteous, deft, deferential service with which each customer was attended. The bearing of the proprietors towards the most casual patron was irreproachable. The furnishings of the restaurant were still plain, although a shade less sketchy than those of the cafe next door. But the food was piquant, often unfamiliar, and the cooking superlatively good. For the first time, New Yorkers were able to order a luncheon or dinner of their choice, selected from a varied bill of fare, have it cooked to perfection and served at the hour they named, wash it down with a sound light wine, and pay a reasonable, set price. Men who had traveled abroad were the first to relish this convenience and opportunity to revivify their palates; and to the stay-at-homes they preached the delights of *potages, ragoûts,* and *entremets de douceur* as prepared by John and Peter Del-

monico. Americans were made acquainted with vegetables new
to them, or nearly so — eggplant, endive, artichokes — and to
surprising ways of cooking others that grew locally but had
been in such slight demand that farmers seldom brought them
to market. The subtle sauces accompanying the dishes hot and
cold, the meats and the desserts, were discovered to be not only
savory but digestible, and the care with which the simplest
dish was put together predisposed even the skeptical to enjoyment.

At the start, when the outcome hung in the balance, John
Delmonico secured a reduction in their combined rent for the
two houses from $537.50 a quarter to $475; but quality told,
and soon the new restaurant caught on and businessmen began
to think little of taking an hour from their preoccupations to
relish an appetizing luncheon immaculately presented. A delicate dish of veal, it was learned, might even be an aid when
broaching a subject equally delicate to a business associate.

Increase of business led the brothers to call again upon the
relatives in Mairengo for hands to assist in the work, and on
September 1, 1831, Lorenzo Delmonico, another son of Francesco, arrived in New York to join his uncles and his brother
François. Lorenzo was a strapping lad of nineteen, but, perceptive as the elder Delmonicos were, neither of them suspected
that the moment Lorenzo walked in the door at 23-25 William
Street the family's prosperity and fame were assured. To Lorenzo the restaurant business came as naturally as swimming to
a swan, and the fundamental elements of his genius — hard work
and conscientious attention to details — he displayed from the
start.

6.

Of that William Street restaurant glimpses have come down
in the reminiscences of New Yorkers who knew it personally.
In 1907, for example, a woman of ninety-six, who had been born
on Rector Street, clearly recalled going "all the way downtown
to William Street" from her "uptown" home on Washington

Street near St. John's Park, where "a French family named Delmonico had opened a shop and won the patronage of the best people. You went up two or three steps from the ground floor, where a few tables were spread. That was the restaurant. Everything was neat and clean and the cooking was the best in town." A sideline of the business remained vividly in her memory. "When the holidays came, the little shop blossomed with fresh importations of French toys and novelties, in addition to the usual line of confectionery. The best things were from Paris, and it makes my mouth water today to think how good they were." These were the thoughts of an old, old New York lady reliving the days when she was twenty-two.

Another glimpse of William Street, showing how it appeared to a harum-scarum, gourmandizing Columbia College lad, was set down in his old age by the man who, as much as any other single individual, confirmed Delmonico's reputation for gastronomical supremacy during the better part of a century — the bon vivant, lobbyist, poet, and "everybody's uncle," Sam Ward. At sixteen, Sam had found himself for the first time free to explore New York unchaperoned, after a Puritanically strict upbringing, and fifty years later he recalled the William Street house:

"I remember entering the cafe with something of awe, accompanied by a fellow student from Columbia. The dim religious light soothed the eye, its tranquil atmosphere the ear. It was a primitive little cafe where John and Peter Delmonico first commended themselves to the city as epicures. I was struck by the prompt and deferential attendance, unlike the democratic nonchalance of Holt's Ordinary, in Fulton Street, or at Clark & Brown's in Maiden Lane, or at George W. Brown's in Water Street . . . I revelled in the coffee, the chocolate, the bavaroises, the orgeats, and petits gateaux and bonbons. The burgundy disappointed us and did not prove comparable to the March & Benson Madeira of those days." The rattle of dominoes on the cafe tables was a sound more pleasing than a clatter of crockery, and the "attractive refections" tempted one to gustatory explorations, such as indulging, on a wintry day, in "a certain hot, rosy whiskey punch, sweetened with currant jelly and heightened by a dash of peach brandy." The cost of a weekly blowout at Delmonico's was half a dollar, but Sam and his friends felt that the price was immaterial — as long as their pocket money held out. At Brown's Ordinary, or at Clark & Brown's in Maiden Lane, they could get a whole dinner cheaper — "upstairs a quarter of a dollar, a shilling in the basement" — but they chose the refinements of Delmonico's instead.

Naturally the eating place appealed to young men-about-town, and many a youth introduced to Delmonico's at this time remained the establishment's loyal liege for life. Such was Abram C. Dayton, a New Yorker who traced his ancestry back to Knickerbocker times. In extreme old age he recalled the charms of Delmonico's in William Street and in recollection shuddered at the assaults that had been made on the city's stomachs by the brothers' native competition in 1830.

"Eating houses, now more politely called restaurants," Dayton remembered, were few in number then, "commonplace in appointments," and notable only as the "stepping-stones by which primitive Gotham gave way to metropolitan New York. They were in the business part of the city, and their patronage was derived from the necessities they afforded, and not from their gastronomical appeal. Dinner [at midday] was the meal they depended upon, and the noon hour their harvest time. The clatter of dishes, the bustle of the hurrying waiters, the steam from the savory compounds, were perhaps appetizers to some . . . but long abstinence was needed for a novice in such matters before he could enjoy a repast [there] . . . Evening, or more properly night, customers were to most of them unknown. Saloons were not the mode for gentlemen, and women would have endured the gnawing of hunger before venturing to enter the most retired one on the list."

The dining room of Clark & Brown, which provided the shilling dinners (a shilling was twelve and one-half cents), specialized in "very rare roast beef in thick slices, or a beefsteak barely warmed through, English plum pudding, and half-and-half ale and strong London Dock brandy." Brown's Ordinary spread out homemade pies "on a long shelf, already cut, and customers helped themselves, bolted the food, and rushed out."

How different was the shop on William Street, where (in Dayton's words) "the courteous manner of the host, coupled with his delicious dishes and moderate charges, attracted the attention, tickled the palate, and suited the pockets of the Knickerbocker youth, who at once acknowledged the superiority of the French and Italian cuisine as set forth by Delmonico. It must not . . . be thought . . . that the new converts from the plain roasted and boiled doctrine to the new rich gravy faith, plunged at once into the vortex of the elaborate and expensive spread. Their visits were at wide intervals and mostly confined to Saturday afternoons, when the good folks were almost certain to be at home laying out their Sunday clothes. Two or three would agree to meet at the cafe . . . Secrecy was indispensable, for if detected we were certain to incur the marked displeasure of our grandmothers, and to be soundly berated, first for our foolish extravagance, and secondly, pitied for our lack of taste by giving preference to 'such vile greasy compounds,' which we were assured would destroy our stomachs; while if we dared to mention the cool, refreshing *vin ordinaire*, that delightful beverage was denounced as a miserable substitute for vinegar.

"Still . . . we repeated our visits whenever we could and were warranted by our limited supply of pocket money, and . . . inducted others into the secret that good things to eat could be had at the cook-shop on William Street. Gradually the little shop had not space to accommodate its increasing patronage."

Of course, there was a minority report. Old eating habits were hard to shake. Philip Hone, no mean gourmandizer, tried the novelties at William Street and was disdainful. "Moore, Giraud, and I went yesterday to dine at Delmonico's, a French restauranteur in William Street, which I had heard was upon the Parisian plan and very good," Hone jotted in his diary on December 18, 1830. "We satisfied our curiosity but not our appetites; and I think are prepared, when our opinions are asked, to say with the Irishman who used lamp-oil with his salad instead of olive-oil, that if it were not for the name of the thing he would as lief eat butter."

Hone lived to revise his estimate of Delmonico's and the "Parisian style" of cooking, and his eventual conversion to the new-fangled sauces and unfamiliar vegetables was typical of the town.

7.

As business improved, the prices on the Delmonico menu advanced, although never was there any deliberate overcharging. Forced by limitation of space to choose which class of customers they should encourage — the few or the many — the brothers elected to cater to those who could afford to pay a little more to get a little more; and never would there be a shortage of people in New York who were ready to pay extra for the extra-best.

The growth of the city, meanwhile, was pacing the restaurant's progress. The Erie Canal had fulfilled the rosiest expectations by increasing the city's commerce many fold, and the population never ceased to shoot up. In 1830, when 25 William Street was opened, New York had 242,000 inhabitants, and within a decade the number would double. The cash flowed into Madame Peter Delmonico's till in a steady stream, and the brothers were able to reduce their indebtedness. Entries in John Delmonico's receipt book show a remittance on May 1, 1830, of "$2,000 on principal and $322.50 interest on bonds of Harris and Wyckoff." A year later there was another payment of $2,262.50 "principal and interest on Wyckoff bond and bond of Samuel Harris." These were considerable sums, and testified to the thriving state of the business even at that early date. Apparently the debt to Wyckoff was wiped out with this second payment, for no mention of it or of the Harris bond appears thereafter.

TOWN AND
COUNTRY GENTLEMEN

A PROPER AMBITION of a bourgeois of France or Italy is to own a country seat, a villa surrounded by formal gardens, and this ambition John and Peter Delmonico had. With the accrual of capital from the William Street business, they purchased, in 1834, a farm of two hundred and twenty acres in Williamsburg, on Long Island. They had a double purpose in mind, for in addition to acquiring a place of *villeggiatura* they proposed to utilize their acres by growing vegetables for the restaurant; the amount and variety of green stuffs they required was not to be found in the markets.

Williamsburg was open country for the most part, and would not be absorbed into Brooklyn until 1855. The Delmonico tract was bounded approximately by what today are Hart Street on the south, Bartlett and Broadway on the north, Marcy Avenue on the west, and Lewis Avenue on the east — an area comprising more than forty city blocks. The Tompkins and Sumner housing developments now stand on a portion of the tract. John Delmonico bought the land with partnership funds for $16,000, and soon construction was begun on a square stone house of imposing dimensions and severe dignity in the European villa style. There also were stables, gardens, and outbuildings suitable to a gentleman's country seat.

John Delmonico's receipt book reflected this new interest. The 1830's were marked by a nationwide wave of speculation, set off by the opening up of the western territories, and with prices going up and profits pleasantly plentiful, New Yorkers were acquiring fastidious dining habits. As early as February 7,

1832, John's receipt book recorded an outlay of $419.90 for "four cases of burgundy (payment in part only) delivered to them from Paris." Other receipts during that and the next year included one for $365.04 paid for coffee; another, "Recd. note of Messrs. Delmonico & Brother on account of champagne bought of us"; $69.85 paid for flour; $933.93 for sugar. The sugar bills were always large, for Peter was a pastry cook and his cakes were an attraction of the house. There were also outlays for glassware and beer, and $160 for a piano; $34 for Parmesan cheese; another $463.86 for coffee; $28.12 for "eau de fleur d'orange"; $165.75 for oil and pork; $162.25 for china; $209.66 for cocoa; and $29.58 for "49 bottles absinthe." Light wines, clarets, and burgundies accounted for sizable payments as the taste of New Yorkers was gently deflected from Madeira and the fortified wines of Spain and Portugal. On August 14, 1833, two bills were settled: one of $214 "for wine," unspecified, and the second "by note in four months of $285.50 for ninety-three cases of wine."

Receipts recorded in 1834 (the year the farm was purchased) covered payments for imported delicacies that were exotic in the New York of the time, and increasingly large outlays for staples of the restaurant — another $839.38 for sugar, for example; $42.50 for "lemons and cornichons"; $233.75 for charcoal; $88.13 for "segars"; $150.32 for almonds; $255.38 for Madeira wine; $55.00 for champagne; $20 for olives; and $75 for "one bbl. Chateau Margaux."

Scattered through the record of these business transactions were receipts for improvements being carried out at the farm. The amount paid for "one pair of mules" was $160 (the same as for a piano); "manure and standing of Horse" cost $92; a bureau and table, $25.25; and "two gold buckles," $40. "Timber delivered at farm at Long Island" accounted for $86.20; and the last receipts entered in 1834 included one for $31.39 for bricks, and another, on the same day, for $27.90 for "brick and soft stone"; and on December 18, $300 for "2 marble columns & capitals and base."

The 1835 bills jumbled $52 for "olives and capers" with $100 for "work done on billiard tables"; $1,718 for "furniture and blinds," and two payments ($300 and $218.17) for carpenter work. There was a notation of $149.69 "recd. of Mr. Delmonico for hay and other articles purchased by him at an auction sale held March 3, 1835," and another receipt reading: "From Mr. Delmonico $75.00 for drawing maps of his farm." As a supreme touch of gentility, on April 25, 1835, $255 was paid "in full for chariotee which we warrant for one year." A chariotee was a pleasure carriage — four-wheeled, much like a buggy, but with a single seat behind — designed for use on country roads, and the builder of this one was James Brewster, the New England carriage maker who had set up shop in New York the year the Delmonicos started in business. Brewster carriages would be as famous for quality for almost as long a period as would Delmonico dinners.

2.

Expenses were mounting in other directions, also, but there was income to pay for everything. Peter's two older daughters, Anna Maria and Josephine, were helping in the business; but Rosa, the next daughter, was still in boarding school. John's receipt book recorded periodic payments ($176.94, $178.86, and $122.16) for "board and tuition of Miss Rosa Delmonico," acknowledged by her French tutor, F. Charagay. Peter's growing family was installed in a house at the rear of 52 Beaver Street, close by the restaurant, for which a rental of $122.50 per quarter was paid. (Presumably during the first few years the family had lived in the upper floors of the William Street house, for there is no mention of any upstairs dining rooms at that address.)

Brother Francesco Del-Monico in Mairengo may have been encountering difficulty in providing for his numerous brood; at any rate, the expanding business in New York called for more hands, and in 1835 John and Peter brought over two more of Francesco's sons — Constantine, aged thirteen, and Siro, eleven.

With them came a cousin, John Napoleon Longhi, who was Siro's age. Constantine — or Constant as he was better known — was old enough to start his apprenticeship in the business, but Siro and young Longhi were packed off to a school in Westport to get more education.

As part of their business expansion in 1834, besides acquiring the Williamsburg farm, the brothers had added a lodging house to their restaurant; this was at 76 Broad Street, where for some time a hotel of sorts had been operated by a Frenchman named Collet. In December 1827 (the year the first Delmonico signboard appeared on William Street) a notice was published in the *New York Evening Post*, which provides an insight into the gastronomical condition of New York then. This advertisement read:

"COMMERCIAL COFFEE HOUSE — No. 76 Broad Street — The subscriber has the honor to inform citizens of the city of New York, strangers, and transient customers, that his *French Restaurant* will be opened on the 11th instant, where at any hour of the day, he will be ready to serve them with Coffee, Chocolate, Soups of every description, Veal Cutlets, Mutton Chops, Partridges, Pheasants, Chickens, Beef a la Mode, Hogs Feet, Oysters, and every dish that constitutes either a breakfast, dinner, or supper. He will constantly keep a supply of the best Wines and Liquors that can be procured; the whole at a moderate price. The patrons of the above establishment may rest assured that Jos. Collet will spare nothing to please them. He hopes by his unremitting exertions, to induce those who call once to call again."

These large promises were followed by a footnote indicating that Joseph Collet had two strings to his bow: "J. Collet will put up to order preserved Meats, Birds of Game, Tomatoes, etc., in a manner that he will warrant them to keep for twelve months, even in the warmest climate. He considers this very important to sea travellers."

The mention of tomatoes is noteworthy, for tomatoes were

among the novelties commonly served by the Delmonicos. Tomato plants had been cultivated in gardens for their decorative
effect, but the fruit had not been considered edible; under the
name "love apples" it had been used for ornament.

Joseph Collet's gastronomical innovations apparently did not
catch on, for within a few weeks he was advertising his establishment as the Commercial Hotel, primarily providing lodgings.

In 1834 the Delmonicos bought out Collet, and at 76 Broad
Street opened a modest hotel to serve mostly foreign businessmen. The outlay necessitated by remodeling the Broad Street
building seems to have somewhat strained the cash resources of
John and Peter, for on November 2 and 16, 1835, receipts were
taken for $600 "interest on bond on property in Broad Street
for $20,000," and $420 "being six months interest on $14,000
at 6% till the 1st instant." The rent of the 52 Beaver Street
dwelling meanwhile had to be paid (the quarterly receipts being
signed by Rufus L. Lord, a leading New York attorney), and
there were other costs incurred by enlarging the business. For
example, $54.55 was paid for "storage of brandy," and $62.50
for a quarter's rent "of house in Third Street." The supply bills
for the restaurant grew steadily larger; the month of October
1835 showed among other outlays, $964.96 for coffee; $363.50
for claret (receipt signed by Archibald Gracie, a shipping magni-
fico), and $352.62 for cocoa, all basic staples.

With another payment of $122.16 on November 23, for
"board and tuition of Rosa Delmonico," the 1835 record was
halted abruptly. For good reason. On the bitterly cold night of
December 16 fire broke out in the Wall Street district, and with
hydrants frozen, firemen were powerless to prevent its spreading. Pushed by a gale, the flames enveloped most of the lower
end of the island, and morning showed block after block of
smoking ruins. William Street suffered heavily, and the Delmonico establishment there was wiped out. Overnight the
brother's chief source of income had been obliterated. But they
would not stay wiped out long.

NEW YORK ACQUIRES
A LANDMARK

WATER AND WINE had played antagonistic parts in the conflagration: the shortage of one had allowed the flames to spread, and a superabundance of the other had helped to quench them. The only source of water was the East River, but the pipes were frozen and even the hose lines turned to solid ice. With gunpowder brought from the Brooklyn Navy Yard, buildings were blown up to clear a fire zone, and among the structures demolished was a warehouse containing a great quantity of Madeira wine. When the casks burst, the sudden flood of wine into the street put out the fire at that point.

The loss caused by the catastrophe was more than $18,000,000; every insurance company in the city was bankrupted. Charred merchandise littered the ruins — silks, laces, prints — "a mountain of coffee" at the corner of Old Slip and South Street, and an entire cargo of tea that had been landed there the day before. Bottles of champagne and spirits jutted out of the muck, and despite patrols of soldiery there was much looting.

With other victims, the Delmonicos faced the stupendous task of rebuilding from scratch. Among newspaper accounts of the holocaust and the steps taken to extricate the city from the disaster, special mention was made of the Delmonicos and their fight. The *Daily Express* said admiringly:

"Mr. Delmonico established a restaurateur [sic] in William Street some years ago, which was the first of any importance known in this city. By great assiduity to his occupation, he soon acquired not only a great run of business from foreigners, but from Americans who were fond of the French style of cooking.

On the memorable night of the 16th December, 1835, his large establishment, which was then in perfect order, was laid in ashes, and he, with his numerous servants and attendants, were thrown entirely out of all business. Not discouraged by the calamities of that night, Mr. Delmonico made immediate arrangements for erecting a building that would afford ample room to accommodate the public."

No time was wasted in contemplation of the wreckage in William Street. The pressing need was to get the business going again, and fortunately number 76 Broad Street had been unscathed. Hastily remodeling a portion of that building into a restaurant, the brothers resumed activities at that location. How promptly the action was taken is indicated by the first entries in John Delmonico's receipt book for 1836. These show that on February 23, two months after the fire, $300 was paid for chairs, and $42.43 "for soap and candles." Thereafter was a steady outgo to meet the costs of construction and renovation — "painting work to date"; "stovepipe, etc."; "copper work to be renewed if wanted"; "mason work"; and $403 for "work done."

Many of these bills John met by giving notes redeemable in three or six months, counting on taking them up by means of the income from 76 Broad Street. Typical transactions were accompanied by receipts reading: "Recd. from Messrs. Delmonico & Brother their note for $1,133 at 90 days for bill of 1st. inst"; and "Recd. two notes of $5,534 each, at 9 and 12 months, in payment of our bills since Feb. 16." Fresh supplies for the restaurant had to be laid in, and by August 1836 the brothers were settling such bills as $261 "for sherry and claret," and $145.05 "for one cask of Madeira." Trade was brisk at their makeshift headquarters; and dinners helped to pay one wine bill, submitted by Williams & Roberts, wine merchants; the invoice for $484.51, dated August 18, 1836, was endorsed as settled, "Mr. Roberts' bill of $116.31 for dinner being deducted."

These were some of the expedients by which the Delmonicos refloated their venture. Their confidence in New York's future was not diminished, and already they had set about their most ambitious undertaking thus far — the erection of a building to house a restaurant first class in every respect, a building constructed for the purpose, and a restaurant that would measure up to the standards of anything in Europe. For New York in 1836 this was a tall order.

The project probably originated with John Delmonico, who always was the more venturesome of the brothers, but Peter lent it loyal support. Early in 1836, therefore, they had bought the plot of ground at the junction of Beaver, William, and South William (formerly Mill) Streets. The price paid for the two separate parcels that formed the triangular gore is not known, but it could not have been small. New Yorkers were gambling in city lots all during 1835 and 1836, and Philip Hone was moved to cry out against the fantastic rise in property values. A lot on William Street, thirty by seventy-five feet, only nine months before the fire changed hands for $51,500. A larger lot, which three years previously had been purchased for $60,000, was divided and sold at about this same time for $225,000. Hone held out against offers of $55,000 for his dwelling at 235 Broadway, opposite City Hall Park, for which he had paid $25,000 fifteen years previously; but in March 1836 he at last yielded, sold the house and lot for $60,000 and joined the fashionable surge uptown, building again on Great Jones Street.

On their Beaver Street site the Delmonicos set about the construction of a building large enough to accommodate the restaurant they had in mind. Work got under way in August 1836. John Delmonico had moved into living quarters at 12 Marketfield Street, virtually around the corner, to be close at hand, and in August he paid a contractor $1,123.75 "for digging cellar in Beaver Street." Thenceforward the expenditures for labor and materials were continuous, receipts for those outlays being interspersed with such routine items as $100 paid for fish, $575 for "fifty baskets of champagne," and $131.28 "for board and tuition of nephews."

By December 1836 construction had progressed to the point

of installing equipment, and $286 was paid "for looking-glass," $32 for carpeting, $350 to an upholsterer "on acct. of work now doing in building at corner of Beaver & Wm. Sts.," and there were recurrent payments for carpentry. Some of the bills were discharged by notes payable in several months. Thus in March 1837 a receipt was taken by John Delmonico for $600 "for carpenter work still doing at Beaver St.," together with one for $500 "for marble for new building," and others of $426.70 "for plumbers work on new building," and $200 and $500 "for portico marble work." Refrigerators were installed at a cost of $25, and there were payments of $26 "for German silver mounting for stair," $10 "for varnishing cases," and $928.83 for gas fixtures installed by the New York Gas Company. At the same time the Broad Street restaurant involved outlays ("$132.25 for truffles"); and there were family expenses, including another $148.56 "for board and tuition of nephews." These were Siro Delmonico and his cousin, John Longhi.

In the midst of business demands, other obligations were not neglected. The Delmonicos from the first had been generous contributors to church and welfare activities. In 1833, when Christ Church, in Ann Street, was declared unsafe, John Delmonico bought for the pastor, Father Varela, a new site in Chambers Street; and in February, 1837, John's receipt book showed him paying $225 "interest on the bond of the church in Chambers St.," and a few days later another $70 payment for the same purpose.

During the spring of 1837, a crisis affecting the entire community threatened to interrupt the building work on Beaver Street. This time it was not fire, but a disastrous business depression, known in history as the Great Panic of 1837. The crash had been brought on by the frenzy of speculation that swept the nation for several years, and was precipitated by President Andrew Jackson's determination to crush Nicholas Biddle's Bank of the United States. There was a rash of business failures; English investors called their loans; and on May 10 New York banks suspended specie payments. Prices collapsed; property that had been selling for tens of thousands of dollars found no buyers at any figure. It may be surmised that the Delmonicos were shaken as badly as anyone; but in the pinch, their frugality and conservatism paid. Somewhere they found reserves of capital to continue their building. And continue it they did, in the midst of national gloom and much suffering in New York, and by the autumn of 1837 the place was ready.

2.

With the shrewdness they displayed in most of their operations, the Delmonicos made a practice of inviting the press to inspect each new building they opened, and by giving these guests a Delmonican dinner secured invaluable publicity. On the evening of September 20, 1837, John and Peter Delmonico were hosts to editors of the New York newspapers in a "preview" of their new establishment at Beaver and South William Streets. The diners comprised "the greatest assemblage of editors on record," according to the lively *New York Herald*, which was itself less than a year old. As might have been foretold, the newspapers for days thereafter rang with plaudits for "Delmonico's new magnificent establishment."

John Delmonico welcomed the guests at the entrance, standing between the marble pillars of the porch. These were the first feature to strike the visitors as marvelous, for they had been brought from Pompeii, where they had formed the doorway of a villa; set into the portico, with the name "Delmonico" across the lintel, they were the oldest bits of architecture in practical use in New York City.

The guests next were taken on a tour of the building, after remarking its favorable location just behind the new Exchange. The structure was three and one-half stories high, of brick and brownstone with marble trim, and the walls were of exceptional solidity. "The first story contains a fine saloon," the conservative *Evening Post* reported, with an "elegantly inlaid" floor of marble set in lozenge shapes. The second floor "saloon" was similarly luxurious, the floor there being laid with the "choicest samples of wood, such as mahogany, bird's-eye maple and black walnut — presenting an appearance far surpassing anything of the kind in the city." At this period, parquetry was almost unknown in New York; on the occasion of a ball wealthy residents would decorate their wide-board floors with designs drawn in colored chalk.

Facilities for private dining, a novelty evocative of Paris, were provided on the third floor, where several small rooms were fitted up for "select parties, free from the interruption of strangers." This amenity the *Post* commended as "an improvement much needed heretofore."

But the wine vaults caused unconcealed astonishment. The cellar was built out under the street in front, one hundred feet long and twenty feet wide. There were stacked "something like sixteen thousand bottles of wine, all neatly separated from each other by niches in the shelves," according to the enraptured *Post*, which compared this treasury of vintages to an arsenal — "and if one may judge from the execution likely to be done by this ammunition, not a few will find themselves crippled by a too near approach — at least in pocket."

The editors bore the risk bravely; none more so than the editor of the *Commercial Advertiser*, who was not there. This had not happened by intention, he informed his subscribers, but "simply because we had forgotten the invitation, which was verbal and not written, as such important matters should be." He revenged himself by lifting from the columns of his competitors a description of the "feasting, music, mirth and wine" that had marked the inauguration.

The *Daily Express*, exuberant in its enthusiasm, if somewhat faulty in its French, regaled *its* readers with a first-hand account of the "rich repast, served in the French style," that had opened the new "Delmonico's Restaurateur." There had been entertainment by actors and singers, much joviality, and speeches in French, Italian, Spanish, and English. "The best of feeling prevailed," the *Express* wound up. "The wines were superb."

CHAPTER IV

A NATION OF FEEDERS

THE TRUE MEASURE of an era must be taken by its own standards, and to think of the New York of 1840 in terms of the New York of 1860 (and still more of 1960) is to distort the picture out of all resemblance. This applies with special force to the history of New York City, because the dominant note of its history has been one of continual change, physical and social.

The fugitive nature of American customs and institutions struck European visitors to this country almost from the start. In 1838, for example, Captain Frederick Marryat, an observant Englishman, writing up his impressions of a tour in the United States, cautioned his readers that "those who would describe America now would have to correct all in the short space of ten years."

With the above in mind, we can appreciate the magnitude of the investment the Delmonico brothers managed — and dared — to sink into their Beaver Street project — for the total outlay was about $100,000. Then and thereafter, decidedly, John and Peter Delmonico were classed among New York's substantial citizens and prominent businessmen.

Mere purveying of luscious cakes and delicious coffee, of course, had not brought this about. Other cook-shops were operating at the same time, but for the most part these gradually disappeared. The Delmonicos and François Guerin started business at about the same time, but a contemporaneous New Yorker, writing long afterward, pointed out the basic difference in the spirit and method of their two enterprises which accounted for their different fates. Guerin "had no taste for display, and very little even for cleanliness. Penurious, lacking in personal ambition, he stuck to his shop, accumulated an immense fortune, and left no record to tell when or how he lived and died. The old sign, 'François Guerin, Confectioner,' has been swept away." John Delmonico, on the other hand, was described as "generous and enterprising; adhering strictly to his original plan, he enlarged and improved when warranted by the demand and growth of the city. A social host, his ambition was to please the public, and to outstrip competition by a lavish yet judicious expenditure. He rose from the obscurity of a petty shop to have his name known everywhere."

Character, in combination with aptitude, foresight, and professional competence, thus determined the Delmonico success. From the first, the quiet dignity of the brothers impressed the class of patrons they set out to attract, and gave even their modest dining room on William Street a tone that set it above a mere eating house. Not content to be purveyors, they were hosts, and their customers were treated like guests.

The difference between a proprietor and a host was defined once by a famous host, Charles A. Stetson, for many decades the manager of the magnificent Astor House which old John Jacob Astor had erected on Broadway opposite the Park at about the time the Delmonicos opened their Beaver Street place.

"A tavern-keeper," said Stetson, "knows how to get to market and how to feed so many people at a public table. A hotel-keeper is a gentleman who stands on a level with his guests." For half a century Presidents and statesmen and financiers stayed at the Astor House and were Stetson's personal friends. Similarly, an anonymous writer, glancing back, in after years, at the long career of the clan of Delmonico, remarked that "no Delmonico has ever thought himself above his business, and for that reason no gentleman has ever thought himself above the Delmonicos."

*

2.

Already the Delmonico influence upon the dining preferences of upper class New Yorkers was apparent. Captain Marryat, who liked Americans and esteemed many of their domestic habits as heartily as he disliked their democratic principles, bore testimony to this during his 1837-38 tour as far west as St. Louis. Like other travelers, he marveled at the quantity of game that was dished up everywhere: in a New York market he saw "nearly three hundred head of deer, with quantities of bear, raccoon, wild turkeys, geese, ducks, and every variety of bird in countless profusion." No theorist, he tasted everything that was set before him and gave his opinion frankly: bear he abominated, raccoon he found "pretty good," and wild turkey he deemed superb.

Forty years before, Anthelme Brillat-Savarin had given the palm to wild turkey during his exile in America at the time of the Terror. The great gastronomer had shot his own turkey on a farm in Connecticut, and had it roasted by the farmer's daughters in a style that was (he said) "charming to look at, flattering to the sense of smell, and delicious to the taste. As the last morsel of it disappeared, there arose from the whole table the words: *'Very good! Exceedingly good! Oh! dear sir, what a glorious bit!'*"

Brillat-Savarin also had been struck by the abundance of food he encountered everywhere. At the same farmer's table where he ate turkey, he and a friend were treated to "a handsome piece of corned beef, boiled goose, and a magnificent leg of mutton," with several vegetables. At the two ends of the table were jugs of cider, and after dinner they were served excellent tea.

Such was rustic eating in America around 1795, before any trace of French cookery had entered native stew pots. With the Delmonicos and their allies (for their success attracted imitators), the transformation set in. Not uniformly or on a wide scale yet, but within a steadily enlarging circle.

With the cooking came a new nomenclature. French is the

language of cooks as Latin is the language of lawyers, and when the cafe in William Street was first expanded into a restaurant, John Delmonico took cognizance of the difficulty many of his prospective customers would have in identifying dishes under French titles; he therefore paid a linguist, Robert Greenhow, $100 to translate the French menu into an English bill of fare, and printed the two side by side on the restaurant card. Since there is nothing quite so effective for giving *tone* to an article of merchandise as attributing it to a foreign source, the trick was soon taken up by other eating houses; and by the time the Beaver Street house was opened, French and English were appearing cheek by jowl on a number of New York menu cards.

3.

What Marryat termed a "very important question, which is that of eating and drinking" in the United States, he explored thoroughly during his 1837-38 tour. He started by quoting James Fenimore Cooper's castigation of Americans as "the grossest feeders of any civilized nation known," subsisting on food that was "heavy, coarse, and indigestible, taken in the least artificial forms that cookery will allow." Cooper had recently returned from an extended stay in Europe, where he had come to appreciate the Continental cuisine. So sweeping a denunciation, Captain Marryat testified, was not justified. In his opinion, "the cookery in the United States is exactly what it is and must be everywhere else — in a ratio with the degree and refinement of the population. In the principal cities you will meet with as good cookery in private houses as you will in London, or even Paris; indeed, considering the great difficulty which the Americans have to contend with, from the almost impossibility of obtaining good servants, I have often been surprised that it is so good as it is. At Delmonico's, and the Globe Hotel at New York, where you dine from the *carte*, you have excellent French cookery; so you have at the Astor House, particularly at private parties; and, generally speaking, the cooking at all the large hotels may be said to be good . . . The bill of fare of the ta-ble-d'hôte of the Astor House is *printed every day*. I have one with me, which I shall here insert, to prove that the eating is not so bad in America as described by Mr. Cooper."

Preserved in his book of impressions of rural and civic life in America in 1838 is this menu:

ASTOR HOUSE, *Wednesday, March 21, 1838*
Table-d'hôte

Vermicelli Soup	Salade de Volaille
Boiled Cod Fish and Oysters	Ballon de Mouton au Tomato
" Corn'd Beef	Tête de Veau en Marinade
" Ham	Casserolle de Pomme de Terre
" Tongue	garnie
" Turkey and Oysters	Compote de Pigeon
" Chickens and Pork	Roulleau de Veau à la Jardinière
" Leg of Mutton	Côtellettes de Veau Sauté
Oyster Pie	Filet de Mouton Piqué aux
Cuisse de Poulet Sauce Tomate	Ognons
Poitrine de Veau au Blanc	Ronde de Boeuf
Fricandeau de Veau aux Epinards	Roast Chickens
Côtellettes de Mouton Panée	" Wild Ducks
Macaroni au Parmesan	" Wild Goose
Roast Beef	" Wild Guinea Fowl
" Pig	Roast Brant
" Veal	
" Leg of Mutton	Queen Pudding
" Goose	Mince Pie
" Turkey	Cream Puffs

Dessert

This was the bill of fare of the Astor House's "ordinary," or standard meal, one of the four daily meals that were included in the charge for a room — two dollars. It was designed to please the traveler possessing normally cultivated tastes. It is note-worthy that in this typical menu, appearing only eight years after the Delmonicos had opened their first restaurant, French and English dishes are mingled, American standbys with foreign novelties. Thus boiled cod uneasily companions *fricandeau de veau aux épinards;* the time-honored roasts (beef, pork, veal) are set off by a *casserolle de pomme de terre garnie;* and oyster pie and *macaroni au Parmesan* consort together. The basis of the menu is its profusion of meat dishes; only four vegetables are even mentioned, and in each case they are mere garnishings. The desserts betray a woeful lack of imagination. Yet the Astor House was the most sumptuous hotel on the American continent, and its dining room was famous.

As the Delmonicos became firmly established, this custom of indiscriminately mixing English and French on bills of fare gradually gave way, and the Astor itself set an example of sticking to plain American terms, rather than try to compete with the repertory of the brothers Peter and John. An Astor House menu of 1849, for example reads:

ASTOR HOUSE, Thursday, October 11, 1849

Game — Roast

Black Ducks	Rail Birds
Lake Ducks	Meadow Hens
Teal	Short Neck Snipe
Widgeons	Broad Bills
Grouse	Wood Ducks
Mallard Ducks	Gray Ducks
Plover	Doe-witches

Venison, Currant Jelly Sauce

Game — Broiled

English Snipe	Robin Snipe
Cedar Birds	Surf Snipe

Soup

Vegetable Soup

Fish

Bass, Genoise Sauce

Roast	*Boiled*
Beef	Corned Beef
Turkey	Beef Tongue
Chickens	Duffield Hams
Ham, Champagne Sauce	

Side Dishes

Oysters, baked in the shell	Small Birds, Madeira sauce
Curried Veal with Rice	Broiled Pig's Feet
Frog, fried in butter	Macaroni with Cheese
Black Fish, barbecued	Rice Cakes, flowered with
Stuffed Tomatoes, baked	Orange
Calf's Liver, fried with pork	Sausages with mashed potatoes
Calf's Head, brain sauce	

Vegetables

Onions	Cabbage
Boiled Potatoes	Sweet Potatoes
Mashed Potatoes	Raw Tomatoes
Pickled Beets	Stewed Tomatoes
Egg Plant	Spinach
Lima Beans	Corn
Squash	

Pastry

Pumpkin Pies	Cranberry Pies
Rice Pudding	Bread Pudding
Charlotte Russe	Almond Cakes

Dessert

Ice Cream, served in forms, molded

The mere number and variety of dishes offered in this bill of fare of 1849, compared with the menu of eleven years previously, is immediately noticeable. Evidently the public would not be content with 1838 fare in 1849; and the spread of the gospel of Delmonico and French cookery is traceable in the list of vegetables, including eggplant, a relative newcomer to American plates. There are wine sauces, and the variety of game is astonishing to modern eyes. Still the pastries and desserts are not to be compared with the dozens of airy confections which first-class pastry cooks like Peter Delmonico and his assistants could turn out.

The wine list was printed on the above 1849 menu card in two columns down either margin, and what was available on call is interesting. Listed were two kinds of Moselle wine, three Sauternes, fourteen Hocks (Rhine wine), fifteen Champagnes, twenty-one Clarets, seven Burgundies, three Ports, fifteen Sherries, and *forty-seven* Madeiras.

4.

Captain Marryat, in his survey of American gastronomy in 1838, drew a distinction between fare like that provided at the Astor House and at Delmonico's and eating houses in cosmopolitan New York City, and what was encountered in the hinterlands. "As you advance into the country and population recedes," he wrote, "you run through all the scale of cookery until you come to the 'corn bread and common doings' (i.e., bread made of Indian meal, and fat pork) in the far west . . . Americans eat a great deal of pork, which renders the cooking in the small taverns very greasy — with the exception of the Virginia farm taverns, where they fry chickens without grease in a way that would be admired by Ude himself; but this is a state secret, handed down from generation to generation, and called *chicken fixings*."

American meats, Marryat judged, were equal to any in England. Terrapin he would pass up any time for turtle, which, however, he also found widely served. He was given many kinds of fish, all good; oysters, "very plentiful, very large," although their flavor was not to his taste; and the canvasback duck justified its reputation as a crowning delicacy. His conclusion was: "The old proverb says, 'God sends meat and the devil sends cooks'; and such is and unfortunately must be the case for a long while in most of America." From too many devilish cooks New Yorkers were mercifully exempt, the author of *Mr. Mid-*

shipman Easy made clear, and Delmonico's he commended without reservation.

The captain also turned his serious attention to a subject which he deemed "of much more importance in America — that of drinking." Up to then he had considered Englishmen and "Switzerlanders" the world's heaviest consumers of potent liquors, but in his opinion Americans surpassed them. To run through the "whole catalogue of the indigenous compounds in America, from 'iced water' to a 'stone fence' or 'streak of lightning,' would fill a volume," he reported. Therefore limiting himself to the single subject of wine, he determined to his own satisfaction, at least, that apparently the American climate and port wine did not harmonize; he came across no port that was more than passable. The stuff labeled "champagne" he figuratively poured down the drain: "The quantity drunk is enormous, and would absorb all the vintage of France, were it not that many hundred thousand bottles are consumed more than are imported." The State of New Jersey, he was told, had "the merit of supplying the American *champagne*, which is said to be concocted out of turnip juice, mixed with brandy and honey." The result, however, was pleasant and harmless, "a very good imitation," and it had the practical advantage of costing only six or seven dollars per dozen.

Where Americans displayed genius, however, was in their Madeiras, he exclaimed. "I may almost say that I never tasted good Madeira until I arrived in the United States," was his judgment, while the prices the best Madeiras fetched astonished him. A really tiptop wine would bring twelve, twenty, or even forty dollars a bottle if sold at auction, he was assured. He doubted that his fellow countrymen would swallow such a sailor's yarn, and to prove his point he submitted the Astor House wine list.

"Even in this list of a tavern, the best Madeira is as high as twelve dollars a bottle, and the list is curious from the variety it offers," he noted.

There were ten separate headings (Moselle, Sauterne, Hock,

Hermitage, Champagne, Claret, Port, Burgundy, Sherry, and Madeira), and one hundred and twelve different wines were available on call, from the hotel's regular stock. The popularity of the different wines was indicated by the choices listed. Thus there was only one Moselle ("Oberemmel"), priced at $1.50 a bottle, and two Sauternes (one of them "Morton's Y Chem"), both of which cost $2.00 a bottle.

The Hocks (fourteen in this list) ranged in price from $2.00 for "Steinberger 1811" to $8.00 for "Prince Metternich, celebrated Castle-bottled, gold seal Johannisberger, vintage 1822." Hermitages were in slight demand, only two being listed — "Red Roche" and "White, 1815" — both priced at $2.00. The ten champagnes ran from "Beaver Sillery" at $2.00 to "Sparkling Hock" at $3.00, and neither of these was champagne at all. Clarets (seventeen listed) started at a dollar a bottle for "Léoville Bordeaux," and moved through "Château Lafite 1828" at $2.50 to a top of $3.00 for "Château Margaux, 1831, Lynch's." * The best of the three Burgundies, Romanée, cost $3.00, and so did the best "White Port," one of the six ports offered. "Ne Plus Ultra" sherry at $4.00 a bottle topped the fifteen listed.

With Madeira, the cellar's treasures were displayed. There were forty-two choices spread before the connoisseur, and the cheapest ("Sea Bird") cost $2.00 a bottle. "Phelps, Phelps, and Laurie, vintage 1811, via East Indies" was a bargain at $2.50; "Vaughan, two voyages to East Indies, vintage 1811, yellow seal" was priced at a tempting $3.00; "Monteiro, 6 years in East Indies, Metior" went for $4.00; and so on up to "Old Calcutta, bottled in Calcutta in 1814, imported 1824," available at $4.50; "Gratz (red seal) bottled in 1806," $5.00; "Essex, Jr., imported 1819," $6.00; "Smith & Huggins (Dyer's white top), bottled in

* During the early part of the last century, the "château" wines of Bordeaux were not bottled at the point of origin ("estate bottled"), but were generally sold in bulk to wine shippers, who blended different cuvées according to their own formulas. The exceptions to the practice were few. Château Lafite's first château-bottled wines were of the great 1869 vintage, and the custom was adopted generally after that.

St. Eustatia," $7.00; "Wedding Wine," at $8.00; and "Gov. Phillips," $9.00. Crowning all was "Gov. Kirby's original bottled, 00," at a royal $12.00 a bottle.

In terms of 1967 dollars, such a price would easily be equivalent to $50 or $60 dollars a bottle; and this wine was not one of those priceless vintages hoarded in the cellars of private homes, but was merely a choice Madeira available to the casual diner in a public hotel.

Captain Marryat was even more astonished, if possible, by the multiplicity of mixed drinks which Americans had evolved than he was by the altitudinous prices paid for Madeira. "I could not remember, or if I could, it would occupy too much time to mention the whole array against one's brains," he protested; but he did feel bound to "descant a little upon the mint-julep, as it is, with the thermometer at 100°, one of the most delightful and insinuating potations that ever was invented, and may be drunk with equal satisfaction when the thermometer is as low as 70° . . . The Virginians claim the merit of having invented this superb compound. They say that you may always know the grave of a Virginian, as, from the quantity of juleps he had drunk, mint invariably springs up where he has been buried."

The custom of inviting bystanders to join in a drink, whether wanted or not, in Marryat's opinion was heathenish; and he provoked umbrage at some of his stops by declining drinks that strangers attempted to foist upon him — not from any desire to appear standoffish, he said, but simply because, "had I drunk with them all, I should have been in the same state as many of them were — that is, not really sober for three or four weeks at a time." The way Americans drank, in his judgment, was "quite a caution," and he found them unanimous in their opinion of water — "it is very good for navigation."

5.

Captain Marryat's strictures upon the diet of Americans generally are given grim support by the remedies for indigestion that were advertised everywhere at that period. Such far-from-simples as "Beckwith's Anti-Dyspeptic Pills," and "Rev. B. Hibbard's Vegetable Anti-Bilious Family Pills," to mention two of the many nostrums, were extolled in the biggest, blackest type the newspapers could provide, with cures for "intemperance" fortified by copious testimonials.

Social conventions helped to militate against the spread of gracious dining habits; it was considered improper for a woman of refinement to enter an eating house. As late as 1835 James Thompson, a confectioner, opened a shop at 171 Broadway "for the sale of cakes and other dainties, to accommodate ladies who were shopping; but for a long time this embryo Delmonico's languished in neglect, even though the sisters of the proprietor, middle-aged women, were the sole attendants and it was on the most frequented part of the promenade." This was the recollection of Abram Dayton.

Gradually this social taboo was eased and then lifted altogether. The increase in the number of the city's hotels speeded the process, for women who traveled were obliged to eat. A "Strangers List" published in 1835 showed that during a period of two hundred and seven days, nearly sixty thousand visitors had registered at New York hotels, for an average stay of three days. To accommodate this influx, hotels proliferated; there had been only eight in the city in 1818; by 1836 there were twenty-eight; and ten years later, in 1846, there were one hundred and eight. The hotels were conducted almost wholly on the American plan — that is, room and meals included in the flat daily charge. At the Astor, engraved cards informed guests that the schedule of meals would be:

Breakfast	7:30 in Ladies Ordinary
	8:00 in Men's Ordinary
Dinner	3:00 in Ladies Ordinary
	3:30 in Men's Ordinary
Tea	6 to 9
Supper	9 to midnight

The quantity of food served at these "ordinaries" amazed foreigners. It was normal to serve for breakfast griddle cakes (rye, buckwheat, and corn), ham and eggs, sausages, fish, chicken, beefsteak, pork, oysters, several kinds of bread and biscuits, coffee, tea, and chocolate.

Europeans positively shuddered at the way Americans bolted their food, wolfing it in silence, and always in the presence of other desperate feeders. The larger the crowd, the keener the appetite, seemed to be the rule. Robert Burford, an English traveler, in his "A Description of a View of the City of New York" in 1834, observed:

"The hotels are numerous, large, and convenient . . . but the meals are taken in the public room, where fifty to one hundred persons sit down at the same time. A vast number of dishes covers the table, and the dispatch with which they are cleaned is almost incredible. From five to ten minutes for breakfast, fifteen to twenty for dinner, and ten for supper is usually sufficient. Each person, as soon as satisfied, leaves the table without regard to his neighbors; no social conversation follows."

Since, in the axiom of Brillat-Savarin, there can be no true dining without the accompaniment of good talk, Americans had much to learn when Delmonico's and a few co-laborers in the field introduced their reforms.

But New York was willing to learn, and visitors from abroad who came expecting utter barbarism were sometimes agreeably surprised. Fanny Elssler, the Viennese dancer, who came to America in 1840 and caused a sensation by her fiery performances, wrote home soon after her arrival in New York telling of her reception. Fanny was accustomed to the utmost in the way of luxurious living that Paris could provide, and she had embarked upon the American tour with misgivings. Her surprise, upon checking into a hotel on Broadway opposite City Hall Park, she recounted under date of May 8, 1840:

"I alighted at the American Hotel, where I had been strongly recommended, and was ushered with great civility into a handsome salon, but was promised an even better one upon the first vacancy. My exertions had made me quite hungry [Fanny Elssler was hefty and muscular], so I ordered my dinner, not a little curious to see something of the mysteries of an American cuisine. I must confess my first dinner astonished me outright. The table was most elegantly garnished with fine linen and beautiful glass — and would you believe it? — I was so positively assured by those who had been here that a napkin was not to be found in the city, that I consequently brought some dozen with me. I found them useless. Four or five courses were served, and nothing could have been better cooked or a better quality. There is 'science' in the kitchens of the hotel, and I began to think that America is not quite so barbarous as fine folks have assured me."

Her good opinion would have been reinforced had she dropped into the Delmonico cafe on Beaver Street, where the chocolate was not surpassed even by that of her own Vienna. And she may have visited Delmonico's, although there is no record that she did. What she would have found made an impression on many New Yorkers, however. Three months after the establishment at Beaver and South William Streets was opened to the public, a seventeen-year-old Columbia student of good family, George Templeton Strong, recorded in the diary he already was keeping: "Went to Delmonico's and drank some of the only good chocolate I ever tasted, so much superior to the stuff that ordinarily goes under that name as champagne to small beer." Strong would remain a devotee of Delmonico's for the rest of his life.

Celebrities from overseas frequented the "Citadel," as the new stronghold of Delmonican fare was soon dubbed. According to legend, one of these was a shabby exile named Prince Louis Napoleon, nephew of the great emperor and pretender to his uncle's throne. The prince had been shipped off to America by Louis-Philippe's government as a nuisance, after one farcical grab at the imperial title. The story told in New York was that Louis whiled away his evenings at Delmonico's, cadging drinks from compatriots and practicing sleight-of-hand with James Wallack, the English actor. That the impecunious prince did borrow right and left (and when he came into power as Napoleon III paid back the loans with right-royal interest) is true; but he did not frequent the Beaver Street house, for it was not opened until after Louis had returned to Europe. Probably he stayed at the Delmonico lodging house at 76 Broad Street, where without a doubt he was welcome, whether he could pay or not, for the Delmonicos hero-worshipped Bonaparte. Young Siro Delmonico's middle name was Napoleon, and so was that of John Longhi, his kinsman. Lorenzo Delmonico revered the memory of the Corsican. During the years when Napoleonic exiles dragged out a weary existence in America, Lorenzo met an officer of the Grand Army who had accompanied Napoleon to St. Helena. Upon the hero's death, this veteran had clipped a lock of hair from his head, and kept it as a talisman. Lorenzo was fascinated by the old man's tales and tried to buy the lock, but the officer would not part with it. As a token of friendship, however, he divided it and gave half to Lorenzo, who had the relic set in a gold locket which was his most prized possession. And the old soldier was lodged and fed at Delmonico's for the remainder of his days.

6.

That New Yorkers took kindly to the ministrations of Delmonico, Sam Ward, the house's most notable would-be historian, made plain in the memoirs he dictated many years afterward. Wall Street's men of affairs, he recalled, were as eagerly converted to "the precepts of Robert Beauvilliers and Carême as their wives and daughters had long been to the fashions of the boulevards. The truffles of Périgord, the vintages of the Côte-d'Or, became a marital set-off to the silks of Lyons and the flounces of Chantilly. From morning until night it was impossible to enter the refectory of the 'Citadel' without seeing a merchant, a banker, or a lawyer, and at the hours of incandescence [in plain words, by gaslight] it was filled with all three. The innocent rattle of dominoes still enlivened the outer cafe. Knots of brokers discussed speculations in their private rooms above, in others of which German bankers and foreign merchants formed daily luncheon clubs."

One of these luncheon clubs had been organized by that same Nicholas Wyckoff who lent money to the Delmonicos at the commencement of their career in America. This club, known as WEDA (Wyckoff's Economical Dinner Association), comprised businessmen who could not get home on "packet day" — the day when they made up their European correspondence, to catch the sailing of the fast mail packets. Since the first WEDA dinner cost $10 a plate, evidently there had been a rise in prices since the William Street cafe and its six-cent coffee.

The trend of the prices can be judged from two bills that have survived, rendered to "J. O. Sargent" in 1840 and 1847, respectively. (Almost certainly this was John Osborne Sargent, a New England lawyer who became associate editor of the New York *Courier and Express*, and published a translation of Horace.) The 1840 bill was for four dinners (plus an incidental charge of 63 cents) at a total cost of $20.76. This works out to an average of about $5.00 per dinner. The meals were served on January 11 and 18, and February 2 and 12, indicating that Sargent was a frequent customer.

The 1847 bill was for six dinners, at a total charge of $55.50. These were served on June 23, 24, and 25, July 25 and 27, and August 2, showing that Sargent had not wavered in his regularity. The average cost per dinner this time was more than $9.00, though this increase might be attributed either to the fact that on two occasions, when the bill came to $17.88 and $12.00 respectively, Sargent had entertained guests, or splurged on wines. The supplemental charges and the cost of wines were what could run the check for a Delmonico repast up and up.

"Those were indeed palmy days," Sam Ward recalled of the Beaver Street house, "when the ubiquitous Louis, the most sup-

ple and indefatigable of head waiters, with the happiest memory
of names and faces, and smiles for all, and appetizing suggestions
for the uncertain palate, now noiselessly placed before a solitary
guest some *plat fin* as tenderly as were it on Sèvres royal, and as
respectfully as though he were serving a monarch — and in the
evening superintended a banquet with all the mastery of a *chef
d'orchestre* directing a symphony of Beethoven."

For the few erudite gastronomers the city contained (Winfield Scott, who had seriously studied the restaurants of Paris,
was one of these) the kitchens of John Lux, the *chef de cuisine*,
produced continual surprises. The Delmonicos were always on
the alert to learn "the latest thing" in Parisian dining, and as Ward
put it: "Today a new *aide cuisinière* [he means cookbook]
brought the last inventions of the Rocher de Cancale, the Trois
Frères Provençaux, and the princely laboratories of Talley-
rand — tomorrow, a new invoice of pâtés of Strasbourg, Tou-
louse or Angoulême, or the arrival of a Clos de Vougeot or
Chambertin, unscathed by its then supposed enemy, the sea." In
Ward's opinion (and he was a qualified judge, for he had revelled
in the best of Europe), these Gallic inventions, when transferred
to Delmonico's kitchens, often proved superior to their proto-
types at Paris, because Delmonico's cooks considered themselves
ambassadors charged with upholding the honor of their national
cuisine; and in fulfilling this mission they were able to draw
upon the greater abundance of fine foodstuffs available in America. Finally, their very nostalgia for France spurred them to
intenser efforts. In Paris, Sam reasoned, a cook had the city he
regarded as his own just outside his door; but in New York the
same chef was exiled from the sights and sounds he loved, and
therefore when recreating a dish just reported from "home"
he would lavish upon it the tenderest artistry, working with the
heart as well as the head.

At the Beaver Street "Citadel" the organizing talents of Lorenzo Delmonico and the culinary ingenuity of Lux combined
to carry off a catering feat that drew widespread notice. The

Prince de Joinville, a younger son of King Louis Philippe, visited the United States with a naval squadron, and Delmonico was asked to provide a spread of refreshments for a grand ball to be given aboard the prince's frigate, the *Belle Poule*, at Newport, Rhode Island. The notice given was short, but Lux and Lorenzo rose to the emergency and provided a supper, hot and cold, that was transported, in large part, from New York, and served in perfect condition. This type of service was brought to perfection by Delmonico's; the restaurant would always excel at it.

As the 1840's rolled in, the Delmonico's position seemed assured. Peter and John were rich and growing richer, their families were well provided for, the outlook seemed solidly secure. Then on November 10, 1842, "a dark shadow fell upon the 'Citadel,' " Sam Ward related: John Delmonico, the real founder of the family's prosperity, dropped dead while deer hunting on Long Island. The shock felt throughout the business community was recorded by Philip Hone in his diary:

"The respectable proprietor of the great hotel and restaurant in William Street died on Thursday morning in a strange and awful manner. He was with a party deer-hunting at Snedecor's, Islip, Long Island. He was placed on a stand up the creek, and a deer coming, he fired. The deer being wounded took to the water, and was killed by one of the hunters on another stand. After some time his companions, going to join him, found him [John Delmonico] lying on his face in the same spot where he had fired, quite dead of apoplexy."

Hone's initial distaste for the French style of cooking had long since yielded to admiration, and he paid the restaurateur the tribute of genuine regret: "Mr. Delmonico was an amiable man, very obliging in his house, and will not fail to be remembered as long as good dinners dwell pleasantly upon the recollections of gastronomes."

CHAPTER V

MORE WATER,
AND MORE WINE

IN THE WORDS OF SAM WARD, John Delmonico was "widely and justly lamented, and was followed to his grave by a long convoy of our most respected citizens." The location of that grave was a gauge of the family's standing, for it was a vault in old St. Patrick's Church, on Mott Street near Prince. Then, and until 1879, that church was the Roman Catholic pro-cathedral of New York. Peter Delmonico had purchased the vault two years previously, and John was the first member of the family to be placed in it. In surrounding vaults, as the years went by, some of the brightest leaders of New York's Catholic society would be interred — lawyers, merchants, and politicians noted in their day.

Philip Hone's sympathy for the bereaved Delmonico family curdled somewhat when John's survivors served notice that private grief would not impede the performance of their duties. Four days after John Delmonico's death, Hone copied into his diary, with strong expressions of disapproval, the "card" which John's widow, brother, and nephew, Lorenzo, had caused to be published in the newspapers, at the same time conveying their thanks to the friends and societies who had attended the funeral, and informing all that the business (which had been temporarily suspended) would resume without change of ownership or policy. "The establishment will be reopened today under the same firm of Delmonico Brothers," the notice read, "and no pains of the bereft family will be spared to give general satisfaction. Restaurant, bar-room [i.e., cafe] and private dinners No. 2 South William Street; furnished rooms No. 76 Broad Street, as usual."

The widow left by John Delmonico was his own niece, Peter Delmonico's eldest daughter, Anna Maria. John also left an infant daughter, seven months old, named Marie Josephine. Anna Maria Delmonico had been active in the restaurant almost from the start, and had eventually replaced her mother, Peter's wife Catherine, as bookkeeper. As John's widow, she inherited, in her own name and her daughter's, a half interest in the partnership; but she survived her husband only until March of the next year, so that her participation in the firm in her new capacity was brief.

It was John's nephew, Lorenzo Delmonico, who assumed the burden of management. Twenty-nine years old, Lorenzo had mastered every turn of restaurant-keeping; his grasp of even the most trivial details of the business would become proverbial. In addition, he had an instinctive understanding of New York City, and unbounded confidence in its future. Peter Delmonico, verging on sixty, assigned control of the firm's operations entirely to Lorenzo, probably with a sense of relief; and soon after John's widow's death, he took Lorenzo into full partnership.

The New York City Directory of 1844 (compiled 1843) listed for the first time Lorenzo Delmonico's name, and also the name of the new partnership, "P.A. & L. Delmonico, hotel, 2 South William and 76 Broad St." "P.A." of course stood for Pierre Antoine, as Peter signed himself formally. The designation of the Beaver Street (2 South William Street) house as a "hotel" was the directory's mistake; only a restaurant was ever conducted there, although on the attic floors there were living quarters which at various times were occupied by members of the family.

2.

Lorenzo Delmonico came on the scene as general-in-chief just as the city was taking another exuberant step towards metropolitan stature. The Forties were a time of great tumultuousness, and also a time of civic achievements. The greatest of these was the completion of the Croton aqueduct system, which at last gave the city an ample supply of pure, wholesome water.

From early times, wells had been the only sources of potable water. Any citizen could dig a well upon payment of $10, but the water procured by this means was brackish. The Tea Water Pump, near the corner of Pearl and Chatham Streets, furnished water of a superior purity that was sold from door to door for a penny a gallon. In 1799 the Manhattan Company had been chartered by the State Legislature specifically to provide the city with a water system; but Aaron Burr, who lobbied the charter through the Legislature, had slyly inserted a clause to the effect that the company might invest its "surplus capital" in any lawful business. The directors of the company, once they received their charter, engaged in the business they had secretly had in mind all along — banking. To comply with the law, they did construct a reservoir in Reade Street that drew from the Collect, a pond on the site of the future Tombs prison, in Center Street. Pipes of hollow pine logs were laid through the lower part of the city; but the supply was never sufficient, and it became progressively inadequate as the city expanded.

The 1835 disaster had given impetus to a program that was then already under way, to bring water from the Croton River, forty miles above the city in Westchester County. The project was stupendous for that time; it required the construction of an enclosed aqueduct forty-five miles long, carried over twenty-five streams in Westchester County, and crossing the Harlem River on the High Bridge, built for that purpose.

Croton water was pure and it was abundant, and when it first flowed through the mains on July 4, 1842, there was rejoicing the like of which the oldest New Yorker could not recall. Parades, fountains spouting in City Hall Park and Union Square, at night fireworks and band concerts for the crowds, and a banquet for the bigwigs at the City Hotel (where nothing was drunk except Croton water, downed with fortitude and bravado, no doubt, if not with the relish of Rhenish) — these marked the festivities. As an ex-mayor and one of the city's most prominent men, Philip Hone drank a glass of the "wholesome temperance beverage" and certified it to be "clear and sweet and soft . . . well calculated to cool the palates and quench the thirst of New Yorkers, and to diminish the losses of the fire insurance companies." He did not go so far as to contemplate emptying his own cellar stocked with several thousand bottles of fine old sherries and Madeiras, except by drinking it dry. Yet he, like many others, believed that morality and virtue could be promoted by water drinking. It seemed indisputable that filth and crime were near akin, as were cleanliness and godliness.

Provided with a proper water supply, the city's upswing gained momentum, and Delmonico's prosperity boomed. Lorenzo now had younger members of the clan helping: Constant and Siro Delmonico were active at Beaver Street, John Longhi was showing promise at 76 Broad Street, and François had become the soul of the cafe, customers insisting that only his deft touch could impart the proper foam to their chocolate or bring out the full aroma of their *café au lait*. François had brought his wife, the former Anna Maria Proce, from Switzerland, and was striking roots in the New World. During the Forties his family increased steadily, and although two boys, Joseph and Theodore, died young and were placed beside their great-uncle in Peter's vault at St. Patrick's, there was another son, Charles Constant, who proved sturdier, and there were also two daughters, Rosa and Giovannina. Perpetuation of the line in America seemed assured.

Peter did not wish to bring his son Honoré into the business. Although Honoré was the same age as his cousin, Siro Delmonico, he showed no aptitude for restaurant-keeping, and Peter proposed to set him up as a gentleman of means, independent of business cares. Peter's property on Long Island was increasing in value rapidly, and there seemed every prospect than Honoré would inherit a fortune. Instead of apprenticing him to the business, therefore, Peter sent the lad to Georgetown University to acquire education and polish at that excellent Jesuit institution.

There was never any dearth of competent help to staff the establishment at Beaver and South William Streets. New York wages were higher than those paid in either London or Paris, and the Delmonicos paid above the average. Waiters in New York, in the Forties, earned $10 to $12 a month, with board and lodging. Boys were paid $6 to $7 a month, ordinary cooks $8 to $10, and dishwashers $4 to $5, with "keep." The work day was twelve to sixteen hours long. The Delmonicos matched and exceeded the wage standards of Paris for their principal employees. At Paris a *chef de cuisine* could command $16 a week in gold, but he provided his own living. A vegetable cook or a roast-meat specialist received a little less. More important than salaries, in both restaurants and hotels, were the perquisites claimed by the employees, according to well established custom. In the restaurant trade, the perquisite was termed the "bijou," or jewel, and it was recognized as legitimate. The "bijou" ranged from the percentages which a *chef de cuisine* collected from suppliers of food-stuffs, to the scullions' privilege of skimming the grease off the dishwater and selling it to soap-makers. There is no reason to suppose that the Delmonicos ran counter to accepted usage.

Lorenzo Delmonico's day was strictly divided. He understood that no matter how masterly a restaurant's service, its success in the long run depends on the quality of its food. Lorenzo did the daily marketing himself. An employee who spent thirty years in the cafe left a description of Lorenzo's invariable routine. Every day, at four o'clock in the morning, Lorenzo would go to the Washington and Fulton markets and pick out "what was good and fine, from meats and game, fish, fowl, terrapin, whatever was in season, and all that makes a fine table beautiful." At eight o'clock he returned to the restaurant in a cab, followed by others loaded with his purchases. He would drink a cup of black coffee, smoke a "Figaro cigar," then take a cab home and go to bed. "Every evening he came back, and sat with his friends, after taking a little supper, till twelve o'clock, when he went home again, like a clock work," said the man who checked this timetable for a quarter of a century.

Merely mentioning the "Figaro cigar" was a bit of under-playing, for, as Captain Marryat remarked of the way Americans drank, Lorenzo Delmonico's cigars were "quite a caution." Black as licorice, an inch thick and eight inches long, they were made to his specifications in Havana. While in the restaurant he smoked almost continually, and friends vowed that towards the close of his life he would consume as many as thirty of these cigars a day. His brother Siro acquired the habit and also was seldom seen without a cigar.

3.

When Lorenzo took over the management, the firm of Delmonico apparently was flourishing. The restaurant was briskly patronized and the Broad Street *hôtel garni* was never empty. However, the casting up of accounts necessitated by John Delmonico's sudden death revealed that although the income was regular and handsome, the partnership's debts exceeded its ready assets. To settle the estate, Peter proposed to sell some of the Williamsburg property. A buyer was found, a Frenchman named Guillame; but when Peter produced the deed to the farm, Guillame refused to go through with the transaction, contending that since John's infant daughter, Marie Josephine (her mother having also died), had inherited half of the property bought with partnership funds, the sale would not be binding without the infant's consent.

The dispute landed in the courts in a law suit that became a classic of the textbooks, and was taught to students for many years as an authority on the question of a partner's interest in firm property. *Delmonico vs. Guillame and Delmonico* finally ended in a decision whereby Guillame was compelled to buy the property, and Peter was obliged to account to his granddaughter for John's share of the partnership. Some of the farm land was retained, however, with the house and surrounding grounds, and Peter lived there in suburban respectability. The vexations of the long litigation strengthened his inclination to take his ease without striving for more wealth, and the way thus was opened for Lorenzo to bring his full talents to bear upon the advancement of the business.

4.

During the Forties, eating houses that catered to New Yorkers in general were of a sort to set off brilliantly any establishment that provided distinguished cookery and superior service. The city's growth was constantly outstripping its capacity to supply the citizens' needs. Business had rebounded from the 1837 stagnation, and as everything grew bigger the tempo of the town quickened; but with growth came also calculated carelessness. In the scramble for dollars that agitated rich and poor, high and humble, there were few persons active in mercantile or financial pursuits who were disposed to spend the midday in leisurely lunching. The gap between gobble-and-run makeshifts and the culinary enjoyments of the well appointed houses had widened as their customers multiplied. A writer for the *New York Weekly Tribune*, surveying the facts in 1848, reported his findings in a series of lively sketches entitled *New York in Slices*.

He estimated that some thirty thousand persons were fed in the downtown eating houses of New York every day. The engorging began punctually at noon, "and from that hour until three or four in the afternoon the havoc is immense. Not a fragment is left. The fare is generally bad enough — not nearly equal to that which the cook at the uptown house above Bleecker Street saves for the beggars (generally her own thirteen cousins, just come over). It is really wonderful how men of refined tastes and pampered habits, who at home are as fastidious as luxury and a delicate appetite can make them, find it in their hearts — or stomachs either — to gorge such messes of stringy meat and tepid vegetables, and to go about their business again under the fond delusion that they have dined.

"But custom, they say, does wonders; and it seems that the fear of losing it makes our merchant princes willing to put up with, and put down, warm swill in lieu of soup, perspiring joints for delicate entrees, and corn meal and molasses instead of *meringues à la crème à la rose.*"

"There are three distinct classes of eating houses [in New York]," this critic went on, "and each has its model or type. Linnaeus would probably classify them as the Sweeneyorum, the Browniverous, and the Delmonican. The Sweeneyorum is but an extension downward of the Browniverous. The chief difference to be noted between the two is that while at Brown's the waiters do actually pass by you within hail now and then, at Sweeney's no such phenomenon ever by any possibility occurs."

Sweeney's "sixpenny eating house" was at 11 Ann Street, and the proprietor, Daniel Sweeney, achieved slippery fame as the father of cheap restaurants. At this emporium of mass mastication a plate of roast beef, pork, or veal could be had for six cents up; rice or corn mush with milk cost nine cents; and fried potatoes or "extra bread" cost three.

"The room is laid out like the floor of a church, with tables and benches for four in place of pews," this picture in pewter unfolded. "Along the aisles (of Greece, if you judge by the smell) are ranged, at stated intervals, the attentive waiters, who receive the dishes ('small plate sixpence, large plate shillin') as they are cut off by the man at the helm, and distribute them to either side with surprising dexterity and precision. Sometimes a nice bit of 'rosegoose, tender' may be seen flying down the aisle without the original wings, followed closely in playful sport by a 'small plate bilebeef vegetables,' till both arrive at their destinations.

"At Brown's we get a bill of fare, with the 'extras' all honestly marked off and priced in the margin. But at Sweeney's we save our sixpence and dispense with superfluities. The bill of fare is delivered by a man at the door, regularly engaged for that purpose, and is . . ." Well, frankly, it was illegible and unintelligible; the writer confined his comment to, "it was certainly as clear and distinct as General Zachary Taylor's political opinions, and does away with a great deal of lying in print."

Sweeney's customers, swarming there to get something to chew on at a rock-bottom price, were heterogeneous: one might espy a professor of languages "dining cheek by jowl with a hodman off duty, or a blackleg from Park Row seated opposite the police officer whose manifest duty it will be one of these days to take him to quod — unless he should happen to have money enough to pay for being let go."

4.

The contrast to this dyspeptic hurlyburly was the type of restaurant available to a limited number of New Yorkers; the "expensive and aristocratic restaurant, of which Delmonico's is the only complete specimen in the United States . . . equal in every respect in its appointments and attendance, as well as the quality and execution of its dishes, to any similar establishment in Paris.

"To dine at Delmonico's, as a correspondent once said of traveling in Europe, two things are requisite — money and French. Of the latter a little will answer; but the more you have of the former the better off you are, as well at Delmonico's as elsewhere."

The reporter then gave a detailed description of the Beaver Street "Citadel," its service and its patrons. The first-floor eating room he passed by, as "appropriated to general and indifferent customers, who come in a hurry and must return to their business as soon as possible." It was in the upstairs dining room that the true aura of the institution could be felt. What impressed one first was the immaculate, intelligent, swift service. "The waiters have been regularly trained to their profession, and, without seeming to observe you, are always at your elbow just at the moment when you are beginning to think about wishing for something. They listen to you with a grave attention which

assures you that you are to receive exactly what you have ordered, and in the shortest possible time."

This phenomenon having produced a preliminary gratification, one was in a mood to order dinner ("and we don't suppose
you to be such a booby as to require any instructions as to what
you will eat"). After that, one might sit back and glance around
at one's neighbors.

"There on your right is an elderly Frenchman dining with his
son . . . At the next table behind them, in an attitude of listless
self-complacency, sits a tall, striking-looking man . . . He has
evidently just finished his breakfast, for there stands the gigantic
chocolate cup, deep enough for him, long as he is, to drown
himself in, and before him lie the delicate remains of the *oeufs
en miroir* with which he has been trifling. Although still under
twenty-five, he is evidently a thoroughbred man of the world
— an epicure, an amateur, a gallant, a dilettante, a critic." This
personage was Richard Grant White, music critic and man
of letters, one of whose sons would be Stanford White.

At another table might be Nathaniel Parker Willis, scribbler
of newspaper gossip, conversing with Parke Godwin, editor of
the *Evening Post* and inveterate joiner — "an Associationist, a
Swedenborgian, a Homeopathist, a Hydropathist, a . . . we
know not what." A few writers, a few wits, an actor or two,
and merchants predominantly; solid comfortable men, who
"dine, pay, go away — bargain, sell — do so tomorrow — and
the next day and the next — from month to month and year to
year, never changing, never growing old, never dislocating
their jaws nor jerking their heads across the room while speaking" — that was the foundation of Delmonico's prosperity in
the 1840's and later. Talent and elegance lent a panache of
smartness to wealth and solidarity — the same day after day,
month after month, year after year. Such a patronage is not
fickle, and Lorenzo Delmonico drew and held its loyal appreciation. In return, he provided unvaryingly what they wanted at
a price they were prepared to pay.

5.

The social position of Delmonico's became clear-cut during the decade at the "Citadel" immediately following its construction. It was a preferred setting for balls, assemblies, and other public entertainments. The upstairs dining room, with its parquetry floor, made a ballroom of handsome proportions, and every catering facility was on the premises. Until well into the 1850's, the Beaver Street house was in demand for social gatherings, and Samuel Ward shone in many a dance at the place which he recalled as being "as gay as the maidens of that day were graceful and attractive, and its young squires gallant and spirited." It was then, he said, that dancing became seriously cultivated by the bloods and debutantes.

Another development was the emergence of Delmonico's as a place for family dinners. A retired United States Army officer in 1929 remembered being taken to Delmonico's in Beaver Street when he was a boy. The family lived not far away, near Pearl Street and the Battery, and he never forgot his enchantment with Delmonico's French pastries. As he described the scene: "At noon business men came and went like bees into and out of the marble-floored lobby, where stood, immediately at the right, a great press with wide but shallow drawers, each with cakes of its kind, surrounded by talking and gesticulating customers untrammeled by waiter or cashier as they helped themselves." Now and then his parents took him to dinner in one of the private rooms upstairs — a room that had "a bewitching wallpaper, with small, gaily colored pictures, no two alike, applied after the manner of decalcomania."

This family patronage created a bond of intimacy between the proprietors of the house and many of their customers. George Templeton Strong, who had been a regular frequenter of Delmonico's since his first cup of chocolate there, considered it proper, upon his engagement to Eleanor Ruggles in 1848, to carry two wedding invitations to Lorenzo Delmonico personally. "Quite took his breath away with the news," Strong wrote with satisfaction in his diary.

The well-fed bustle nearly came to an end on the night of July 19, 1845. Shortly after midnight, a tremendous explosion occurred in a building on New Street. People were knocked out of their beds, and Staten Islanders thought it was an earthquake. In a few minutes fires broke out in half a dozen buildings; they raged all night, sweeping down Beaver Street almost to William, destroying everything on New Street, annihilating buildings on Broad Street from number 20 clear to the river, and eating their way along the south side of South William Street almost to the junction with Beaver. Leaping across Broadway, the flames destroyed the fine homes extending from Morris Street past Bowling Green to the Battery. Even the Croton water supply could not cope with such a conflagration, and three hundred buildings were lost before the fire burned itself out.

The "Citadel" escaped, but narrowly; cooks and waiters had spent the night on the roof, beating out embers and wetting down the walls, and the blaze was stopped just short of the building. But 76 Broad Street was demolished. Again there was widespread distress in the commercial world, and several insurance companies went bankrupt; but again the city rebounded from disaster. Twenty-four days after the fire, Philip Hone, wandering through the ruins, where his insurance investments had vanished in the holocaust, remarked new stores rising on every hand, and one in South William Street already completed as high as the eaves.

In this crisis Lorenzo Delmonico reacted as his uncle John had in 1835: instead of repining, he branched out boldly, confident that he read New York's future aright. He contracted with Gardiner O. Howland to erect a hotel on the corner of Broadway and Morris Street, just above Bowling Green, on the three Broadway lots numbered 21, 23, and 25, and took a ten-year lease on the building at an annual rental of $15,000. The work went forward so expeditiously that on May 27, 1846, "P.A. & L. Delmonico" advertised in the newspapers that their "new hotel in Broadway, corner of Morris St.," would be opened on the first of June. "No pains have been spared to render it one of the most comfortable in the city, and persons in search of a permanent home, as well as strangers merely passing by, will find all their wants attended to with the strictest attention," the announcement read.

This modest notification appeared amid headlines telling of battles in Mexico, where General Taylor's troops were making history at Palo Alto and Resaca de la Palma. Business was booming, and contractors were getting rich.

Number 25 Broadway was the only real hotel ever operated by the Delmonicos. It brought no satisfaction to Peter Delmonico; according to Sam Ward, he never even entered the place; he was averse to new ventures. Ward wrote of the aging Peter: "He was punctual and methodical in his presence at the cafe and the performance of his supervising duties. But after the hour of noon he would accept the challenge of any friend to a game of dominoes, in which he excelled. Towards five P.M. he took his absinthe and went home, where the improvements progressing around his garden, and the certainty that his cheaply bought acres would soon become streets yielding him a thousandfold, not only made any misgiving impossible as to the future, but imparted the rosy glow of gratified hopes to his reveries. The 'Citadel' and his Williamsburg possessions amply satisfied his ambitions, and his motto was, 'Let us have peace.'"

Peace with comfort, of course, for no Delmonico ever decried prosperity.

Assured that the house of Delmonico was in safe hands with Lorenzo in charge, in 1848 Peter sold his interest in the business to his nephew, and retired. This made Lorenzo the sole owner. The grand days of Delmonico's fame were to come under his guidance.

Part Two

LORENZO THE GREAT

CHAPTER I

EPICURES AND
ELEGANCE

LORENZO DELMONICO did not believe in partners. He believed that any enterprise, to prosper, should be under the direction and control of one executive, and as far as Delmonico's was concerned, he was that executive. He had assistants and managers trained in his methods and obedient to his wishes, but from roughly 1845 until 1881 he was the central administrator, and in himself virtually personified the institution that bore his name. In the annals of the family he richly deserves to be styled Lorenzo the Great, for it was he who (with the able seconding of his brothers and his nephew) lifted Delmonico's into international renown.

About the time Lorenzo was assuming responsibility, two entries, at dates only seven weeks apart, in the journal or daybook kept by G. T. Strong, took note of two parallel streams of development along which New York itself was moving — a sharp increase in the number of its wealthy families, and a simultaneous increase in the number of its poor. These twin trends boded both well and ill for the city's future, and the brief observations of young Strong might have served as warnings of problems and pitfalls that would vex the city for years to come, and at the same time would give it greatness.

On November 4, 1845, Strong wrote: "The Boston steamer in today brings news of the total failure, or something nearly as bad, of the potato crop in Ireland. A frightful amount of misery will be caused by it, I'm afraid, coupled as it is with bad harvests in England."

Thus was registered the first premonitory shock felt in New

York from that upheaval which would pour into the tenements of the East Side a horde of starving Irish — a flood that no force or foresight of the period was capable of coping with, or diverting into productive channels, except after incalculable distress and years of time.

Along with this impending tidal wave of immigration, another, born of the exuberant times, was gathering force, and it, too, was reflected in Strong's diary. On December 23 and 24 of the same year he recorded his attendance at two balls. The first, at Mrs. Mary Jones's, the diarist termed a "very splendid affair — 'the ball of the season' . . . Two houses open, standing supper table — 'dazzling array of beauty and fashions.' Polka for the first time brought under my inspection. It's a kind of insane Tartar jig performed to a disagreeable music of an uncivilized character." The next night found him at "Mrs. Baker's rout — or whatever its name may be in the dialect of the élite." There was "a jam unprecedented, the invitations out being reported by some as one thousand and by others as 2,500." He got another dose of the dizzy waltz and the discordant polka, and came to the conclusion (by no means original with him) that the city's rich had a great deal of time and money to spend upon frivolous amusements. And that would be another trend of the city in the tumultuous years ahead.

2.

Delmonico's Hotel on Broadway was successful from the start. Favored by visiting celebrities, especially Europeans, it was the first considerable hotel in New York to be conducted successfully on the European plan — all meals à la carte, no "ordinary," and guests paying separately for room and board. The New York Hotel, which had been erected in 1844 at the tremendous cost of $500,000, had adopted this system and was managed by a French cook, S. B. Monnot; but it was so far uptown — at 721 Broadway, between Washington Place and Waverly Place — it was slow to attract customers, despite the allurements of six stories of height, two hundred rooms, and the first hall baths. It would catch on later as the headquarters of aristocratic Southerners.

An innovation of the Delmonico Hotel reflected Lorenzo's sensitivity to changing public tastes. At 25 Broadway the cafe, on the Parisian model, was for the first time overshadowed by the bar. Oldtimers like Sam Ward deplored such a concession to the hurrying tempo of the times, and lamented that "there was no display of confectionery in glass cases, or of pastry, upon the counter of the coffee room of Morris Street. The gloomy American system of tippling at the bar, like railway passengers tossing off a glass of ale during the 'ten minutes for refreshment,' left the marble tables, at which friends used to sit and chat as well as drink, comparatively unoccupied." However, he absolved Lorenzo Delmonico of any personal deterioration in taste; a bar was preferred by American customers, and the minority clinging to the old ways had no option but to yield as gracefully as they might.

3.

Among the many famous names on the registers of the Delmonico Hotel was that of Jenny Lind, who landed at New York in 1850 to begin her triumphal tour under the ballyhooing of Phineas T. Barnum. New Yorkers serenaded her, paid fantastic prices for tickets to hear her sing, gaped at her gowns, and gossiped about her piety. Whenever she entered or left Delmonico's there was a crowd on the sidewalk to cheer her. However, the legend that she sent her coloratura cascading across Bowling Green in *al fresco* free concerts is contrary to the fact; Barnum, who was all business, saw to it that people paid to hear his profitable nightingale.

Another eminent frequenter of the hotel, one who did much to authenticate Delmonico's gastronomical supremacy, was General Winfield Scott. Long a patron of the restaurant, Scott reserved rooms at the hotel upon his return from the war in

Mexico in 1852. (Another Army officer, a lieutenant of dragoons as obscure as Scott was renowned, made straight for Delmonico's Hotel when he landed at New York early in 1850, bringing the first official report of the gold being scooped out of the streams of California; his name was William Tecumseh Sherman, and in *his* days of greatness he would be a pillar of Delmonico's.)

Winfield Scott was without a peer as a gourmet on the American continent, in his own estimation, at least; and he certainly was not without qualifications for such a position. To his attainments as a soldier, his contemporaries and posterity have rendered justice, and on the fields of gastronomy he was no less all-conquering. Vain and pompous in manner, although a genuine hero, he rated his mastery of every aspect of the art and science of alimentation fully equal to his prowess as a strategist.

During a stay in Paris just after the fall of Napoleon, he had delved into the secrets of the three superlative restaurants of that era — Véry's, Le Rocher de Cancale, and Les Trois Frères Provençaux — the same academies of gastronomic learning where Sam Ward would pursue his researches a few years later. Scott stood over six feet three and was magnificently proportioned; and his appetite was as awesome as his presence. Brought up near Petersburg, in Virginia, his introduction to the higher pleasures of the table had come from a refugee from Haiti, an old Frenchman who dwelt in a cottage in the town. Too poor to afford a servant, this epicure cooked and carved for himself. Young Scott striking his fancy, the veteran often invited him to share his simple but delicious dinners. A partition, about five feet high, shut off the kitchen space from the dining table in the tiny cottage; and Scott, while waiting for the dinner to be cooked, could see his friend's head bobbing up and down behind this barrier as he supervised the saucepans. The food being cooked, the old gentleman discarded his apron, pulled on a rusty dress coat, and coming to the other side of the partition dispensed the hospitality of his house with grace and dignity.

"It was then and there," Scott told his aide, Lieutenant Erasmus Darwin Keyes, "that I received my first and best lessons in cooking, and in conduct at the head of the table."

Scott's duties took him and his aide on inspection tours to all corners of the nation, and often Keyes was favored with discourses upon the importance of gastronomy to one's own, and to the country's, well-being. His chief's culinary erudition and trencherman capacity alike caused the younger man to marvel, for the general was equally at home in the theory and the practice of eating wisely and well. Wrote Keyes, decades afterward: "I know of no flesh of beasts, or edible fishes, or fowl, or herb, or root, or grain, the preparation of which for food was not many times the subject of [Scott's] conversation."

Fanny Elssler's pleasant surprise at the high quality of the food served at the American Hotel in 1840 was due in part to General Scott. The American Hotel was operated by W. D. Cozzens, who had formerly run Tammany Hall, the hotel that gave its name to the Democratic organization which met there. Cozzens also conducted a hotel at West Point that was much frequented by New Yorkers.

About 1837, Scott, on a visit to West Point, put up at Cozzens's hotel, and growled about the bread — "not fit for dogs to eat." Volunteering to show the baker how to turn out a wholesome article, the general marched to the bakehouse, issued his orders, and went away. The next summer, again visiting the Point, he tried the improved bread at Cozzens's urging. "Not as bad as it was," he gave his verdict; "now it *is* fit for the kennel!" Another trip to the bakehouse and a post-graduate drilling of the baker produced the desired result; and from then on Cozzens's hotels were noted for their fine bread. And Keyes could testify from his experience that previous to that time the bread served generally throughout America was "vile."

A favorite vegetable with General Scott was the Swedish turnip, although he seldom found it cooked to suit his taste — neither too much nor too little. Once, when returning from the Northwest, he and Keyes stopped at a hotel in Cleveland where the turnips were cooked to perfection. Taking one on his plate, the general regarded his aide earnestly, and tapping the turnip with his fork, proclaimed with all the majesty at his command, "Young gentleman, we are now in a civilized community!"

As a Virginian, the general was particular about the hams he ate; none would do but those cured near Petersburg, taken from hogs that had run wild in the woods. Every winter he would have a barrel of these hams, packed in the ashes of the smokehouse fires, shipped to his quarters, and none others were permitted on his sideboard.

Fond of fish, he tried every variety that came under his notice, and there were only two kinds that he deemed unfit to eat — porgies and gar. The whitefish of the Great Lakes he especially prized — above all, those taken from the upper lakes, Huron and Superior. The rules for serving whitefish he laid down with military exactitude: "They must be cooked *done*, and immediately rolled up, one after another, in a napkin, doubled and heated almost to scorching. Then they are to be served and eaten immediately, unrolling the napkin as the fish are wanted." When in appetite, he was capable of finishing off an entire roll of whitefish prepared in this manner.

Like other epicures, Scott ranked the canvasback duck of Chesapeake Bay and the Maryland terrapin as the supreme native delicacies. His table eccentricities were the talk of his subordinates. Keyes once offered to wager with several of the younger officers that if they would invite the hero to dinner, and serve terrapin prepared by his favorite cook, he would without fail do two things. First, leaning his left elbow on the table, and taking up some of the terrapin on his fork, he would hold it about six inches above his plate, and exclaim: "This is the best food vouchsafed by Providence to man!" Second, while leaning on the table in the same attitude, he would silently pour wine from one glass into another. Why he did this, no one knew. Keyes could get no bet: the officers knew their commander too well.

Winfield Scott and Lorenzo Delmonico were friends over a long course of years, in a personal as well as in an alimentary sense. The general detested dining alone, and was known to invite a perfect stranger to his table and pay for his dinner, in order to have company. Not infrequently Lorenzo Delmonico shared the old warrior's table, but in the relationship of a friend dining with a friend, and Scott's loyalty to Delmonico's ceased only with his death.

4.

The surge of the city towards the northern reaches of Manhattan was speeded by the rapid filling up of the lower sections with shoals of immigrants, Irish and German. A new center of social elegance sprang up around Lafayette Place, Astor Place, Bond and Great Jones Streets, and in the blocks on Broadway just below fashionable Grace Church, at Eighth Street. Lorenzo Delmonico observed the trend and felt that it would continue. There were many indications of this. For example, on January 2, 1852, the committee appointed by the Board of Aldermen to study "alternative proposals for laying out a new park in the upper part of the city" submitted its report. This set forth the belief of the committee that "the city of New York is now, and probably will ever be, the metropolis of America; it is already one of the first cities of the world in point of population, wealth, commercial importance, and beauty." What the committee foresaw in the near future was plainly put: "The island city, steadily increasing at a ratio of 10% per annum in population, must soon be closely inhabited throughout its entire length."

This was a daring prediction at a time when northern Manhattan was half a day's journey away, over a bone-cracking, rutted road that ran through the straggling village of Harlem and across Washington Heights.

The choice before the aldermen was between a tract of land located centrally between the two rivers, and an irregular plot on the East Side, extending from Sixty-sixth to Seventy-fifth Streets, from Third Avenue to the East River. The more central location was preferred by the committee because of its accessibility from both sides of the island, and because of its greater acreage, which would give wider scope for landscaping, and would permit the inclusion of a winding carriage drive several miles long, along which the opulent of the city might display their tastes in horses, women, and apparel.

Such straws in the wind coincided with Lorenzo Delmonico's analysis, and in 1856 he made a move which was reprobated by some of his customers as foolhardy — he moved uptown with the tide, to the corner of Broadway and Chambers Street, opposite the City Hall. In vain friends warned that he would be losing the best part of his trade by deserting lower Manhattan and the patronage of men congregating near the Exchanges; these men were too busy to take the time to journey a mile farther north for luncheon — and besides, who would buck the traffic on Broadway at noon?

Lorenzo Delmonico listened to the well-intentioned counsels, but he read the portents differently. It seemed to him that plainly an era had closed and another was opening. On the national stage the scene-shifters had been active: where, in 1856, were the three giants of the Senate whose voices had helped to guide the nation for half a century? Webster, Calhoun, Clay — all were gone, and new men had taken their places, men of a different generation. Webster had been a guest of Delmonico's (although he preferred the Astor House), but Webster in 1856 was a memory. And in New York the new forces were at work; business was developing beyond the immediate vicinity of the "Citadel," where brokers and bankers poured a rivulet of gold daily into his cash box; he merely proposed to cater to the new generation in a new location, and perhaps add a fresh clientele to the one of whose loyalty he was sure.

Sam Ward, in prose almost apocalyptic, recorded Lorenzo's pondering; picturing him as "the young Napoleon of our future army of restaurateurs" who looked out from the "Citadel" and "saw as in a vision the unfolding resources of the mighty West attracting the industries and population of Europe, and based his calculations upon one of the few categories in which the rule of three may be trusted as a guide to human fortunes. 'Man must eat to live — the population of this city must infallibly grow by the law of arithmetical progression — *ergo*, while I continue to purvey attractively for their primary necessities, my business and gains must increase in the same ratio.' "

How highly Ward rated Lorenzo Delmonico's prescience may be judged by his bracketing the restaurateur with three other New Yorkers who reaped immense fortunes by providing basic necessities in a constantly growing market — John Jacob Astor, who built houses; A.T. Stewart, who sold clothing; and Cornelius Vanderbilt, who provided transportation.

"At the end of two lusters," wrote Sam, "the new outlaying fort [number 25 Broadway] had achieved its mission and an expanding city required a house of refection above the Park," by which he meant City Hall Park. "Its population, numbering but one hundred seventy-five thousand when the 'Citadel' was completed, had increased from three hundred seventy-one thousand at the inauguration of the Morris Street corner, to six hundred twenty-nine thousand in 1855, when Lorenzo rented and fitted up the corner at Chambers Street and Broadway which had formed part of the old Irving House; where John Howard made (and retired with) a rapid fortune out of the returning California gold rush Argonauts." Sam's population figures were approximately correct.

Lorenzo Delmonico signed a twenty-one year lease of the property mentioned at an annual rental of $25,000, later raised to $30,000. The Delmonico Hotel on lower Broadway was closed, to reopen shortly under different management, operated by Paran Stevens, a Bostonian who had hotel interests in the South. As the Stevens House it would become enshrined in New York's affections. This was reflected in lines tossed off by the poetizer Godfrey Saxe, often quoted by after-dinner speakers of the period. The following is a sample:

> And now Mr. Brown
> Was fairly in town,
> In that part of the city they used to call 'down',
> Not far from the spot of ancient renown
> As being the scene
> Of the Bowling Green . . .
> And he stopped at an inn that is known very well,
> Delmonico's once, now the Stevens Hotel;
> And to venture a pun which I think rather witty,
> There is no better inn in this inn-famous city.

Against such puns the Stevens House remained proof until 1919, when it was torn down to make way for the Cunard Building on its site.

5.

Not everybody believed that Lorenzo was taking a rash step. Hardly had he signed the lease when he was offered $75,000 for it; but the renovations were under way, and he clung to his bargain. The Irving House, on the northwest corner of the intersection, had indeed earned a fortune for its original proprietor. Built in 1848, it was the first in New York to boast of "bridal suites," and its furniture was reputed to have cost $150,000. Lounging around its entrance any day might be seen a cross-section of the floating population of the city — prosperous merchants in town on buying expeditions, Southerners puffing Havanas, slouching Western men straight from the gold fields. Across Broadway rose the six-story marble "dry-goods emporium" of A. T. Stewart, where the richness of the stock startled visitors. A young woman from England was quite overcome at Stewart's in 1854 by the sight of "lace collars at 40 guineas each, and flounces of Valenciennes lace, half a yard deep, at 120 guineas the flounce! Damasks and brocades for curtains and chairs at almost fabulous prices . . . I saw some brocade embroidered in gold to the thickness of half an inch, some of which had been supplied to the St. Nicholas Hotel at £9 a yard!"

This St. Nicholas Hotel was another eye-opener for European travelers. Completed five years after the Irving House, it stood on the west side of Broadway between Broome and Spring Streets, a dozen blocks north of Chambers Street. Sir John Acton, the future historian, marveled at its mirrored dining room, where forty waiters maneuvered in uniform and unison at the headwaiter's command; at its six hundred rooms and three hundred employees, its conveniences and its elegance. Another Britisher exclaimed in letters home that "every chimney-piece and table slab is of marble . . . every carpet is of velvet pile . . . chair covers and curtains are made of silk or satin-damask . . . the looking-glasses are in frames worthy of Windsor Castle . . . the embroidery on the mosquito nettings itself might be exhibited to royalty!"

Crowded Broadway caused that young lady from London who was startled by Stewart's even more amazement. "A journey from one end to the other of this marvelous street is a work of time and difficulty," she wrote home. "Pack the traffic of the Strand and Cheapside into Oxford Street and still you will not have an idea of the crush on Broadway. There are streams of scarlet and yellow omnibuses racing in the more open parts, and locking each other's wheels in the narrower — there are helpless females deposited in a sea of slippery mud, condemned to run a gauntlet between cartwheels and horses' hoofs — there are loaded stages hastening to and from the big hotels — carts and wagons laden with merchandise — and 'Young Americans' driving fast-trotting horses, edging in and out among the crowd — wheels are locked, horses tumble down, and persons pressed for time are distracted. Occasionally the whole traffic of the street comes to a deadlock, in consequence of some obstruction or crowd, there being no policeman at hand with his incessant command, 'Move on!' "

This human tide flowing past his new location Lorenzo Delmonico viewed with satisfaction. The law courts were just across the way, commerce filled the streets all around. Henceforth, the "Citadel" would supply luncheon in the financial district, and the Chambers Street establishment would become a separate stronghold, with its own patronage.

The premises were fitted up to deal with the different classes and purses that filled the neighborhood. As Sam Ward saw the setting in memory: "While dry goods clerks and lawyers' scribes lunched at one counter in the outer room, contractors, aldermen, and pothouse politicians drank *à l'Americaine* at the opposite one. Within, there was a great dining room for the small dealers and the more thrifty of the large ones from the neighboring streets; and the really superb and luminous *salle à manger* overhead was frequented by men of distinction in every pursuit and profession, save the Church." There, from the day of opening, one might see civic leaders like A.T. Stewart himself, or John Van Buren, the hard-drinking, arrogantly handsome son of the former President, or the Irish lawyer and orator, Charles O'Conor, who had married into Knickerbocker society, or a host of similar celebrities.

The restaurant was the resort of a busy, haranguing, expansive crowd at midday, while at night a different type of customer filled the tables. "The stock broker exuberant with a successful coup essayed for the nonce to become a *viveur* under the tutelage of some traveled client. The banker brought his latest *accredité* to taste one of those magnums of Château Margaux which had acquired under our climate a velvetiness unknown to its own growers. The journalist, the political tadpole, and the embryo statesman were seen, each dipping his nose into the soup. Henry J. Raymond (founder of the *New York Times*) was a liberal patron of the new Church of the Dietetic Evangel. At his table ate and sat the migratory senator, and the sages of local or State politics." This was Ward's recollection of the evening scene. In one corner might be detected the "wily and witty" William R. Travers, whose stammering *bons mots* were repeated around town; nearby a smooth-talking broker might be attempting to convince an investor that, "excellent as the dinner was and rare the wines, there were higher joys to be tasted in the realization of the little 'corner' he was nursing in the Street."

Socially the place also caught on, almost at once. Chambers Street was closer to the new fashionable residential district than was Beaver Street; one could stroll of an evening down Broadway from Bond Street, and pass nothing but fine houses, handsomely appointed shops, and massive public buildings. Chambers Street became the place for social dining. The politicians and the law clerks might usurp it during the day, but in the evening the "best people" took over — people who knew how to dine. True, other restaurants provided good cuisine, but Delmonico's had a cachet of its own. No competitor could match its superb service, and if the prices were high, the ability to pay was not lacking. And there was no distinction of names or numbers in the quality of the service. "The solitary gourmet was as sedulously cared for as were the luxurious parties in the private rooms," Sam Ward testified. "Young bloods from the New York Club and old stagers from the Union revelled, the one in truffles and Burgundy, the others in simpler viands and less gouty wines; while the merry laugh of well-matronized maidens musically thrilled the air." So ran his memories. "Some traveler has said that our best American hotels were the 'palaces of the people,' and he might have added that Delmonico's was their Paradise." The Chambers Street house in Ward's opinion "combined the resources of any six of the most famous hotels . . . and I should hazard little in wagering that during the . . . years of its joyous existence it took in more money than any six of its contemporaries in Christendom.

"Thus," concluded he, "by the spacious conveniences of their new location, a more varied and brilliant career was opened to the second generation of the family."

6.

Family cooperation was a main prop in carrying through Lorenzo's new enterprise. Siro Delmonico was in charge at Chambers Street, assisted by young Charles Delmonico, the son of François. That older brother of Lorenzo had succumbed in 1853, and was interred in the Delmonico vault at St. Patrick's. Constant Delmonico, the fourth brother, had had charge of the Delmonico Hotel, and when that place was closed he was put in command at the "Citadel." Supervising all operations, and performing the marketing, was Lorenzo Delmonico.

The care of François's children had devolved upon Lorenzo as acting head of the clan in America. The girls, Rosa and Giovannina, were receiving a careful education, while Charles, although still in his teens, was already showing remarkable aptitude as a restaurateur, and Lorenzo listened with respect to his nephew's suggestions.

Charles was responsible for a policy which in later years he credited with having contributed as much as any single factor to Delmonico's success. The sort of man who patronized Delmonico's, Charles said, was not the sort that liked to be dunned about a bill; so the rule was laid down that bills should be presented only when a customer asked for one. At the same time, Delmonico's became the easiest place in town to get credit. Should a customer conspicuously neglect to request a statement of his account around the first of each month, Delmonico's managed to dispense with his presence and his business by a simple but effective method of blacklisting.

The blacklist also was credited to Charles. The existence of this private credit rating and social directory was never acknowledged, and there is no record of any person's claiming to have seen an actual list of names. However, the reality of the blacklist was never denied, either, and in any case its effectiveness was undisputed.

The way it worked was insidiously simple. If a customer had the misfortune to be "listed," whether as a dead-beat or because of brawling and disorderly conduct (Delmonico's would not countenance rowdyism, and anybody who was unable to carry his liquor was eventually carried out for good), the victim would not be informed. On the contrary, the next time he appeared he would be welcomed with special suavity, ushered to a table with every sign of consideration, and an obsequious waiter would take his order with flattering attention. As a public restaurant, Delmonico's could not refuse to serve any person who came in looking respectable; but in the case of a "listed" undesirable, nothing would happen after he had given his order. This alone was odd in a house where dispatch was the essence of the service. The unwanted guest might sit and sit, waiting for his dinner, meanwhile being subjected to the subtle torture of inhaling tantalizing aromas from the food being served at the tables around him, but nothing arrived to appease his hunger. He might summon the headwaiter, who would listen to the complaint with expressions of sympathy, would take the order afresh, and move off in the direction of the kitchen "to see what might be the trouble." Still nothing would happen, except more waiting. If the luckless customer at length demanded to see the proprietor, one of the Delmonicos would purr with sympathy and depart in the direction of the chef's office "to see what might be the trouble." By this time the most obtuse victim would be smelling a rat in place of *poulet roti*, and gathering himself up, the luckless wight would stalk out of Delmonico's, never to darken its Pompeiian-pillared portico again. Men incurring this rebuff, it was said, were marked with a social stigma almost as ineradicable as that attached to being caught cheating at cards, in one's own club.

CHAPTER II

A MASTER MOVE
AND THE MASTER CHEF

LORENZO DELMONICO'S CARE for the offshoots of his family found new outlets while he was bringing the business to greater stability and expansiveness. In 1854 he married Clemence Chanon Miège, a widow with two grown daughters. These daughters, Marie Zéphine Romaine and Aline Augustine Clemence Miège, Lorenzo considered as his own, and after Aline was married to Georges Renault, their son and daughter would become Lorenzo's grandchildren in effect.

Clemence Chanon was the daughter of the director of the porcelain factory at Sèvres, France, where she was born. She had come to America at sixteen, and was married shortly thereafter to Pierre Augustus Miège, an importer of fine chinaware. At his death she was left a comfortable income, and devoted herself to activities of the French community in New York. At the time of marriage to Lorenzo Delmonico she was thirty-eight years old (three years his junior), and in her habits and character thoroughly French. For a dozen years the Delmonico home would be at 100 East Fifteenth Street.

The Delmonicos also had remained active in the affairs of the French colony. They had helped generously in organizing the city's first French congregation, St. Vincent de Paul, in 1841, and a close friend of Peter Delmonico was the Rev. Anthony Cauvin, a priest from Nice, France, who founded Our Lady of Grace in Hoboken. This parish Father Cauvin built up from a small Sunday school, in which among his assistants was a Davis family; James Davis, Jr., taught the boys the catechism, and Rose Anna Maria Davis, the girls. Through Father

Cauvin the Brooklyn Delmonicos and the Davises became acquainted, with the result that in the mid 1850's Honoré, Peter's son and heir, married Rose Anna Davis.

Peter was serene in retirement. Like a prudent Swiss, he prepared for the inevitable, and in 1859 drew up his will. How excellently he had prospered in his adopted land was revealed when the testament was read after his death on April 10, 1860. To his granddaughter, Marie Josephine, the only child of his brother John and his daughter Marie, Peter left the stone dwelling in Williamsburg, "with the lots of land upon which same is erected and its appurtenances, gardens, stables, and outbuildings situated in Delmonico Place . . . with the household furniture, plate, pictures, and books and other articles of housekeeping, family use or ornament, and all my horses, carriages, cows, stable furniture, and implements contained therein." Williamsburg had been absorbed into the city of Brooklyn in 1855, and this property, enormously increased in value since the time of its purchase, was the legacy of John Delmonico's daughter; the only restriction imposed being that Peter's wife, Catherine, should retain the use of the house and grounds during her lifetime.

Marie Josephine Delmonico had become the wife of Frank Otard, as he was known in New York, although in Europe he used his title, Baron Otard de la Grange. He was connected with the cognac house of that name, and although he and his wife made their home in Switzerland, both were much in America and remained in close touch with the New York Delmonicos.

Other clauses of Peter's will divided property in Brooklyn among his children — lots of land ("thirty-eight lots of land as designated" . . . "five lots of Myrtle Avenue" . . . "the lot on Flushing Avenue" . . . "to my son Honoré six lots of land forming a triangle in the block bounded by Throop and Tompkins Avenues and Floyd and Stock Streets") and remittance of numerous debts ("to my daughter Annette, wife of Jean Canavello, I also remit the debt which she herself owes and amounting to the sum of $2,140, or thereabouts" . . . "I give and bequeath to my daughter-in-law Rosanna [sic], the wife of Honoré, the mortgage which I hold upon the house of her father in Hoboken, New Jersey, for the sum of $3,000 and accrued interest"). There were gifts to Father Cauvin and his church, and bonds and mortgages in great number left to children and grandchildren.

To Lorenzo, Peter left all his "real and personal estate in Switzerland . . . subject to payment by him of all claims against the church of Mairengo." One mortgage he reserved from the general distribution — the $50,000 mortgage he held on the restaurant property at Beaver and South William Streets; the interest and income of this mortgage he directed to be paid to his wife, and after her death to his son Honoré and Rose Anna Davis Delmonico.

The will was that of a man of affluence and conservatism, and it attested how far the family had come from the deal tables of the little pastry shop on William Street. Peter's will was drawn by the attorney who would counsel the Delmonicos in their private and business affairs for years, S. L. M. Barlow, one of New York's wealthiest and politically most influential citizens, and a gourmet of renown. Peter's choice of executors stressed the bonds of mutual trust and exclusiveness that knit the Delmonicos so tightly; Charles Delmonico, Peter's grandnephew, and Frank Otard, his grandson-in-law, being charged with the responsibility of administering the estate.

Peter Delmonico had been laid in the vault at St. Patrick's only a year when his widow, Catherine Giannini Delmonico, followed in 1861. With her death was severed the last of the strongly personal links with Mairengo; although Lorenzo and his brothers had been born there, they had grown to maturity in America and considered themselves what they were — New Yorkers.

2.

Peter's death left Lorenzo completely freed from the limited concepts of the firm's founders, and in the year when Peter died he undertook another speculative expansion — a move farther uptown, to Fifth Avenue at Fourteenth Street. In this venture he was encouraged by young Charles Delmonico.

Lorenzo was a businessman wholly, having few outside interests. There is no indication that he took active part in the political turmoil of the period. His meticulous supervision of every detail of the restaurants absorbed all his energies; his daily marketing schedule remained unvaried. He still rose before dawn, was among the first arrivals at the Washington market, and personally selected all the food supplies for both restaurants. He still drank his cup of black coffee on his return from the shopping, smoked a strong cigar, and went home to bed, reappearing at the restaurant in the evening and remaining until nearly midnight. His headquarters were, and would continue to be, at the Beaver Street house, where he maintained a tiny office just off the main-floor dining room, but he was often seen at Chambers Street. Like many Swiss, he was strongly imbued with a feeling for locality, and of a fine evening might be seen standing on the steps of the "Citadel," gazing meditatively up William Street towards the spot, less than a block away, where the Delmonicos had struck their roots in America.

At the time of Lorenzo's death, a member of the Manhattan Club, who had eaten his bachelor dinner at the Beaver Street house a quarter of a century previously, recalled the peculiarly personal relationship that existed between the head of the business and his regular customers. Their interests and the interests of their sons and grandsons Lorenzo watched over paternally but unobtrusively, for he possessed tact, this witness remembered.

"Lorenzo knew what to avoid talking about and what to bring to the fore. His knowledge of catering and of wines and of the fitness of all things pertaining to banquets or small dinner parties belonged, if I may be allowed the phrase, rather to the regions of philosophy than of merely practical experience. And he carried his executive watchfulness into many outside matters. For instance, I remember Jack N. . . . , who has been sleeping in the family vault at Trinity many years now, telling me that Lorenzo once drew him aside and said: 'Jack, I couldn't help hearing from my little room what you said to your friend. Don't embark in that speculation; and I will tell you why.' The reasons he gave saved Jack from a loss of $30,000. I have seen Lorenzo use a handsomely mounted cane that Jack gave him as a little memento of that caution."

In his own affairs Lorenzo was not so cautious, and it was rashness, as some thought, to consider moving uptown upon the wave of fashion then cresting at Union Square. The decision was made just as the Civil War was breaking out, and was carried through during the gloomy early stages of that struggle. The time seemed inauspicious for making heavy financial commitments. New York City's prospects seemed precarious; the best commercial minds foresaw only catastrophe in the wake of Southern secession, for the city lived by its commerce, and much of this was with the South. At the commencement of the war, New York merchants and commission houses held the notes of Southern customers for millions of dollars, all of which would be uncollectible in the event of prolonged fighting. And it was in the midst of this unsettled, foreboding atmosphere that Lorenzo Delmonico set about converting a mansion on the corner of Fifth Avenue and East Fourteenth Street into the most luxurious restaurant New York had ever seen.

The house, on the northeast corner of the intersection, had been the home of Moses H. Grinnell, a shipping magnate, who had such little faith in the success of Lorenzo's enterprise that he rented the place for a mere $7,500 a year. The three-story building, of brick with marble trim, was dignified and aristocratic-looking, the roof topped by an array of stately chimneys. A narrow lawn and flower beds bordered both frontages. The entrance was at number 1 East Fourteenth Street, one block west of Union Square.

Throughout 1861 carpenters, masons, painters, and upholsterers made the necessary alterations in the mansion, and on

April 8, 1862 — one year after Fort Sumter had been fired upon — an announcement appeared on the front pages of New York newspapers, stating simply:

DELMONICO'S
Corner of Fifth-Av. and 14th St.
WILL BE OPENED
Wednesday, April 9, 1862

The main news headlined in the press that day concerned the siege of Yorktown, where General George B. McClellan's Army of the Potomac was attempting to push upon Richmond; and, in the West, the battle of Pittsburg Landing (the opening phase of Shiloh) and the death of the Confederacy's most valued military leader, General Albert Sidney Johnston. In the midst of these momentous happenings, the *New York Daily Tribune* found space to chronicle an event of importance to New Yorkers — the inauguration of a new Delmonico restaurant. Following the sagacious custom, Lorenzo invited the press to a preview feast on April 5, and the *Tribune*'s representative waxed florid in prose (as probably also in complexion) when penning his report. After noting that "merchants, bankers, and the legal profession especially," had long enjoyed the "elegant and liberal cuisine" of Delmonico's, he launched into this gusty tribute:

"As New York spreads herself, so must the House of Delmonico dilate. Before Fifth Avenue was built, there was the downtown Delmonico; when it was achieved, there were the Chambers Street and Broadway Delmonicos; and now that Central Park is undertaken, precedent to a line of noble mansions to its walls, Delmonico has spread up to the corner of Fifth Avenue and Fourteenth Street, into the splendid dwelling of Mr. Moses Grinnell — which [the reporter, like many after-dinner speakers, having presumably stayed not his hand upon the bottle, was powerless to stay his periods] — which [we resume], with certain extensions, will henceforward be the cynosure of those having the ability and taste to draw distinctions between eating and dining — the one being animal and the other human or divine."

Doubtless glowing with satisfaction over this jet of verbosity, the reporter got down to particulars:

"This new Delmonico is under the charge of Mr. Charles Delmonico, long known for his amenity and kindness to the guests who dine upstairs at the Chambers Street establishment. The interior is very elegant. The rooms are spacious and beautifully decorated. There are numerous apartments for dining parties, besides the general dinner and breakfast halls. It has been furnished, at great expense, completely; including sumptuous dinner services, and all that imperial array which the proprietor so well understands."

Next, favoring the *Tribune*'s subscribers with an extract from the encyclopedia about Antonin Carême ("The great author and practitioner in the charming art of preparing food for Man"), the reporter bestowed this benediction: "Who would know Carême must be an habitué of Delmonico. Carême was in his glory on the inauguration of the new Fourteenth Street and Fifth Avenue house — by means of a dinner given to a few persons, on Saturday evening, who were considered able to understand his French as interpreted by Mr. Charles Delmonico." Among these enlightened few, of course, the reporter numbered himself; and his paean of praise continued with the sounding of the note that would recur constantly in connection with Delmonico's: "The service is splendid. The waiters noiseless as images in a vision — no hurry-scurry of preparation. The dishes succeed each other with a fidelity and beauty like the well composed tones of a painting or a symphony. It was a brilliant overture to the noble opera henceforth to be played there" — daily and on Sundays.

In support of his lyricism (and perhaps as an easy way to fill out his column) the reporter appended the menu of the invitational spread which had been served to the publicity-commanding press. Here is that bill of fare as printed, and few newspapermen today would be capable of navigating its windings from "potages" to "entremets":

Delmonico's, Fourteenth Street — April 5, 1862

MENU

Potages

Crème de volaille à la Rachel

Variés   *Hors d'Oeuvres*   *Variés*

Timbales à la Monglas

Relevés

Truites de Long Island   Filet de boeuf à l'Andalouse

Entrées

Côtelette de pigeon à la Noaille
Filets de volaille à l'Imperiale
Mayonnaise de homard à la ravigotte

Sorbets

Cardinale au vin du Rhin

Rôtis

Canvas-back duck   Bécasses bardées

Entremets

Asperges   Petits pois

Dessert

Millefeuilles Pompadour   Croquenbouche d'oranges

Napolitaine

etc., etc.

One fact of importance that emerges from the well-fed scribe's juicy ramblings is that the Fourteenth Street house, from its inception, was in charge of Lorenzo's nephew, Charles Delmonico. This was a mark of exceptional confidence in Charles's ability, for he was barely twenty-two. As the first member of the family to be born and reared in the business, among uncles and cousins active in the management, Charles seemed a predestined restaurateur. Affable in company — a good fellow among good fellows, and himself one of the city's gilded youth — possessing unfailing tact and a fine feeling for the social proprieties — Charles Delmonico was perfectly equipped to make the Fourteenth Street establishment the brilliant center of New York life that it speedily became. And not through his own management alone; for in this widening of Delmonico's sphere of dominance and prestige, he was to have the cooperation of the man who probably was the greatest cook America ever knew, one who moved among the great chefs of France as peer and equal — Charles Ranhofer.

3.

As Lorenzo Delmonico perfected a great business enterprise, Charles Ranhofer carried the already preeminent cuisine of Delmonico's to a summit of perfection and kept it there for nearly thirty-four years. He was not at Delmonico's when the Fourteenth Street house opened, but was then presiding over the kitchen of an establishment nearby, a restaurant called the Maison Dorée, that had been launched in 1861 by a man named Martinez. Situated on the south side of Union Square between Broadway and Fourth Avenue, the Maison Dorée was to provide Delmonico's with the only serious competition the latter was to know until the close of the century. Its cuisine was without a superior in the city, and some connoisseurs even rated it better than Delmonico's. The credit for this was due principally to the good fortune of Martinez in securing the services of Charles Ranhofer.

For a generation prone (to their great impoverishment) to regard an eminent cook or accomplished gourmet with the condescension accorded a male ballet dancer, a glance at the education by which Charles Ranhofer prepared himself for his most complex, exacting profession, may inspire respect. He was born to his calling on November 7, 1836, in St. Denis, France, where both his grandfather and his father were noted cooks, the latter being the proprietor of the Restaurant de Commerce. At the age of twelve Charles was sent to Paris to learn pastry-making. He completed his apprenticeship at fifteen, and was engaged as head baker by a Parisian restaurant. After a year he was taken into the service of Prince Hénin of Alsace, and there received the training in the kitchen of a great household which laid the foundation of his skill in the management of banquets, dinners of state, and similar entertainments on a grand scale. When the prince's *chef de cuisine*, Mollard, resigned, Ranhofer succeeded to the position.

Reports of the opportunities in America induced the young man to find out for himself, and he first came to New York in 1856. He was then twenty years old, and the conditions he found appalled him: except for himself, he discovered only one cook in New York whom he deemed fit to bear the title — Felix Délice, who was at Delmonico's.

"It is a wonder that you have not ruined the nation's digestion with your careless cooking and hasty eating!" Ranhofer lectured stomach-bogged Americans. "I must teach you something."

But there was more which he felt he should learn, and he took service with the Russian consul, who lived in Astor Place, where he mastered the Russian style of service. This, while akin to the French and closely resembling the American service, embodied important differences. Next he went to Washington, where he was employed by a noted dinner-giver, M. Duvernois. Thence he traveled to New Orleans, and studied Creole cookery in the kitchens of two restaurants operated by Guenedon and Lefevre.

Thus equipped, he returned to France and spent the winter of 1860 in the Tuileries, in charge of arrangements for the grand balls that were making the court of Napoleon III and the Empress Eugénie the talk of Europe. With this crowning finish to his culinary education, Ranhofer arrived in New York again in 1861, and assumed the management of the kitchen of the newly opened Maison Dorée. That restaurant's vogue was immediate. On July 19, 1861, G. T. Strong wrote in his diary: "Dined with Charley Strong and George Allen at the 'Maison Dorée,' a new and very nice restaurant established in Penniman's house on Union Square." Strong, a long-time devotee of Delmonico's, was qualified to pass judgment, and his verdict was in every respect favorable.

It may be that Martinez's success on Fourteenth Street, so far uptown, had determined Lorenzo Delmonico to plant his banner there; at any rate, his answer to the challenge of the Maison Dorée was the Fifth Avenue establishment. And soon after its opening, Charles Ranhofer transferred his talents there. Lorenzo Delmonico once recalled for an interviewer his first meeting with the redoubtable chef.

"He was perfect in dress and manner, and his attitude was such as to make me feel that he was doing me a great favor by coming into my employment," said the great restaurateur. "He gave me plainly to understand that he would be 'chief' indeed. 'You are the proprietor,' he said. 'Furnish the room and the provision, tell me the number of guests and what they want, and I will do the rest.' That was the way it was. And it has been a good thing for Charles, and for me, too."

For thirty-four years, with one short interruption, Ranhofer would dominate Delmonico kitchens. Never was there a more unbending autocrat in his own domain. He brooked no interference, and a word from him, or a mere motion of the hand, was not to be disregarded with impunity.

"I am responsible," he would say, "and things must be done as I direct."

The respect in which he was held by fellow cooks was unbounded, and he was never known either to miscalculate the extent of his authority, or to overrate his powers. The saying in New York for many years was that Charles Ranhofer was the city's first chef, and there was no second.

CHAPTER III

DINNERS AND
DIPLOMACY

WHEN HE JOINED FORCES with Lorenzo Delmonico in 1862, Charles Ranhofer was aware that he was allying himself with what was, take it all in all, the finest restaurant in America. Already "Delmonico" was accepted as a synonym for the best. As caterers, the house had attained a place of acknowledged supremacy before ever the Fifth Avenue branch was thought of. If some single feat of culinary prestidigitation had been needed to confirm that reputation it was provided in October, 1860, when the Prince of Wales visited the United States, and was honored by a grand ball at the Academy of Music on East Fourteenth Street which eclipsed every previous social entertainment in the city's history. So great was the crush, the floor of the stage gave way (fortunately injuring nobody seriously), but the dance went on.

According to some newspaper accounts, in the stampede to the supper tables more champagne and ice cream was dribbled upon the fine raiment of the guests than was gobbled — but spilled or not, the fare provided by Delmonico, all agreed, befitted the awesome elegance of the great event. In a pavilion offstage — a tent surmounted by the triple plumes of the prince's crest — the royal party ate from a blue-and-gold dinner service specially made for the occasion, and drank from glasses to match. The buffet offered a *consommé de volaille* to start; advanced to galantine of turkey and suckling pig (*cochons de lait à la Parisienne*); moved into the game course with grouse, pheasant, *bécasses et bécassines;* and terminated with a gallimaufry of tantalizing desserts. The obligatory setpieces portrayed *La Reine*

Victoria et le Prince Albert, the *Great Eastern* (largest ocean liner afloat), *Silver Fountain,* and other architectural triumphs in sugar-paste and isinglass. The service inside the pavilion was provided by a line of waiters in livery, posted behind the tables, and all was carried off impeccably, clinching Delmonico's prestige as the city's caterers *hors concours.*

The opening of the Fifth Avenue restaurant marked the dividing line between Delmonico's as purely a restaurant — foremost of its class, which was the foremost — and Delmonico's as a social institution, influencing the manners, tastes, and customs not only of the city but of the nation for decades to come.

The Fourteenth Street Delmonico's did not attain full splendor at once. The war was dragging on, with defeat meted out monotonously to the Northern forces. McClellan pulled back from the Peninsula, his attempt to take Richmond by that route thwarted, and Lincoln was compelled to inform the country that the struggle would be long and hard. At home there was sorrow caused by the mounting casualties, while abroad intervention by Great Britain and France on behalf of the Confederacy hung in the balance; Napoleon was itching to meddle, and many English leaders were inclined to egg him on. Confederate sea raiders like the *Alabama* were almost wiping out United States shipping, and the cost of imported goods soared out of sight. Foodstuffs took the same inflationary route, and before long butter would be selling for fifty-five cents a pound, beef for thirty, coffee for sixty-five, and tea for a dollar and a quarter. The paper currency issued by the government in its effort to meet the enormous costs of the war created havoc with the already dislocated finances of business houses and unloosed the plague of "shin plasters" — paper substitutes for coins, and scrip handed out by merchants in lieu of change. Delmonico's issued scrip like the rest, and the socially eminent Maria Lydig Daly, doting wife of Judge Charles Patrick Daly, was exactly one-half right when she wrote in her diary that the country's "finances are crazy and its government is crazy." But then, the consort of a prominent Democrat could hardly be expected to discern virtue in either the person or the policies of the creature in the White House whom she called "Honest Ape."

2.

There is no record of the direct involvement of any Delmonico in the war, but the restaurant could not escape the effects of the upheaval. One reason why the Maison Dorée was able to draw away some of Delmonico's regulars undoubtedly was the tension between hostile political factions in the city. When Fort Sumter was attacked, New Yorkers rallied almost unanimously to the Union's support; but since that crisis, patriotic fervor had become diluted with doubt, and there was an intense dispute going on about how the war should be fought. The newspapers fanned this clash of opinion. (Someone observed, regarding these armchair strategists, that "all the great editors want to become great generals.") Northern Democrats generally backed the determination to preserve the Union, but took exception to the methods advocated by the extreme Republicans known as Radicals. New York was honeycombed with Southern spies, and the New York Hotel, so long favored by the cotton aristocracy, was a nest of Copperheads; many of its guests were constantly shadowed, and not a few were seized and locked up on suspicion of aiding the enemy.

In the upper levels of society the cleavage was as sharp as it was in the slums. When the Union Club (the oldest club in the city, of which Philip Hone had been a founder, and where he had dined with satisfaction although execrating what a French cook could do to turtle soup) permitted some of its secessionist members to resign, instead of kicking them out, a group of ultra-Unionist members formed their own club, the Union League, for the express purpose of furthering the war effort by every possible means. George Templeton Strong was active in the Union League, and the favoritism for Delmonico's displayed by prominent New York Democrats, whose patriotism Strong believed to be lukewarm or less, quite likely first sent him to the Maison Dorée, where the Republicans gathered. At the commencement of hostilities, Strong had joined his friends in recruiting a regiment of infantry. The first meeting had been held at the "Citadel" in Beaver Street two weeks after Sumter; but the atmosphere proved too mixed for Strong's group, and they shifted their base of consultation to Martinez's establishment on Union Square. Upon the tablecloths of that restaurant were sketched the plans for the Sanitary Commission — the Civil War's Red Cross and USO — of which Strong would become the hard-working secretary.

From the Maison Dorée the diarist kept a vigilant eye upon "the gang of [August] Belmonts and [S.L.M.] Barlows and [Samuel J.] Tildens" in their "surreptitious" meetings in a private room at Delmonico's; and he was elated when their confabulations were "undermined, caught, and haled into the light" by the *Evening Post*.

This division of loyalties and patronage between the rival restaurants would last throughout the war. In 1864 Strong celebrated Sherman's capture of Atlanta at the Maison Dorée. But two months after Appomattox he returned to Delmonico's, at a dinner given by his father-in-law, Samuel Ruggles, in the Fourteenth Street house. About that time the Maison Dorée closed, Martinez presumably retiring upon his laurels and wartime profits. The matchless ports and sherries in the cellars of the defunct restaurant were bought by Lorenzo Delmonico, and for years afterward these treasures would be doled out to favored customers. Some of the wines were more than a century old, and nowhere in the United States was there anything to equal them.

In 1871 the Maison Dorée building was leased by a political wire-puller intriguingly named Sheridan Shook, an habitué of Delmonico's, and reopened as a hotel and restaurant under the old name, but it had no connection with the original establishment of the Sixties.

3.

In the midst of wartime tumults and alarms, high life and
low life in New York City went on much as usual. Man must
eat, and at intervals between the prosecution of private business
and the stimulation of patriotic zeal, dinners on a grand scale
were given at the uptown "social" Delmonico's. There was
plenty of money around, war contractors were making and
spending it riotously, and New York had progressed in appreciation of culinary refinements; many of the generation coming to the fore in civic and national affairs had been accustomed
to polished dining since their youth. The worldwide tone of
entertainments was being set by the ornate official hospitality
dispensed in Paris of the Second Empire, and throughout the
Sixties state dinner succeeded state dinner at Delmonico's under
the Parisian direction of chef Ranhofer, all in the grand manner.

The menu cards for these affairs were works of art, or sometimes models of pretension — printed in gold on silk, engraved
on silver leaf, mounted on satin enclosed in Russian-leather fold-
ers, embellished with delicate watercolors. One surviving specimen is electroplated on zinc, clasped in a velvet-covered case
— the accompaniment to a banquet of metal manufacturers.
At the foot of each bill of fare appeared the signature, in fine
type, that was the hallmark of highest quality — "Delmonico."
It hardly is to be wondered that these menu cards were preserved as relics of great events.

Wartime diplomacy enlisted the support of Delmonico's in
carrying out the subtle designs of Secretary of State Seward, an
ardent devotee of the house. One such diplomatic maneuver,
disguised as a banquet of courtesy, was the civic ball tendered
to Rear-Admiral Lessoffsky and the officers of the Russian fleet
that dropped anchor in New York Bay in November, 1863.
Russia was the only major European power openly favoring the
North in the war, and the visit was timed to impress that friendliness upon France and England. The Delmonican refreshments

served at the ball were certainly a change from sea rations. This
is how the Russians ate at the Academy of Music on the evening
of November 5, 1863, in the city of New York:

BALL
Russian Fleet

Rear-Admiral Lessoffsky, Russian flagship *Alexander Weosky,*
51 guns
Captain Kopytor, Russian screw frigate *Peresvat,* 48 guns
Captain Bontakoff, Russian screw frigate *Osliaba,* 33 guns
Captain Lund, Russian screw sloop *Vitioz,* 17 guns
Captain Kremer, Russian screw sloop *Variag,* 17 guns

MENU

Hors-d'oeuvres

Huîtres à la poulette   Huîtres en marinade   Bouchées de gibier
Canapés de filets d'ortolans   Snit-mitch à la Russe

Grosses Pièces

Saumons au beurre de Montpelier   Truites à la Régence
Filet de boeuf à la Mazarin   Pâtés de canvas-back ducks
Galantines de cochon de lait   Pâtés de gibier sur socles
Jambons de Westphalie   Galantines de dindes
à la moderne   aux truffes

Entrées

Salade de volaille à la Russe   Canetons Rouennaise
Côtelette de pigeons   Bordures d'escalopes de homards
à la macédoine   Aspics de filets de soles
Chaudfroid de filets de faisans   Victoria
Pain de gibier à la Royale   Timbales à la Renaissance
Terrines de Nérac   Bécassines à la Geoffroy

Rôts

Cailles aux feuilles de vignes   Bécasses bardées
Faisans piqués   Grouses

Entremets Sucrés et Desserts

Savarins au Marasquin   Biscuits Moscovites
Gateaux de mille feuilles   Babas glacées au rhum

Charlottes Sibériennes	Charlottes New York

Meringues panachées et vanillées

Gelées macédoine au champagne	Pain d'abricots à la Bérisina
Gelées Dantzic Orientale	Blanc mager rubané au chocolat
Gelées de poires à la maréchale	Bavarois aux fraises
Gelées au Madère	Biscuits glacées à la rose

Gâteaux assortis   Petits fours   Compotes   Fruits

Pièces Montées et Glacées

Pierre le Grand	Washington
Alexandre II	Lincoln
Le berceau des Palmiers	La rotonde d'Athènes
La fontaine moderne	L'Ermitage Russe
L'Arc de Triomphe	Cornes jumelles d'abondance
Sultane à la Parisienne	Le Pavillon des aigles
L'aigle Américain	Pouding Nesselrode

LA LIONNE

Colombus	Corbeille jardinière	Les Dauphins
Diana	Madeleine	Mousse aux amandes

Bombe spongade   Citron et fraise   Ceylan au café   Vanille Chocolat

Fourteenth Street and Fifth Avenue   *Delmonico*

All which may serve as an example of how gastronomy can be made to serve two purposes simultaneously: in this case, to give delight to friends (the Russians), and to give potential enemies (the French and English) an indigestion.

4.

International attention was focused upon dinners at Delmonico's in the following year, and by one of them an emperor's ambitions received a setback. This dinner occurred on March 29, 1864; it was a testimonial banquet tendered by representative New Yorkers to Mattias Romero, minister of the Republic of Mexico to the United States. The event was staged to demonstrate the hostility of Americans to Louis Napoleon's attempt to foist upon Mexico a puppet emperor in the person of the Archduke Maximilian of Austria. The popularity of the cause was so great, the attendance overflowed four large rooms of the Fourteenth Street restaurant.

After "full justice had been done to the large variety of sumptuous dishes" (to quote one of the promoters, Wall Streeter Henry Clews), toasts were drunk to "the President of the United States" and to "Don Benito Juarez, Constitutional President of the Mexican Republic." Since Juarez had been driven into exile by French troops, who claimed to have conquered all Mexico, the significance of this formal recognition was plain. To make it plainer, even to Frenchmen who might speak neither Spanish nor English, the French invasion of Mexico was denounced belligerently and bilingually by speakers who pledged that Americans would never permit "the heel of European despotism to place its imprint upon the soil of our Western continent." The ceremonies concluded with the toast: "The daughters of Mexico — fair as her sons are brave." This drew "enthusiastic and prolonged applause," while the orchestra struck up "Viva Republica."

This far from subtle intimation of what was in store for him and for his puppet, Maximilian, Napoleon disdained to notice — that is, until the issue of the *New York Herald* containing a full account of the proceedings reached Paris, when the newspapers were hastily confiscated and burned. On April 10, at Miramar, his castle on the Adriatic, Maximilian was proclaimed Emperor of Mexico. Shortly thereafter he set out for his sullen empire, weeping copiously, not to return alive.

Although Napoleon could not foresee that tragic dénouement, before the year 1864 ended he had begun to entertain doubt regarding the absolute wisdom of his course; after all, it began to appear that the North might win its war — and Louis never backed a loser if he could help it. Consequently, and by no coincidence, in November of that year a French flotilla visited New York on an errand of good will. The city's welcome was tempered by frigidity, and although Admiral Renaud was honored by a banquet of protocol at Delmonico's, for this affair a single dining room was large enough to accommodate the mere twenty-six carefully screened guests. No report of any toasts except those demanded by etiquette reached the press, and the menu, of course *soigné*, was noticeably lacking in those flattering allusions to the guest of honor and his nation that are customary on such occasions. Oblique references to imperial France were *saumon à l'Imperiale* and *consommé royale*, but these seemed to be cancelled out by *croquettes à la Victoria* and *punch à la Régence;* for Victoria was not the name of the Empress of the French, and the only regency the Napoleonic dynasty would ever know was to be the brief regency assumed by Eugénie at the very moment of the dynasty's disintegration. The point of these menu ambiguities was not lost upon a mind as subtle as that of the master of the Tuileries; the dinner to Admiral Renaud was a culinary success, but it was a diplomatic triumph.

5.

Entertainment of celebrities had become common at Delmonico's; scarcely a leading figure of the war years failed to make an appearance there sooner or later. President Lincoln stayed at the Fourteenth Street Delmonico's (on the top floor there were rooms for bachelors) when he came to New York for hush-hush consultations with General John A. Dix, Thurlow Weed, and Henry Ward Beecher. When the President asked Lorenzo Delmonico for his bill, he was told that the privilege of serving the nation's chief executive in such trying times was ample payment. Whereupon Lincoln gave Lorenzo a pocketknife as a memento, remarking humorously: "In Washington where I live there are many mansions, but no cooks like yours. But our hospitality is. Drop in and see us."

It was not long afterwards that Lincoln's funeral cortège wound solemnly up Broadway to Union Square, and Delmonico's, like all the buildings along the route, was shrouded in mourning.

Lincoln's successor was guest of honor at a much discussed dinner at Delmonico's in 1866. The issue of the hour was the reconstruction of the South, and President Andrew Johnson was under fierce attack by the Radical Republican majority in Congress. Johnson was a Tennessean, and during the war had been widely popular in the North as the only senator of a slave State who refused to secede. Since the war, the extremists of the Republican party in Congress had been at loggerheads with the President over treatment of the defeated South, and a group of influential New Yorkers believed that whatever bias the President might be feeling towards the section whose representatives were making things hot for him might be mollified if he could experience Northern hospitality and friendliness. Johnson had been invited to dedicate a statue to the late Senator Stephen A. Douglas at Chicago, and an invitation was sent to the White House urging the President to stop in New York on his way west.

He reached the city on August 29. Escorting him was a prestigious entourage — General Grant and Admiral Farragut, members of the cabinet, several ladies, including Mrs. Welles, Mrs. Farragut, and the President's daughter, Mrs. David T. Patterson, and a brigade of newspaper reporters.

At City Hall Mayor Hoffman extended the city's official welcome, and the illustrious parade moved up Broadway to Twenty-third Street through dense crowds, greeted by incessant cheers. Turning at Twenty-third Street, the procession passed smartly down Fifth Avenue to Delmonico's at the corner of Fourteenth. Lorenzo Delmonico was waiting at the portal to receive the President and his party, and with a committee of dignitaries he conducted them to the reception rooms on the second floor. Immense throngs milled around the building as two hundred policemen struggled to preserve order. Most of the Presidential suite were put up at the Fifth Avenue Hotel, but Johnson was assigned a private apartment on Delmonico's upper floor.

A platform had been set up outside the Fifth Avenue side of

the building, and from there the President reviewed a brilliant military show. Then came the important feature of the visit, the banquet and speeches. Everything contributed to produce harmony. The banquet went off flawlessly. The mayor presided, with Johnson seated on his right, and the Russian, Mexican, and Brazilian ministers among the hundreds of notabilities present. The combined geniuses of Delmonico and Ranhofer had perfected the emollients that smoothed away partisan rancors, and nothing was lacking or stinted in the cuisine, service, or setting. The menu was a far cry from the "country fixin's" Andrew Johnson had eaten as a poor tailor in East Tennessee; but though word has not come down to us about how the President reacted when confronted with the curleycues of culinary French and the princely parade of wines, there is little question that he made his way with aplomb through a thicket of *potages, poissons, entrées, and entremets,* and although little addicted to wine, sampled the Amontillado, Clos-Vougeot, and Madère Faquart. Here is the traveling map that was provided for that gastronomic safari:

Dinner given by the Citizens of New York
To His Excellency
PRESIDENT JOHNSON
In honor of his visit to the city, Wednesday, August 29, 1866

MENU

Potages

| Amontillado | Consommé Châtelaine | Bisque aux quenelles |

Hors-d'Oeuvres
Timbales de gibier à la Vénetienne

Poissons

| Hochheimerberg | Saumon Livonienne | Paupiettes de kingfish Villeroi |

Relevés

| Champagne | Selle d'agneau aux concombres | Filet de boeuf à la Pochantas |

Entrées

Suprême de volaille Dauphine
Ballotines de pigeons Lucullus
Filets de caneton Tyrolienne
Château Margaux '48   Côtelettes à la Maréchale
Riz de veau Montgomery
Boudins à la Richelieu

Sorbet à la Dunderberg

Rôts

| Clos-Vougeot | Bécassines Bardées | Ortolans farcis |

Entremets de legumes

Petits pois à l'Anglaise   Tomates farcies
Aubergines frites   Artichauts Barigoule

Tokai Impérial   *Entremets sucrés*

Pêches à la New York
Abricots Siciliens

Macédoine de fruits   Moscovites aux oranges
Bavarois aux fraises   Gelée Californienne
Crème aux amandes   Meringues Chantilly
Beauséjour au Malaga   Millefeuilles Pompadour
Gâteau soleil   Biscuits glacés aux pistaches

Madère Faquart   *Fruits et desserts*

Pièces montées

Monument de Washington   Fontaine des Aigles
Temple de la Liberté   Trophée National
Casque Romain   Colonne de l'Union
Char de la Paix   Rotonde Egyptienne
Cassolette Sultane   Corne d'Abondance

Fourteenth Street and Fifth Avenue   *Delmonico*

Sorbet à la Dunderberg was a felicitous touch, topical and
patriotic; it gratified both municipal and national pride, for the

Dunderberg was the name of the Navy's newest acquisition, the largest ironclad afloat, just completed in a New York shipyard. Of course, with the war ended it was a white elephant, but what of that?

After the dinner Johnson spoke in a warm vein, expounding his political program, and was generously applauded. Later, in response to the shouts of the throng outside, he came out on the balcony and spoke even more warmly, ripping into his Congressional enemies with a vigor that brought roars of approval. The occasion was a triumph for the President, and by midnight, as the newspapers expressed it, he was in "extremely high spirits." Calling for his body servant (a former slave who had grown up in the President's household and was enormously vain of his position as "Mr. Johnson's first servant") to "come to bed," the President signified that he was ready to retire. Lorenzo Delmonico indicated that after the valet had assisted the President to undress, he would be shown by a waiter to a separate room; but Johnson would have none of that.

"No, he won't!" he reportedly cried. "I'll undress myself and that boy sleeps in my room tonight, I'll tell you!"

And so it was. To the bewilderment and slight scandal of New Yorkers unfamiliar with Southern customs, the President and his Negro servant that night shared the best room in Delmonico's. At least, this was the story told for years afterwards across the tables at Delmonico's.

6.

Content as the President had reason to be with his entertainment, the New York press was not so. It transpired that reporters had not been admitted to the banquet room until the speeches began, and the *Tribune* (an anti-Johnson paper) strongly reprehended this affront, although willing to attribute it to the "inexperience of the committee in charge." Nevertheless, the *Tribune* pointed out sourly, "the initiatory ceremonies" were by this blunder "lost to history," and of course lost to the

Tribune's readers. Other newspapers echoed the complaint, averring, moreover, that their reporters had been segregated in a side room and condemned to eat "broken meats" from the tables of the banqueters.

The *New York Herald* used this opening to advertise its own disdain for special favors. Professing to have perused with astonishment the strictures of its rivals upon the fact that their reporters had been "kept waiting like lackeys" in an antechamber, and had then been insulted by being offered "the unconsumed viands prepared for the invited guests," the *Herald* wondered whether reporters attended public banquets "for the purpose of eating and drinking, or with a view to perform their duties to the journals they represent and the public? . . . For our part," the *Herald* continued blandly, "we can say that [our] reporters . . . are sent to public dinners exclusively for the purpose of reporting the speeches . . . They are supposed to dine beforehand."

In consequence of this shutting out of the press, only one newspaper — the strongly pro-Johnson *World* — gave its readers a first-hand account of the banquet and setting.

"The tables were magnificently decorated, every beautiful device in sugar and fruit and cake being brought into use, and grand bouquets burdening the air with odors," ran this description. "Silver candlesticks filled with candles, which were not used, were set at intervals on the tables, and a sweetly smelling little bouquet was furnished by the wine glass of every guest. The [menu card] was a triumph of exquisite execution. Neatly enclosed in an illuminated cover, and bearing on the front the United States coat of arms, and on the back the Flag, it contained inside the following interesting reading for *bons vivants* . . ." And the *World* published the full menu, commenting jocosely:

"All this of course was quite unintelligible to many of the gentlemen present (because it was in French), but as the articles were brought without asking, it was quite satisfactory. Yet it might be mentioned that most of the articles were as unintelligible after being placed before the guests as before, being so enveloped by the mysteries of cookery that it was quite impossible to tell what they were. Most of the guests, however, were quite indifferent as to what they were, for the reason that they were all very good."

How the *World* succeeded in thus appeasing the hunger of its subscribers for details was no mystery to the initiated. The *World*'s editors were Delmonico regulars of long standing. Although they had not been invited, for they were politically obnoxious to the arrangements committee, they had been apprised of the menu of the banquet as soon as it was decided upon, and were intimate friends of Siro, Charles, and Lorenzo Delmonico.

The day after this Delmonican feast, President Johnson and his party left New York for Albany, on what was to become the uproarious "swing around the circle." There is no record that Andrew Johnson ever dined at Delmonico's again.

CHAPTER IV

WHEN DICKENS ATE
CROW AT DELMONICO'S

AFTER LORENZO DELMONICO'S DEATH in September of 1881, the *New York Sun*, in an editorial headed "What Lorenzo Delmonico Did," gave its opinion that he "did more than build up a great business and accumulate a large fortune. He gave an impulse to good cookery throughout the country, and raised the standards of hotel and restaurant kitchens. By his success he excited emulation, and the consequence has been a great and general improvement in cookery . . . Mr. Delmonico, therefore, rendered a great service during his long life in this country, and his name will not be forgotten for a hundred years at least."

The *Sun's* tribute was not unique; it merely crystallized what had been said again and again, and would be repeated by contemporaries for years to come. But on what grounds could it be contended that Delmonico's, as an institution, had exerted a decisive force in elevating the eating standards of Americans?

Fortunately, a yardstick exists by which can be measured with accuracy the evolution of New York taste and practice in the era before Delmonico attained a commanding position, and the period a quarter of a century later, when Delmonico had taken over undisputed leadership in matters pertaining to public hospitality. In each case the occasion was the same — an honor paid to a foreign guest; in each case the city put its best foot forward; in neither case was there the slightest question about the setting that must be chosen; and in both instances the guest honored was the same, Charles Dickens. The contrast between the two events is illuminating.

*

2.

In 1841-42, Charles Dickens toured America giving readings from his works. He was then twenty-nine years old, and already famous as the author of *Pickwick Papers, Barnaby Rudge, Nicholas Nickleby, Oliver Twist* and *The Old Curiosity Shop,* all of which had appeared within five years. Everywhere on the tour he was lionized by American admirers; flattered, fawned upon, and all but smothered under social attentions. In New York a "Boz Ball" at the Park Theater degenerated into a riot from which he emerged bruised and breathless. Then a committee of prominent New Yorkers tendered him a banquet. The date was February 18, 1842, the place was the City Hotel, and Washington Irving presided. Among the vice-chairmen were Philip Hone, Gulian Verplanck, James de Peyster Ogden, and John A. King, than whom no more distinguished men could be found in the city. The occasion demanded the best on the part of the caterer, and what was served exactly reflected the ruling taste of the time. In fact, the "Dickens dinner" was spoken of for years afterwards as a model of gastronomy.

Selection of the City Hotel for the festivity was almost automatic, for it enjoyed semi-official status as the most suitable setting in New York for civic celebrations. The hotel had been built in 1793; it occupied the block on Broadway between Thames and Cedar Streets, and was designed for substantial comfort rather than display — a plain, five-story structure, with windows bare of curtains, floors waxed, and furniture utilitarian. The dining room, however, was spacious, airy, and well lighted, and was much used for balls and concerts, and for half a century New York's social life centered at the City Hotel. Lafayette was entertained there in 1824 and had remarked favorably upon its comforts. Its wine cellars were noted, its cuisine was considered unexcelled, and its eminent propriety in every respect was unquestioned. The Dickens dinner in 1842, we may be sure, was the finest that civic pride could provide, and the bill of fare reflected the best taste of cultivated New Yorkers at that period. The Delmonican revolution, although well advanced, had not been generally accepted yet; its time was to come.

Bearing these factors in mind, let us look into this feast of feasts provided by men of education, wealth, and familiarity with the refinements of life, who represented the best of New York society.

Journalistic style in 1842 tended to be as effluent as the diet of the day was diffuse, and the New York newspapers reporting the grand doings at the City Hotel on February 18 conformed to the conventions and language of the time; in accordance with the custom devoting only a few lines, a paragraph or two, to the dinner, although printing the text of the after-dinner speeches in three and four columns of fine type. All the accounts agreed, however succinctly, that the banquet was "in a style not surpassed by any ever partaken in this city" (*Daily Tribune*); and that "the tables were sumptuously furnished with all the delicacies of the season, and the room was elegantly decorated and arranged" (*Evening Post*). These are generalizations. But there was one newspaperman present, James Gordon Bennett, the irreverent editor and owner of the *New York Herald*, who had an eye for detail and a taste for exactitude. Also, he understood perfectly well that the buyers of his paper could do without the speakers' flowers of rhetoric, but would like to be told how the town's bigwigs guzzled when they foregathered in exalted state. As a matter of curiosity, and as a gauge of New York's sprightliest journalism in 1842, let us follow, in part, Bennett's racy description:

"A most splendid affair it was, done by Gardiner, one of the best caterers in New York, at a cost of $2,500. The large room . . . was decorated by Platt Bros., of Gold Street, in the most neat and chaste style imaginable . . . nothing gaudy or showy, and no tinsel. Above all, they have our thanks for not using any of that miserable trash called bunting, which so often defaces

the most splendid public rooms in this city. On the present occasion there was none of this, but everything was chaste to a
degree . . .

"The head of the table was at the west end of the room. Four
long tables ranged down the room parallel with each other, and
each of these tables held twenty-seven persons on a side, making
a total of two hundred sixteen seats at these four tables; which,
with four vice-presidents, one at each end of the four tables,
swelled the number to two hundred twenty. To these must
be added a cross table at the head, at which seats were placed for
seventeen persons, making a total of two hundred thirty-seven
persons that sat down to dinner."

The mathematics were correct, and Bennett's readers could
envision the arrangement of the room easily.

"The chair was taken by Washington Irving. On his right,
Dickens, on his left, the Rev. Mr. Bellows."

Mayor Morris also graced this table, although Governor
Bouck and Lieutenant-Governor Dickinson had declined, plead-
ing (with a little political cattiness) that they were required at
Albany "to do the State some services."

Bennett next described the illumination, which was of unparal-
leled brilliancy.

"On each of the four tables were placed four splendid candelabras, each containing seven wax candles; there were also three
golden candelabras on the cross table at the head; three golden
candelabras on the white pedestals at the extremity of the room
between each table; one hundred thirty gas lights in the four
splendid chandeliers; and ten handsome side lamps with three
lights in each, making in all three hundred sixteen lights in that
one room."

As for those approved decorations, chaste but not frigid:

"Facing the main entrance . . . were two beautifully painted
transparencies, in richly carved antique frames; these represented Pickwick addressing the Pickwick Club, and Ralph Nickleby introducing Kate Nickleby to his friends." There were

also "twelve marble busts on richly carved antique brackets; four at the top or west end of the room, in each compartment of the wall, behind the chairman; four between the windows at the bottom of the room; one over each transparency; and one on the wall on each side of the main door." The grouping of these figures Bennett found somewhat heterogeneous: at the head of the room, Seneca, Franklin, Washington, and Dickens; at the bottom of the room, Shakespeare, Byron, Scott, and Milton; on the south wall, Diana and Apollo, paired; and on the north wall, John Marshall and Demosthenes observing reciprocal silence. All present in the room, mute or masticating, were warranted to be of the first distinction, mortals and immortals hobnobbing convivially; and Bennett congratulated the arrangements committee (name by name) upon their "good sense and taste in excluding all other decorations as out of keeping and irrelevant to this most interesting occasion" — especially bunting.

The company sat down at seven o'clock, and were honored by the semipresence of a number of ladies, who sat in a group around Mrs. Dickens and through the open door of an anteroom were permitted to "witness the festivities as far as was consistent with propriety," although they could not snatch a bite. This violation of strict decorum was considered daring, but Bennett was all for the innovation.

3.

Coming to grips with the solid business of the evening — the bill of fare — the *Herald*'s eyes and ears noted that (after a "short but effective grace" spoken by Dr. Bellows) all fell to with "a perfect literary and promiscuous appetite. And a most magnificent dinner it was. Gardiner — numerous as have been his excellent public dinners — never gave a better one."

Bennett appended the complete menu, and this is the printed record of what New Yorkers extolled as the finest of table fare in 1842, spelling included:

When Dickens Ate Crow

BILL OF FARE

Dinner in Honor of
Charles Dickens, Esquire

At the City Hotel, New York, on Friday, February 18, 1842

First Course

Soups

Potage à la Tête de Veau
Potage à la Julienne
Potage aux Huîtres

Fish

Boiled fresh Trout
Boiled Bass, caper sauce
Broiled fresh Shad,
    à la Met d'Hôtel

Second Course

Cold Dishes

Boned Turkey in jelly
Boned Chicken, Grenade, in jelly
Oysters, aspic in jelly
Chicken Salad
Ornamented Westphalia Hams
Hare Patties

Roasts

Roast Sirloin Beef
Roast Saddle Mutton
Roast Goose
Roast Veal
Roast Larded Turkies
Roast Capons

Boiled

Boiled Leg of Mutton, caper sauce
Boiled Turkey, oyster sauce
Boiled Chicken, celery sauce
Boiled Fresh Rump-Beef, pickle sauce
Boiled Beef à la Mode
Stewed Terrapin

Entrées

Jardiner de Gibier	Jardiner with Game
Timballe de Poulette	Tamball with Chicken
Macaroni à la Italienne	Macaroni, Italian style
Vol-au-Vent, aux Huîtres	Oyster Pies
Riz-de-Veau, l'Oseille	Larded Sweet Bread with Sorrel
Filet de Boeuf, piqué à la sauce Tomate	Larded Fillet Beef with Tomato sauce
Croquette de Volaille	Chicken Croquettes
Canard aux Olives	Ducks stewed with Olives
Fricandeau à la sauce Tomate	Fricandeau with Tomato Sauce

Poulet aux Turbot,
   aux Petits Pois   Turben Chicken
                                         with Green Peas

Poulet aux Turbot, aux Petits Pois — Turben Chicken with Green Peas
Petites Pâtés à la Bechamelle — Small Gravy Patties
Ragoût de Terine — Stewed Terrapin
Pâtés de Poulet aux Truffes — Chicken Patties with Truffles
Pigeons aux Petits Pois — Stewed Pigeons with Peas
Epaule d'Agneau, à la sauce Tomate — Shoulder Lamb with Tomato Sauce
Rognons de Veau, sautées, au vin de Madère — Veal Kidneys with Madeira Wine
Côtelettes de Mouton, grillées, au jus — Mutton Chops, bread-crumbed, with gravy
Pâtés des Pigeons aux Truffes — Pigeon Patties with truffles
Pigeons sautés au champignons — Stewed Pigeons with mushrooms

Third Course

Game

Roast Canvas Back Ducks — Roast Bear
Roast Wild Turkies stuffed with Truffles — Roast Saddle Venison

Fourth Course

Pastry

Cranberry Pies — Charlotte Russe
Mince Pies — Blanc Mange, rose color
Jelly Puffs — Almond Blanc Mange
French Puffs — Madeira Jelly
Plum Puffs — Ice Cream
Apple Puffs — Plum Puddings, blazing

Pyramids

Ornamented Pyramids — Spanish Macaroni
Chrystallized Candy — Jumble Macaroni
Cocoanut Candy — Temple Pyramids

Fifth Course

Fruit

Apples — Hickory Nuts
Oranges — Raisins
Almonds — Prunes
Figs — Madeira Nuts

"Literary and promiscuous" describes this agglomeration of things good and dreary to eat. The keynote was abundance — profusion — over-abundance — a prodigality of edibles, crudely grouped and offering little basic variety. No one could sample everything, and no one was expected to; Falstaff would have belched at the challenge. Three soups, two of them thick — three fish dishes — six meats roasted and six boiled — nineteen entrées and four kinds of game, including "roast bear" — the modern stomach quails. Vegetables are sparingly employed (green peas, olives, mushrooms), and as garnishes, such as tomato sauce, sorrel, celery sauce, truffles. The pastry division was puffed up with "puffs" in four flavors ("puffs" were a schoolgirl's delight), while the season being February, there could be no fresh fruits, like melons or berries.

But already this unimaginative fare had become subject to the ameliorating influence of Delmonico. For four years the "Citadel" had been setting a wholesome example at Beaver and South William Streets, and ripples of change were invading the City Hotel's kitchen. In this festive bill the entrées are listed in French and English, in imitation of Delmonico's elegance. There were among the diners those who were able to read a menu in French, but others, of the older stamp, preferred to "know what they were eating" and have their victuals plainly labeled in plain American. For the one class "ragoût," was more ingratiating than "stew", and "petites pâtés à la Bechamelle," despite the faulty French, was more appetizing than "small gravy patties."

"The viands were all of the first quality and truly delicious in the matter of cooking," the *Herald* testified. "Boz was in high spirits, laughed heartily, drank wine with . . . everybody that asked him, and that was over a hundred. The company was at its height at twelve o'clock. Dickens left at 12:30. The whole affair went off with immense éclat, and reflects the highest credit upon Mr. Gardiner, on whom alone devolved all the details of the dinner, from first to last."

4.

Charles Dickens went home and produced two books based on his experiences in the United States —*American Notes* and *Martin Chuzzlewit*. Both stirred up a tempest of condemnation among his pristine hosts; they were denounced as travesties of American manners, ungenerous if not downright libels, and a shabby return for the welcome the author had received. In *Martin Chuzzlewit*, New York's supposed feeding habits were lampooned savagely. The patrons of a high-class boarding house were represented as all but trampling each other in their rush to the dining room at the sound of a gong announcing the meal — "like lunatics . . . horror and agitation on their faces." Diving wildly into their chairs "in a confused heap of arms and legs," they fell to voraciously, according to Dickens. "Very few words were spoken, and everybody seemed to eat his utmost in self-defence . . . the knives and forks working away at a rate that was quite alarming." Poultry, pickles, oysters vanished down "the gaping gullets — a solemn and awful sight to see. Dyspeptic individuals bolted their food in wedges; spare men with lank rigid cheeks, unsatisfied from the destruction of heavy dishes, glared with watchful eyes upon the pastry. But there was one comfort. It was soon over."

This coarse — and many Americans felt spiteful and vicious — exaggeration of acknowledged defects — such as over-haste in eating, a habit that has never changed, and a deleterious one — was indignantly spurned.

5.

Twenty-six years after he had feasted at the City Hotel, Charles Dickens returned to America on a second reading tour. The time was 1868, and he found New York unrecognizable, so great were the changes. "The number of grand houses and splendid equipages is quite surprising," he wrote home. "There are hotels here with five hundred rooms and I don't know how many boarders." He put up at the Westminster, a quiet hotel on Irving Place, where the waiters were French and he felt that he "might be living in Paris." Haggard from illness and husbanding his energy for the public appearances, he accepted no social invitations. But he ate privately at Delmonico's, close by on Fourteenth Street, and the waiters remarked that he dined well and drank better: after polishing off a bottle of champagne he would call for brandy and toss off a tumblerful. Not surprisingly, his chief malady was a painful form of gout.

At the close of his tour, he made one exception to the rule of no entertainments. This was in favor of the New York Press Club, which was eager to do honor to one member of the craft who had gone on to fame and fortune. So on April 18, 1868, Dickens was the guest of the press of New York at a gala banquet. The place chosen was the only place by that date deemed proper for such an occasion — Delmonico's at Fifth Avenue and Fourteenth Street.

Lorenzo Delmonico regarded that dinner with particular pride. Although it was neither the largest, nor the costliest, nor the most striking in its composition, it gave him special satisfaction. And no wonder, for the two hundred and four guests were the dispensers of publicity on a nationwide scale, quite ready to tell the world what they liked — and they liked Delmonico's. The banquet cost about $3,000, and the tickets sold for $15 apiece. Horace Greeley presided, and the guest list included every editor of note in New York and cities as far west as Chicago, plus a sprinkling of privileged outsiders whose connection with publishing was dubious.

Now fifty-six years old and worn by toil, Dickens kept the guests waiting an hour until he could summon strength for the ordeal. At six o'clock he arrived, limping and leaning on a cane, and the banquet got under way in a setting vastly different from the "chaste" severity of the City Hotel, which had long since been demolished.

The great dining room exuded luxury. Deep-pile carpets muted the footfall of the waiters, damask draperies framed the windows, the gas lights in the chandeliers were softly shaded, the tables flashed with crystal and silver on snowy linen and were bright with flowers. Over the chairman's table were the flags and arms of England and the United States, and this was the only touch of formal grandeur.

The unabashed *New York Herald* had expressed doubt "whether even a menu by Delmonico could tempt Dickens from his snug retreat in the Westminster to the excellent wine to which he was indebted for his goutiness"; and in reporting the proceedings the paper made clear that had the great man not shown up, the dinner would have completely misfired, having been composed "with considerable wit, the point of which would be lost without the presence of the guest of honor. Oysters on the half shell, sure, but these were the only things that were not dignified with some literary name."

The *New York World*'s reporter approved the setting, saying: "No pains were spared to make the occasion as pleasant, informal, and social as possible. Delmonico, than whom none knows better how to work up a banquet into the domain of art, brought all his energies to bear upon the matter . . . The tables were magnificent, with the most consummate commingling of flowers and confections. Connoisseurs in these things declared that the display surpassed anything in the history of banquets. It certainly did in the ingeniousness of designs. Confections were converted into . . . tempting pictures of the most familiar characters of the great novelist. Sugar was not ashamed to imitate him, and even ice cream had frozen into solid obeisance. Sairy Gamp and Betsy Frig and Poor Joe and Captain Cuttle blossomed out of *charlotte russe,* and Tiny Tim was discovered in *pâté de foie gras* . . . Not only did [Delmonico] make it a Dickens dinner, he made it dinner of Dickens."

While an orchestra, "carefully screened in an adjoining apartment," dispensed melodies, Horace Greeley introduced the honor guest, and Dickens responded in his best form. In his speech also, he made public reparation for his peevish strictures of a quarter of a century before. Speaking to men who, he knew, would carry his words to the whole nation, the novelist first denied that he proposed to write another book about the United States; and then went on:

"What I have intended, what I have resolved upon (and this is the confidence I seek to place in you), is, on my return to England, in my own person to bear, for the behoof of my countrymen, such testimony to the gigantic changes in this country as I have hinted at tonight. [At this point the stenographic reporter interpolated, "Tremendous applause."] Also, to record that wherever I have been, in the smallest places equally with the largest, I have been received with unsurpassable politeness, delicacy, sweet temper, hospitality, consideration, and with unsurpassable respect for the privacy daily enforced upon me by the nature of my avocation here and the state of my health. [Applause.] This testimony, so long as I live, and so long as my descendants have any legal right in my books, I shall cause to be republished as an appendix to every copy of those two books of mine in which I have referred to America. [Tremendous applause.] And this I will do and cause to be done, not in mere love and thankfulness, but because I regard it as an act of plain justice and honor. [Cries of Bravo! and cheers.]"

This dish of crow not prepared by Delmonico was downed by Dickens with fortitude and aplomb.

6.

But the proof of the banquet lies in its elements and their interrelation; and this gastronomical-literary celebration of 1868 furnishes material for a direct comparison with the banquet tastes of cultivated New Yorkers in 1842. This is the 1868 menu which Charles Ranhofer prepared:

M E N U

Huîtres sur coquilles

Consommé Sévigné   Crème d'asperges à la Dumas

Hors-d'Oeuvres Chaud

Timbales à la Dickens

Poissons

Saumon à la Victoria   Bass à l'Italienne

Pommes de terre Nelson

Relevés

Filet de boeuf à la Lucullus   Laitues braisées demi-glace

Agneau farci à la Walter Scott   Tomates à la Reine

Entrées

Filets de brants à la Seymour

Petits pois à l'Anglaise

Croustades de riz de veau à la Douglas

Quartiers d'artichauts Lyonnaise

Épinards au velouté

Côtelettes de grouse à la Fenimore Cooper

Entrées Froides

Galantines à la Royale

Aspics de foies-gras historiés

Intermède

Sorbet à l'Américaine

Rôts

Bécassines   Poulets de grains truffés

Entremets Sucrés

Pêches à la Parisienne (chaud)

Macedoine de fruits   Moscovite à l'abricot

Lait d'amandes rubané au chocolat

Charlotte Doria

Viennois glacé à l'orange   Corbeille de biscuits Chantilly

Gâteau Savarin au marasquin

———

Glaces forme fruits Napolitaine

Parfait au café

Pièces Montées

Temple de la Littérature   Trophée a l'Auteur

Pavillon International   Colonne Triomphale

Les armes Britanniques   The Stars and Stripes

Le Monument de Washington   La Loi du Destin

Fruits	Compotes de pêches et de poires	Petits fours
	Fleurs	

Dessert

Fourteenth Street and Fifth Avenue   *Delmonico*

A glance suffices to differentiate this composition from what was regarded as the ultimate in the way of grand-scale dining in 1842. The mere profusion of the City Hotel bill of fare has been replaced by economy, order, balance, and smooth progression of the courses. Elaborate, yes, but the total number of dishes has been cut from the sixty-odd of 1842, not counting nuts, fruits, or "pyramids" (sweetmeats in elaborate forms), to about thirty, again excluding desserts and setpieces. Two soups (the conventional thick and thin) replace the three of 1842; there are six main entrées, instead of the nineteen listed in 1842; the heavy boiled meats are eliminated, with their sauces. Symmetry has been imposed upon variety, the meal charted along a definite line of development; it is no longer a superfluity of abundance. The sauces contain shadings that the palate could catch, and among vegetables are newcomers that would have puzzled the gourmands of 1842 — braised endive with the *filet de boeuf à la Lucullus,* and artichokes. The clumsy crutch of two languages has been thrown aside, for New York's educated diners had passed that primer stage. There are a multitude of literary allusions, as there had been in 1842 — a soup named for Dumas, chopped lamb *à la Walter Scott,* grouse *à la Fenimore Cooper, consommé Sévigné, timbales à la Dickens.* The international motif appears in *petits pois à l'Anglaise,* to counterpoise the *sorbet à la Américaine.* The setpieces distribute honors evenly — the *British Arms* flanked by the *Stars and Stripes;* the *Temple of Literature,* by that reliable standby of eggwhite, gum arabic, and confectioner's sugar, the *Washington Monument.* And not only are the diners carried by easy transitions from course to course, they are so wafted in a way to reanimate flagging appetite. The concluding stages, especially, are beyond the scope of the simple pastries of 1842, when two versions of that insipidity, blanc mange ("rose color" and "almond"), were a pale alternative to repetitious "puffs," "cranberry pies," and "plum puddings, blazing." "Madeira jelly" (1842) would melt with confusion before *"corbeille de biscuits Chantilly"* (1868), and those jolly "apple puffs" would be country cousins beside *"lait d'amandes rubané au chocolat."*

Plainly there had been a fundamental alteration in New Yorkers' notions of what was fit to grace a banquet table, and for that change the Delmonicos were primarily responsible. Although their restaurant catered to the few, their patrons comprised those who set the tone of society and determined the tastes and fashions that gradually permeated other sections of the population. Because those at the top of the social scale ate better, those on the lower levels, aspiring to rise by emulation, in time also ate better. Delmonico's influence was not of a decade only, it remained continuous for nearly a century. Other restaurants appeared, throve, set high standards, and disappeared; Delmonico's stayed, a fixed star in the firmament of good dining. Generations submitted to its mild authority. For millions who never set eyes on the entrance of a Delmonico restaurant, "salad" (to name but one instance) came no longer to mean the "mess of greens" dank and listless under a smothering of vinegar and sugar. In all the printed talk about Delmonico's that appeared from border to border, there is no suggestion, even facetious, that the name and dyspepsia were associated. "Delmonico" meant well-being. As Dickens discovered in 1868, even crow, at Delmonico's, could become a dish not impossible to engorge with equanimity.

John, Peter, and Lorenzo Delmonico in 1840, in the cafe at Beaver and South William Streets. John, with the tray — slight, active, dark; Peter, with the cigar — solid, light brown hair, genial; Lorenzo, at the table — the shrewd businessman.

New-York Historical Society

Peter Delmonico in retirement — the man of property in Brooklyn.
Courtesy of Mrs. Henry A. Campbell

Lorenzo Delmonico, nephew of John and Peter, in the 1860's.
Museum of the City of New York

Clemence Delmonico, wife of
Lorenzo, in the early 60's. Born
in France, she rarely uttered a
word in English.
urtesy of Mrs. Henry A. Campbell

Charles   Constant   Delmonico,
nephew of Lorenzo, inherited
the business and conducted it
until 1884. The ideal restaurateur.
Courtesy of Mrs. Henry A. Campbell

Charles Crist Delmonico. Trained for Wall Street, he entered the business at the death of his uncle, Charles Constant, and was the active manager until his death in 1901.
Courtesy of Mrs. Henry A. Campbell

Charles Crist Delmonico ("Young Charley"), nephew of Rosa. A drawing from *The Illustrated American*, 1891.
Museum of the City of New York

Rosa Delmonico ("Aunt Rosa"), sister of Charles
Constant. She owned the controlling interest in the business after her brother, Charles, died, and managed the
restaurants from 1901 until 1906.

Courtesy of Mrs. Henry A. Campbell

Josephine Crist Delmonico, sister of
"Young Charley," the last of the family to own the business. After the
death of her Aunt Rosa, the restaurants were really run by the staffs.
Courtesy of Mrs. Henry A. Campbell

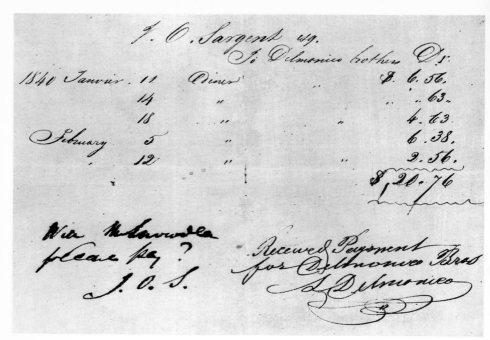

A Delmonico bill of 1840, signed by Lorenzo.   *Museum of the City of New York*

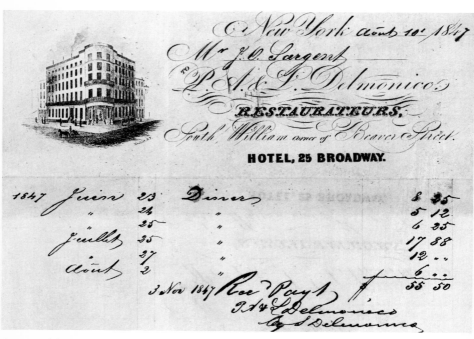

A more elaborate bill of 1847, signed by Siro   *Museum of the City of New York*

"Little Philippe" — of notable exploits.
Museum of the City of New York

"John" (John Klages) — the spirit of the cafe.
Museum of the City of New York

Dining at the Madison Square restaurant in 1891.

Sketch from *The Illustrated American.*
Museum of the City of New York

DELMONICO'S TWEN

(Reproduced from THE SPIRI

W. H. VANDERBILT.   JOE MORA.   SIR JOHN RAE REID.   HORACE POI
B. HOUSTON.   BEN WENBURG. CAPT. WM. CONNOR, ROSCOE CONK
        WRIGHT SANFORD.   CHARLES DELMONICO.   JOHN GAR

Delmonico's cafe at Madison Square, 1877; some well-known habitués.

EARS AGO.

7.)

LLIAM TURNBULL.   FRANK WORK.   CIRO DELMONICO.
GEORGE DEWEY.   JAMES R. KEENE.
F. GRAY GRISWOLD,   T. J. EDMONDSON,

Sketch from *The Spirit of the Times.*
Courtesy of Mrs. Henry A. Campbell

The Delmonicos' country house at Williamsburg (later a part of Brooklyn).
Courtesy of Mrs. Henry A. Campbell

CHAPTER V

BULLS AND BEARS
AND DELMONICO'S

To PLACE THIS 1868 TRIBUTE to Charles Dickens in its time perspective — on the day of the dinner, counsel for President Andrew Johnson in his impeachment trial before the United States Senate wound up their case; while in New York the "battle of Erie" was raging, with Jim Fisk, Jay Gould, Cornelius Vanderbilt, and conniving Uncle Dan'l Drew each trying to outsmart the others and milk the railroad for his own enrichment, in the process trampling on every precept of good faith and honesty.

The Flash Age was in full go. It was an age of gaudiness which had not taken on even the meretricious glitter of the Gilded Age, the next in line. New York was a stamping ground for war profiteers bent on making a splash with their money and boosting their wives and daughters up the social ladder. The vulgarity of this new wealth repelled and frightened the old-line Knickerbocker aristocrats, yet it could hardly be avoided. The likes of Fisk and Vanderbilt laughed at moralizers, and exemplars of social propriety stood aghast, uncertain whether to wither the interlopers with their wrath, or to join the crowd, capitulate to the might of cash, and profit by the change. Manning the dikes against the threatened flood of new-rich seemed a task beyond the power of any but the most determined, and most of the defenders eased their consciences with supercilious but ineffectual ridicule, and inwardly resigned themselves to eventual defeat.

At the Dickens dinner, the writer for the *New York Herald* (not Bennett himself, for he lived, old and misanthropic, in hermit-like seclusion in his upper Manhattan mansion) had alternately praised and poked fun at the sculptured setpieces, seeing in them an epitome of the age. These eight creations, he pointed out, were "of curious sugar manufacture, most of them labeled 'Dickens' in very large red letters at the top, and all stuck full of 'Dickenses' in small caps and brevier from top to bottom"; while the statuette atop the *Temple of Literature*, blowing "an inaudible trumpet undoubtedly was meant to represent the goddess of fame. The deity of a hundred tongues was attired in tinsel of the latest fashion, thus typifying modern fame most particularly."

The times were riding for a fall, but it would not come for a while yet. Meanwhile, without lowering standards, Delmonico's profited from the outpouring of new riches. When a contractor, who had made millions by palming off shoddy upon soldiers, turned to spending of his sudden wealth, he bawled for the best, and the best was what Delmonico's purveyed. The three restaurants — at Beaver Street, Chambers Street, and Fifth Avenue — alike benefited, but in different ways.

At Fourteenth Street the cafe was called "the best club in town," because there one saw everybody who mattered. Many men preferred the cafe to their own clubs — the Union, Union League, Manhattan, New York, and others, situated nearby. The *New York World* found the cafe "the resort of more native and foreign notabilities than perhaps any other place in the city. There distinguished literary and political persons stop daily to sip the matutinal cocktail, the anti-prandial sherry-and-bitters, and the evening 'pony.' There the Wall Street magnates drop in on their way uptown to sip the insidious mint-julep, or quaff the foaming champagne cocktail. There the Frenchman, Spaniard, and Italian may have their absinthe, the American his Bourbon straight, the Englishman his half-and-half. Morning, noon, and evening the place is alive with a chattering, good-natured, oft-imbibing throng of domestic and imported celebrities."

The restaurant was acknowledged to be "beyond all question the most palatial . . . on this continent." A stream of fashion flowed "through its spacious apartments from morning to eve-

ning. To lunch, dine, or sup at Delmonico's is the crowning ambition of those who aspire to notoriety . . . Indulgence of the
whim may be expensive to a moderate purse, but the panorama
once seen and carefully inspected will amply repay for the outlay of money."

Picturing the scene for those who could not participate in it,
another chronicler of the late 1860's stressed the amazing Delmonico service, the perfection of the food, the tables crowded
with notables and their satellites. One conspicuous change from
earlier times was the presence of women in large numbers in the
restaurant; never, of course, in the cafe, and never without a
male escort.

"On entering from Fourteenth Street," wrote this observer,
"one cannot fail to be impressed by the absence of bustle and
confusion; no boisterous commands are heard, and the waiters
glide about as noiselessly as ghosts. An air of luxury surrounds
you as the attentive *garçon* stands motionless before you and
respectfully awaits your wishes. The order once given, you have
ample time to survey the scene. At an adjoining table . . . a
gray-haired, soft-speaking gourmand, who gloats over his
carte . . . A freshly fledged millionaire, who furtively glances
about in dread (lest he should not be seen), as he *points* to the
highest-priced item, having no remote idea what it is . . . A
puffy dowager, perspiring at every pore . . . Beside her the
'Belle of the Period' (ridiculously got up) . . . Two country
girls, all eyes, forgetting to eat. A party of prinked-up young
men, sporting gaudy neckties and flash jewelry . . ."

New times produced new manners, and Delmonico's accommodated itself to the era without forfeiting its identity and peculiar excellences: sumptuous setting, superb service, and cooking
without a peer.

2.

Wherever the Delmonicos located a restaurant downtown,
there was sure to be the center of business; wherever they located uptown, *there* just as infallibly would be the center of

fashion and gaiety. In 1865 this was exemplified again by the launching of a Delmonico branch at 22 Broad Street. Lorenzo Delmonico's young cousin, John Longhi, was put in charge of this outpost. Siro Delmonico was managing the Chambers Street establishment; Charles, Lorenzo's nephew, was in command at Fourteenth Street; and Constant had the responsibility for the Beaver Street house. The new Broad Street restaurant was almost next door to the Stock Exchange, the busiest point in town at noon.

Each Delmonico's specialized in serving a distinct clientele. The Fifth Avenue house drew the world of society; the Chambers Street restaurant attracted the politicians, lawyers, merchants, and judges around City Hall; the "Citadel" catered to bankers and shipping men and brokers; and 22 Broad Street developed its own enthusiastic custom among the stock speculators of Wall Street. Because the premises ran through from Broad Street to New Street and formed a convenient shortcut for hurrying clerks, it was never empty during business hours. Casual customers were accommodated at a counter, and the big spenders could spread themselves in private rooms upstairs. There Jim Fisk, the most engaging of money pirates, entertained, and Jay Gould, his mousy partner in thievery, lunched ascetically on soup and weak tea. Dan'l Drew snatched a bite at the counter downstairs while cogitating new ways to fleece the unwary, never omitting to say grace over his sandwich.

Fisk was seldom seen at the uptown Delmonico's, mainly because "Del's" did not welcome the sort of women he liked to have for dinner companions. But when "Jubilee Jim" wished to impress a crony or a lamb who was being led to the shearing, he did not hesitate to call upon the town's most versatile caterers.

"Charley," he once accosted the head of the Fourteenth Street place, "I want a tiptop stand-up lunch, with flowers and all that sort of thing, to be served in my offices at six-thirty." It was then four-thirty, and Fisk's Erie Railroad headquarters were on the top floor of his opera house at Eighth Avenue and Twenty-third Street. Charles Delmonico glanced at his watch.

"It can be done," he said, "but it will be an expensive job."

"Who said anything about the cost?" roared Fisk. "You do it and I'll pay for it." And he waddled away.

Delmonico's did it, and Jim paid the check with a smirk of satisfied vanity: it totaled $1,500.

At 22 Broad Street Boss Tweed started a custom that caught on with men-about-town — "opening wine." To "open wine" meant to uncork champagne for everybody present. The number of "dead soldiers" carried out of 22 Broad Street in the course of its existence would tax the calculations of a computer. The bar there never knew a drought, good times or bad. When a broker "hit it right," he hurried to Delmonico's to treat himself and his friends to a celebration; if he "hit it wrong," there was no consolation like a bottle of the best at "Del's." Whichever way the market veered, Delmonico's came out ahead. The restaurant did not try to "corner" the Wall Street trade; it was content to take the cream and leave the skimmings to other houses and the myriad hole-in-the-wall lunch rooms that peppered the district then as now.

Yet all the patrons of Delmonico's on Broad Street were not high rollers. A man who was a clerk in the 1870's remembered to his dying day the wonderful iced coffee he got at the counter there on sizzling hot days. There was no ice in it; made strong, it was creamed and sugared, then chilled in an ice-cream freezer, from which the waiter dipped a frosty glass upon request.

It was often said that no homelier building existed in New York than the grimy, five-story brownstone at 22 Broad, with the dingy sign "Delmonico" above its doorway; but by the bulls and bears of Wall Street it was cherished. It was their corral; and the schemes that were hatched there, the companies that were floated, the financial battles that were planned in its up-stairs rooms, would form a *chronique scandaleuse* of Wall Street's wildest days.

3.

Meanwhile, the Chambers Street restaurant entered upon a new cycle of prosperity as Tweed and his gang mulcted New York City. Judges of the Supreme Court, lawyers, and political satraps of all degrees of crookedness foregathered there in the recondite privacy they were willing to pay for. Men famous in their time frequented the upstairs rooms at Chambers Street; their names would constitute a "Who's Who" of New York in the Sixties and Seventies. Some who are still remembered were Horace Greeley; Henry J. Raymond of the *Times*; A. T. Stewart; James T. Brady, the courtroom spellbinder; William M. Evarts, witty and learned leader of the bar and future Secretary of State; John Van Buren; Fernando Wood, the city's copperhead mayor who recommended that New York secede from the Union; Astors and Vanderbilts in assorted lots; crusading clergymen like Henry Ward Beecher and T. De Witt Talmadge, from conscience-bound Brooklyn; Daniel Sickles, a rake of marital and martial notoriety; Samuel J. Tilden, near-President of the United States; Chester A. Arthur, an actual though accidental President; Roscoe Conkling, the posturing "Adonis" senator and mastermind of New York republican politics; and of course the potentates of the Tweed Ring, their aides and abettors without number. Peter B. Sweeney and Richard B. Connolly, Tweed's right and left hands in the public till, and the "Elegant Oakey" Hall, Tweed's cover-up mayor, who wrote poems and drafts on the municipal treasury with equal verve — these were habitués. Should Sweeney yearn for a tranquil hour, he would repair to Delmonico's and recoup from the fatigues of forgery by a regimen of delectable dishes and mellow bottles. The last time he was there, before taking to ignominious flight, he all but closed a deal with Lorenzo Delmonico whereby the latter would purchase the Sweeney house on Thirty-fourth Street.

But during the high-roller days of Tweed's ascendancy, horrid catastrophe lay in the indeterminate future, and pranksters in private rooms drank to the tricks with which they lightened the drudgery of thieving at City Hall—such fantasies as drawing checks to fictitious characters: $65,000 to "T.C. Cash," or $66,000 to an imaginary "Phillippo Donnoruma," alias "Philip Dummy." For men who could steal $6,000,000 in a single working day, Delmonico prices were a bagatelle. For his daughter's wedding in 1871, Tweed gave Charles Delmonico the curt order: "My daughter is to be married a month from now; get me up a good dinner for five hundred people." He did not inquire the cost, and Charles was authority for the published statement that the "simple collation" worked out at $25 a plate, for a total of about $13,000. The day after the wedding Tweed strolled into Charles's office and paid the bill without a flicker. Had he not rented the entire Metropolitan Hotel to accommodate his guests, and then laid out half a million to have the place redecorated? And were not the gifts to the bride valued according to the *New York Herald* at $700,000?

Henry J. Raymond, a politically active editor, gave many dinners at Delmonico's Chambers Street restaurant and mapped journalistic campaigns there. Room number 1 upstairs was the preserve of lawyers, of whom the jovial Brady was a bellwether. Whenever he chalked up another courtroom victory, it was his pleasure to celebrate in room 1 with congenial spirits, human and liquid both fully uncorked. Rooms number 9 and 11 were consecrated to the politicians, Republican and Democratic, for there was no factionalism at Delmonico's. The unwritten rule was that the first party arriving could establish itself in number 11, and those coming later would convene in number 9. In this way next door to each other, the leaders of the opposite parties mapped their election strategies.

A. T. Stewart, whose immense store stood just across Broadway, liked to entertain at Chambers Street, and the food and wines he set before his guests were the rarest and most delicate; but he would dine soberly on a chop.

Siro Delmonico, who presided over all this activity, was more

gregarious than his brother Lorenzo. He was the Boniface in-
carnate: "sun-beaming," was the descriptive phrase of a subor-
dinate who worked beside Siro for years. Siro was always ready
to join in a drink or a conversation, and he possessed to the full
the family traits of unerring courtesy, deference, and strict attention to business. Siro's addiction to fierce black cigars was
more pronounced even than Lorenzo's and the image of Siro
without a cigar clamped between his teeth was all but unimagi-
nable to his many friends. The habit was undermining his health,
and doctor after doctor told him so. Periodically he was
racked by paroxysms of coughing, but nothing would induce
him to cut down his consumption of tobacco.

4.

Siro Delmonico had relieved Lorenzo of daily marketing,
leaving the older man free to supervise the operations of the
four restaurants. At the "Citadel" Lorenzo was a familiar sight,
sitting in his little office keeping a vigilant eye on the tables and
the cash drawer, and now and then exchanging greetings with
customers passing in and out. The patronage was in constant
flow, the tables were never empty. Lorenzo, said Sam Ward,
had "staked his fortune upon the growth of the city . . . Those
who fell by the wayside were replaced by newcomers. Men
might break or disappear or die — but . . . his cisterns were
always open to every falling drop of prosperity."

Unknown to most of his associates, this blooming career almost went to wrack during the free-spending Sixties. The episode was disclosed generally later, and would be retold many
times. Prudent in counseling others, Lorenzo was not always
well-advised in his own dealings outside the business of the restaurants; but so punctual, prompt, and exact was he in all his
transactions, the revelation that he had come a cropper in the
chanciest of all speculations startled intimates who had known
him for years.

It happened during the gambling in oil stocks that followed
the successful drilling of petroleum wells in western Pennsyl-

vania. Lorenzo Delmonico contracted the fever, and invested in a company formed to prospect for oil in Brooklyn; wells were being sunk everywhere, and Brooklyn seemed as likely a spot as any. As his commitment increased, Lorenzo was induced to accept the firm's presidency; and so entire was his confidence in the venture that, when he left on a holiday trip to Europe, he gave his brother Constant power of attorney to advance any funds the company might require.

The visit home was a great occasion for Lorenzo. In 1851 his father had died, in his seventy-third year, but Lorenzo's mother, Rosa Longhi Del-Monico, was still living, settled comfortably in a cottage he had bought for her on the outskirts of Mairengo. There were many cousins, and sisters whom he had not seen for years, although they had received evidences of his generosity periodically. As a gift to the village, he had built a new schoolhouse, and the town fathers invited him to attend the dedication of the building. Mairengo turned out in a body to honor its distinguished son. There was a parade, followed by speeches and fireworks, in the midst of which arrived an urgent message from New York saying that the oil company was in dire straits; by mismanagement (it was said at the time, and apparently credited) the firm had contracted debts beyond its capacity to pay, and no oil has yet been discovered in Brooklyn.

Lorenzo hastened home, cast up the balance, and realized that he was ruined — wiped out. To meet his obligations at least in part, he put up the restaurants for sale. Wall Street was consternated. "Delmonico's is an institution, and must not be allowed to perish," was the consensus, and on the day of the auction not one bid was offered. Lorenzo was enabled to continue the business, furnished capital by his monied customers, and in a short while — thanks partly to the splurge of spending just after the war — he had paid his debts and went on to earn another fortune. His loss in this escapade was said to have been half a million dollars. He never strayed out of familiar paths again.

* * *

5.

By the 1870's, Delmonico's was secure once more, and with
his return to solvency Lorenzo moved to 211 East Fifteenth
Street, in a neighborhood of numerous old New York families,
like the Fishes and Rutherfurds. The commodious house at 211
was around the corner from Stuyvesant Square and St. George's
Church, and there Lorenzo and his wife established themselves
in dignified style. There was no display, but every appurtenance
of luxury. The only real indulgence Lorenzo permitted himself was a fondness for fast trotting horses, and even this was
moderated by his innate conservatism.

The Delmonico family had been undergoing changes that
drew more and more of Lorenzo's attention to domestic affairs.
In 1864 Honoré's youngest daughter, a child of two, had died,
and almost immediately afterwards Rose Anna Delmonico, worn
down by the double strain of nursing the sick child and giving
birth to twins, also succumbed. Then one of the twins died.
The triple bereavement shattered Honoré. Placing his four remaining daughters in a convent in Manhattanville, he retired to
Hoboken, where he lived with his wife's relatives. In February,
1868, he died, and was laid beside his wife, his parents, and John
Delmonico in the vault at old St. Patrick's. His fortune was
dissipated, and his orphaned children remained in the care of the
nuns until they came of age. Thenceforward the descendants of
Peter Delmonico would have no connection with the restaurants,
although they would persist as a family and would outlive the
members who were active in the business.

Charles Delmonico made his home with his sister, Rosa, at
229 West Fourteenth Street, close by the Fifth Avenue establishment. His other sister, Giovannina, had married a diamond
merchant named Theodore Christ, who maintained offices in
Maiden Lane and London. Three children were born to the
couple — Lorenzo, Charles Delmonico, and Josephine Otard
Christ. In 1869 the family moved to Paris, and during an epi-
demic of cholera (it is said) both parents died there early in

1870. Charles Delmonico Christ was a boy of ten when this happened; his brother Lorenzo was a year older, and his sister Josephine was a year younger.

Before his death, on May 6, Theodore Christ had executed a hasty will in his apartment at number 6 rue Lepeletier, naming Charles Delmonico, the children's uncle, their guardian. Charles moved immediately to bring the children back to New York, dispatching Rosa Delmonico, the children's aunt, to France to unsnarl the red tape. After exasperating delays she obtained the consent of the Paris court to take charge of the orphans and their inheritance. The "procuration," or legal instrument of authorization, was issued on July 19, 1870 — the day France declared war on Prussia. Rosa made her escape from the hysterical capital and got safely to New York. There the children were taken into the home that Charles and Rosa shared, and the brother and sister, neither of whom ever married, reared them. In time the name Christ was altered to Crist (perhaps to put a stop to sour punning), and as Crists the children grew up in an atmosphere of restaurant gossip and concern.

Lorenzo Delmonico, who had no children of his own, extended his watchful care to the three orphans. Already he was turning in his mind the best expedients for perpetuating the house his uncles had established, and which he had raised to such a peak of prosperity and prestige.

CHAPTER VI

OF BLUEBLOODS

THE IRRUPTION of a "petroleum and shoddy aristocracy" eager to spend its war profits was threatening to obliterate old-line New York society with its traditions of hierarchy, decorum, and responsible conservatism. "Rough, illiterate, vulgar creatures" were swarming around, demanding consideration on the strength of their moneybags, while the established families muttered about Vandals and Visigoths and "conquest by barbarians." Something would have to be done to preserve their own security, they felt; but until the Seventies, after the city had somewhat cleansed itself of its Fisks and Tweeds, no planned campaign of resistance was settled upon. Then the defenders of the old order found their general, one who could turn back the ruffian horde and hold it at bay (or at least at arm's length) for a while longer. The name of this strategist of the social battleground was Samuel Ward McAllister, although few knew him by his full name. He was a cousin of Delmonico's Sam Ward, and had been named for that engaging gourmet's esteemed banker father.

Ward McAllister is a curiosity of minor history. He also is a curiosity of Delmonico history (which is not minor), for there he planned and executed his grand design to outflank and outwit the clamorous new-rich. So well did he succeed, his name is remembered still, though usually with a pejorative smile.

Ward McAllister was a little man who was fascinated by the pomps and pageantry of social ritual. He had perfected himself in the niceties of precedence and etiquette during a residence in provincial France, and upon returning to New York in the

Sixties he found a chaos that shocked him. Thenceforth he applied his energies to correcting the situation, bringing to bear a power of concentration and a devotion worthy of the noblest cause — and he could conceive of none nobler than his own. "Ascending order" (what in the jargon of a later time might be called the "escalation of rank") must be reintroduced into the tottering social structure to avert collapse and ruinous confusion, he saw clearly. This would require time, but he had no other interest to divert him from the Herculean task.

In person McAllister was pudgy, in manner pompous. His Vandyke mustache and beard were worn with a portrait air, and he carried himself with a swagger that he fancied to be negligently majestical, but was more like the bearing of a complacent butler. His ideas were vain and petty, but within their framework logical. Above all, he did not deplore, he acted; and because of his alacrity in filling a vacuum, society rallied to him and for more than a decade trooped as he directed, like docile geese. There was a time when he was exactly what he claimed to be — New York's "Autocrat of the Drawing-Rooms." And his influence was felt not only in New York, but elsewhere, especially in the newer parts of the nation; for the press, which found him irresistible, so spread his fame that upon occasional jaunts inland he drew spectators from miles around to stare at the "biggest dude of them all." If this sounds a little unreal, so was social life in the Gilded Age and the Age of Extravagance that followed.

Upon the topics of food, wine, and table service Ward McAllister was an authority, for he had been drilled in those branches of social learning by his cousin, Sam Ward — and Sam Ward was the epoch's grand panjandrum of gastronomical erudition. McAllister pitched upon Delmonico's as the pivotal point of his scheme of social retrenchment.

Charles Delmonico, in command at Fourteenth Street, already enforced his own rules to safeguard the house's reputation for correctness. No lady was permitted to dine at Delmon-

ico's without a male escort. That was the general rule at all
first-class restaurants; but at Delmonico's no two persons of the
male and female sex, married or single, could dine together in
a private room with the door closed. This rule applied to everybody, and cost the restaurant some business; but Charles Delmonico allowed no exceptions and was able to enforce it. August Belmont, one of the oldest and most valued customers of
the house, and Mrs. Belmont once arranged a dinner for four
in a private room. Owing to a misunderstanding in the date,
their guests failed to appear; and after waiting an hour in the
lobby, Belmont told the waiter that he and his wife would go
ahead with the meal as ordered. With considerable embarrass-
ment, Charles Delmonico was forced to tell the great banker
that he could not permit them to be served upstairs, unless they
would leave the door open. He knew perfectly well that they
were a domesticated couple of the highest respectability; but
he was adamant. Belmont stalked out in a rage and swore he
would never set foot in the place again. But after thinking the
matter over, he realized the propriety of Charles's action and
forgave him. The rule held.

2.

Charles Delmonico was able to obtain compliance with rules
that were at times restrictive because he had been reared with
the city's gilded youth; he was one of them. From their teens
on, these heirs-apparent had hung out at "Del's," and Charles,
unlike his uncle Lorenzo, was sociable. No one was more truly
born to his occupation ("always polite, civil, considerate, gentle, and deferential," a contemporary called him), and his customers accepted him on their level, as they accepted Lorenzo
for different reasons. This equality of position led to the one
known exception to the rule of no sanctioned fisticuffs in any
Delmonico establishment. It concerned James Gordon Bennett,
Jr.; and Charles himself was responsible for it.

Young Bennett was a sport-about-town who combined the

worst traits produced by a pampered upbringing and too much money. Of his complete sanity there is still doubt; of his boorishness upon occasion there is none. Leopold Rimmer, who at the time was head waiter in the Fourteenth Street cafe, often told the story in a thick Austrian accent.

"Very few people know why Mr. James Gordon Bennett's nose is broken," he would begin. "One nice summer day in the Sixties, a party of young chaps was lounging in the cafe, waiting for the race results from Jerome Park." In the group were young Bennett, Edward S. (Ned) Stokes, who would achieve dubious fame by shooting Jim Fisk over the favors of their shared inamorata, Josie Mansfield; George Lawrence, a man-about-town; Ben Wenberg, a character who would miss immortality by the narrowest of flukes; and Charles Delmonico.

"About two in the afternoon they had luncheon and champagne. They were happy, and chatted about this and about that. All at once, Mr. Bennett slapped Mr. Stokes's face — why, I don't know — and Mr. Stokes wanted to kill Mr. Bennett; but the other gentlemen would not have it. So Mr. Charles Delmonico suggested to have it out fair and square. They took their coats off and went out into the hall. In a twinkling Mr. Bennett was on the floor, and athletic Mr. Stokes hammered away on Mr. Bennett's nose like a sledgehammer, when the other guests took him away and satisfaction was given. We had to bring Mr. Bennett upstairs and send for a doctor to have Mr. Bennett's nose fixed up. And," this old employee would conclude, "he has the mark on his nose today yet."

For this sole instance of permitted fighting at Delmonico's Charles undoubtedly was reprimanded by Lorenzo, and there is no record of any recurrence. Bennett continued to be received, until the day when he committed the unforgivable grossness of mistaking his fiancée's fireplace for a comfort station, and was horsewhipped in front of his own club, ostracized by society, and found it best to betake himself to Paris permanently. Stokes, also, was not penalized. He continued to frequent Delmonico's, and on the day he murdered Fisk got up courage for the deed in the bar. While awaiting trial in the Tombs he had his meals sent in, but they did not come from Delmonico's.

3.

To return to the seemly campaigns of Ward McAllister: in his words (and no one could write about inconsequentialities as inconsequentially as he), the way was paved for a major stroke by the assemblies, or subscription dances, that were given during the late Sixties at Delmonico's Fourteenth Street, under the patronage of established matrons. These McAllister described as "large balls, and embraced all who were in what may be termed General Society." By "General Society" (with capital letters) he indicated a wider circle than the nexus of social distinction which he believed to be the soul of the city.

In 1870, a further step was taken which McAllister applauded, for it fixed Delmonico's as the place for social gatherings *par excellence*. Archibald Gracie King was a banker of impeccable antecedents, and he broke with the tradition that one must entertain in one's home and (in McAllister's carefully italicized wording) gave "the first *private* ball at Delmonico's to introduce his daughter. It was superb. The Delmonico rooms were admirably adapted for such an entertainment. There were at least eight hundred people present, and the host brought from his well-filled cellar his best Madeira and Hock." Thereafter entertaining in public rooms became the thing, and hostesses marveled that they had ever tried to herd a hundred guests into a house occupying the average New York City lot with its twenty-five-foot frontage.

The King ball gave McAllister his cue, and he moved into the arena with a series of cotillion suppers at Delmonico's. During these, while presiding at the table surrounded by influential dowagers, he inculcated his thesis that society must unite in its defense, or be elbowed aside by the vulgarian mob. By 1872 his labors were bearing fruit, and he deemed the time ripe for a bold stroke. With two fellow alarmists, he originated the most famous, the most exclusive, and most arbitrary band of social dictators New York ever groveled before — the Patriarchs.

McAllister reasoned thus: let society itself set up a "board of directors" who would pass upon the pretensions of any aspirant to recognition. To insure that their decisions would be respected, these directors must be men of the right background: rich, but not simply rich; socially immaculate as to pedigree (McAllister's yardstick was "four generations to make a gentleman" in America); and sufficiently few in number to emphasize their exclusiveness. The list of Patriarchs he censored himself; they numbered twenty-five, and included not a single new-rich name.

McAllister was as intrepidly fatuous in discussing his stratagem as he was fearless in carrying it out. He was facing a problem that seemed to admit of no solution, and he solved it by evolving a paradox. In a democracy such as the United States, he pointed out, an aristocracy is a violation of the principle upon which the structure rests. However, "in a country like ours, there was always strength in union; [and] to bind together the solid, respectable, element of any community, for any project, was to create a power that would carry to success almost any enterprise."

The tightly bound band of the Patriarchs, and those who accepted their authority, he designed to be that power in the social sphere; and he happily figured himself as the power behind the power, an autocrat indeed. So bland was his assurance (and so lacking in leadership otherwise was society), both the press and his social peers bowed to his assumptions and acted upon them with a singular unanimity for an appreciable number of years.

The roster of Patriarchs included two Astors, two Livingstons, and members of the Duer, King, Rutherfurd, and Schermerhorn clans — all splendidly old line New Yorkers. "New money," as we have remarked, was rigorously shut out. The group carried on their functions of assent or veto by annual balls, three each season. To be invited to these balls was to be "in," and never to be invited was to be hopelessly "out." Each Patriarch was allowed to invite four ladies and five gentlemen, and the responsibility for inviting only the "right" guests was placed squarely upon each Patriarch individually. McAllister set up an ingenious system of control by which any Patriarch who should become lax in his standards of selection could be set straight by the force of the "public opinion" of their private world.

"Should any objectionable element be introduced," the Autocrat elucidated, "it would become the duty of the executive committee [of which he was the chief member] to at once let it be known by whom such objectionable party was invited, and to notify the Patriarch so offending that he had done us an injury, and pray him to be more circumspect. Thus all society, knowing the offense he had committed, would so upbraid him that he would go and sin no more."

By this device McAllister utilized the fundamental principle of political democracy — the tyranny of majority opinion — to nip any tendency towards social democracy. The Patriarchs were all men in their prime or conspicuously past it, and there was little likelihood of their erring upon the side of social promiscuity; nevertheless, McAllister was aware that the strength of his unique association lay in maintaining its exclusiveness, and he achieved and maintained that by a triumph of casuistry.

"We knew then, and we know now," he subsequently wrote, "that the whole secret of these Patriarch balls lay in making them select; in making them the most brilliant balls of each winter; in making it extremely difficult to obtain an invitation to them, and to make such invitations of great value; to make them the steppingstone to the best New York society; that one might be sure that anyone repeatedly invited to them had a secure social position; and to make them the best managed, the best looked-after balls given in this city."

All this was accomplished with the aid of Delmonico's setting and suppers. Blessed by the Patriarchs, Delmonico's restaurant became a social stronghold, to penetrate which became the ambition of every snob in the United States. The door was open and the crowds came. They met but did not mingle, or mingled but did not mix, and Delmonico's thrived.

The press was of two minds how to take the portentousness of McAllister, who was always available for interviews and uttered his solemn social truths with an explosive hesitancy of speech that was not quite a stammer, but often robbed his pronouncements of their intended dignity. At times the affectations of the prosy poseur were ridiculed, although for a long while his power was admitted. When one paper published a versified tribute containing his self-appointed title, the plump old beau cherished it like a patent of nobility — paradoxically, of course, democratically bestowed. The doggerel ran, in part:

> There never was a sight so fair
> As at Delmonico's last night;
> When feathers, flowers, gems, and lace
> Adorned each lovely form and face;
> A garden of all thorns bereft,
> The outside world behind them left. . . .
> And by whose magic wand was this
> All conjured up, — the height of bliss?
> 'Tis he who now before you looms —
> The Autocrat of Drawing-Rooms.

At least one effect of Ward McAllister's reign was gratefully received by the reporters of social doings: it relieved them of the odium of drawing their own lines of eligibility and discrimination. Whether they agreed with McAllister's rulings or not, under his social autocracy they were never left in doubt as to who was "in" and who was "out."

CHAPTER VII

OF BLUESTOCKINGS,
AND BACKSTAGE

DELMONICO'S ACQUIRED another distinction in the late 1860's when it offered a shelter, and the sanction of its respectability, to a group of insurgent women. The Dickens dinner had provoked more than admiration of the novelist's jaunty way with a dish of crow. There were no women joining in the "tremendous applause and three cheers" which (according to the stenographic reporter) greeted that performance. Not that they might not have cheered and bravoed with the men, but they had not been wanted at the board where bottles gurgled and the smoke of Delmonico perfectos blued the air. In a word, they had been snubbed, rebuffed, and shut out, or so they declared.

As soon as it was known that Dickens had accepted the invitation of the Press Club, there was a rush for tickets, and not a few men whose connection with publishing was purely hypothetical enrolled their names upon the list of guests. The banquet, originally commissioned for one hundred and seventy-five covers, actually was served to two hundred and four.

The invitation sent to Dickens was signed by a committee of which the chairman was David G. Croly, managing editor of the *New York World*. Jennie June Croly, his wife, wrote fashion notes and reviews of plays and concerts for the *World*. Through her husband, she applied for a ticket at the regular price of $15, believing that she was eligible to attend as a member of the working press, in whose name the dinner was being given — "the press of New York." Her application elicited only laughter, and when she indignantly reported the slight to other women journalists they took up the issue and themselves applied for tickets. There were distinguished names among them, including the very successful author signing herself "Fanny Fern," who was one of the highest paid writers of the time, and in her private capacity was married to another member of the dinner committee, the author, James Parton. Although both Croly and Parton urged the acceptance of their wives' request for tickets (they were naturally under pressure at home), the committee did not even reply to the ladies' letters.

This cavalier treatment made Jennie June Croly fighting mad. She consulted the other resentful ladies, and they decided upon retaliation: in the words of Phoebe Cary, another popular author, they "tipped the teapot" and organized their own club, from which men would be excluded. This defiance caused hilarity among the men, who of course had clubs to meet every interest — literary, social, patriotic, sporting, musical, financial, scientific, or dining. No such thing as a club for women existed or was believed to be either possible, permissible, or proper. There were no garden clubs, no bridge clubs, no associations of professional women, not even church or missionary societies carried on solely by women.

Impervious to ridicule, the group proceeded with their plans simultaneously with the final arrangements for the Dickens dinner. Meeting in each other's houses, they debated the form their club should take, and fished for a name that would set the group off from anything it might be compared with. "Bluestocking" was suggested, but rejected because it sounded too "literary"; they wished their club to have the broadest possible scope. Finally a name was adapted from a word picked out of a botanical dictionary, a word meaning "an agglomeration." In this way "Sorosis" was born.

Meanwhile, news of the rebuff to the ladies had reached Horace Greeley, and he served notice that he would not preside at the banquet unless the women were "treated fairly." Greeley

was all-powerful on Newspaper Row, and the committee, finding its hand forced, informed Mrs. Croly that *if* she induced
enough women to buy tickets so that they would not feel "out
of place" and "ill at ease," their presence and their dollars would
be accepted. The grudging notification reached Jennie June
Croly three days before the date of the banquet, and only added
fuel to the ladies' indignation; they declined to attend, but went
ahead blithely with preparations for their own initial meeting.
This was to be held just two days after the Dickens affair.

But a difficulty arose: they could not find a suitable meeting
place. Several assembly rooms and restaurants declined to lend
their premises to anything so risky and outré as a parcel of
women congregating (for what purpose one could only con-
jecture) without male overseers. Mrs. Croly suggested that
they try Delmonico's. The Press Club (all male) had been
meeting there for several years; so why should not Sorosis
(all female)? Lorenzo Delmonico was appealed to, and without hesitation he instructed Charles to place a private room at
the new club's disposal.

On April 20, 1868, Sorosis held its first meeting in the great
Fourteenth Street house, and the members enjoyed a Delmonico luncheon at a dollar apiece. Dickens had been invited to be
present — as a non-speaking guest only — but he found good
reasons for not appearing. However, everything passed off in
so satisfactory a style, and the women were treated with such
consideration that they chose Delmonico's as their regular meeting place thereafter.

2.

That small beginning was the impetus which, in the course of
the next half century, spread women's clubs across the land and
culminated in the formation of the General Federation of
Women's Clubs. Sorosis was the "seed-sower" for that movement, and Delmonico's was its habitat. The members did not
spend much money there, but the presence of the club drew in-

ternational attention, from which the restaurant benefited. The
newspapers (in the main man-powered) never wearied of pok-
ing fun at the man-less club, whose members discussed topics of
the day with an assurance that could hardly help being absurd,
unblushingly exploring the touchiest subjects, such as, for example, "The Distribution of the Income in a Family"! For years
the Sorosis would be pelted with soggy jokes and subjected to
"vulgar would-be wit on the part of men"; but it steadily grew
in size and influence. The spectacle of the members arriving
for their monthly luncheons was looked forward to by many
of Delmonico's regulars, and there were both nods of approval
and gasps of outrage in the restaurant as the ladies tripped
briskly up the stairs to talk about Lord knew what in their
sanctuary above. A few women of wealth and social eminence
joined the group, but most of the members were in the professions or in business for themselves, and doing very well, thank
you. On occasion they could comport themselves with draw-
ing-room charm and demonstrate to doubters that they were
not social misfits or soured in mind and spirit. Once a year they
gave a banquet at Delmonico's to which men were invited, and
the brilliance of these affairs, the elegance of the hostesses, their
fetching gowns, and the fact that some of the members were
positively ravishing beauties never failed to perplex their mas-
culine guests. Why, then, the men perpetually wondered, must
they, in their mysterious conclaves, descend to discussions of
politics, surely a subject too sordid for feminine consideration?

The sole objective of Sorosis was to bring together women
of ability and inquiring minds who were interested in the world
around them, and provide an outlet for their intelligence, which
heretofore had been cooped up within the confines of the home
and social and family preoccupations. The members were not
reformers and not philanthropists, although many philanthro-
pies and reforms were aided by Sorosis. They persistently refused to be drawn into the controversy over "women's rights";
if a speaker violated the rule prohibiting allusion to that topic,

she was called to order promptly. Thus the members of the club avoided being tagged political agitators. In their exchanges of views and ideas, the members touched upon any subject that caught their fancy — art, medicine, science, music, the stage, the upbringing of children, female education, the value of calisthenics, and management of the family budget — and they were perfectly capable of scoring off the males who ridiculed them.

One venturesome man, named Robert B. Roosevelt, applied for membership in Sorosis, and was rebuffed with a deftness that sent chuckles of appreciation rippling clear across the ocean. Jennie June Croly, who was president of the club at that time, replied that the application had been laid before the membership committee, and had been rejected — not, she added in candor, for any reason of "character, position, or personal merit," but solely because of the "unfortunate fact of your being a man. We willingly admit," the letter continued blandly, "that the accident of your sex is upon your part a misfortune and not a fault. Nor do we wish to arrogate anything to ourselves because we had the good fortune to be born women. We sympathize most truly and heartily with you, and the entire male creation, in their present and prospective desolation and unhappiness; but that is all we can do. Sorosis is too young for the society of gentlemen and must be allowed to grow . . . For years to come, the reply to all male suitors must be, 'Principles, not men.' "

This pert saucing of the gander by an independent goose appealed to the editors of *The Queen*, London's leading magazine for women, and they commented with relish upon "how the rules of exclusion from societies, on the simple ground of the sex of the applicant, can be made to work both ways. It is not a little droll to observe, applied to a man, the little courtesies and the utter rejection which women have been made to experience when they have presumed to request admission to societies of men. There is the same complacent expression of superiority arising from secured position, and there are the same patronizing airs which are so pleasant to exercise and so unpleasant to encounter. There is the same softening of rejection by the assurances of personal esteem . . ."

Within a year Sorosis had a hundred members, and eventually the number would swell to five hundred, and branches would spread to other cities. In 1875, at a "May Festival" held in Delmonico's main banquet room to celebrate the club's seventh birthday, an editor who in 1868 had scoffed that Sorosis "wouldn't last a year," was among the guests, and again — although it was not on the menu — diners at Delmonico's were treated to the sight of a literary gentleman gallantly downing a dish of crow.

3.

Six years after Sorosis was founded, another club, which was to become as widely known and enjoy even greater longevity, was born at Fourteenth Street and Fifth Avenue. This was the Lambs. Prime mover in forming the club was Henry J. Montague (real name Henry John Mann), an English actor. "Young, brilliant, and fascinating," he exuded charm. Early in the last century, Charles and Mary Lamb, both enthusiasts for the stage, had gathered around them in London a circle of stage folk, and a remark often heard backstage after the final curtain had been, "Let's go around to the Lambs'." After Charles Lamb's death, a group of actors formed a club and named it in memory of their friends.

In 1874 Harry Montague was playing in New York, and like many other successful actors regularly dropped in at Delmonico's for an after-performance snack. Just before Christmas in that year, he proposed to other homesick theatrical exiles that they form a supper club on the model of The Lambs at home. Four actors joined him at once — Edward Arnott, Harry Beckett, George H. McClean, and Arthur Wallack. They adopted the name and titles used by the London Lambs (calling their president the "Shepherd," the vice president the "Boy," and the secretary the "Collie") and established their meeting place in the Blue Room of Delmonico's. The club grew in numbers and in popularity, and met in several places before it moved to its present home on West 44th Street in 1905 — to a building designed for it by another Delmonico regular, Stanford White.

Charming Harry Montague was the American theater's first matinee idol. A New Yorker who knew him well recalled that once Montague showed him a bushel basket filled with the *envelopes only* of love letters women had sent him. His nature was sunny and carefree, and he gave free rein to oddities that provided copy for the newspapers. One trick was to stroll along Fifth Avenue with a violet dangling from his mouth, an action that in any other man would have suggested effeminacy, but in him was accepted. And no scene he portrayed on the stage was more dramatic than that of his early death.

Although he was ill with tuberculosis, in 1881 he took his play "Diplomacy" on tour, reaching San Francisco late in July. During a benefit performance there, he collapsed on the stage. He was carried to his dressing room, suffering a severe hemorrhage, and when he could be moved, was taken to the Palace Hotel and put to bed.

Next afternoon, feeling better, he got up and dressed. Disliking to be alone, he invited several members of his troupe — men and women — to take dinner with him in his suite. They found him in gay spirits. As they were sitting down, the doctor arrived and went with Montague into the bedroom. In a short time the doctor departed, saying that he wished to consult a specialist. Montague followed him into the parlor, where his friends were already at table, and slapping his chest, exclaimed: "It's all right, boys; there is nothing the matter with me. The verdict is *not guilty!*"

Three minutes later he began to choke, blood streamed from his mouth, and he staggered into the bedroom, where almost immediately he died.

The theatrical world was shocked. His body was sent to

New York, and the funeral, held in the Little Church Around the Corner, on East Twenty-ninth Street, drew every actor and actress of any importance — and many who were not important — in New York. The crowd was so great that forty policemen were required to control it.

Harry Montague's memory is perpetuated by a memorial window in that "actors' church," and by a portrait in the clubhouse of The Lambs. The club was his legacy to his profession, and in its regulations there linger to this day traces of its Delmonican origin. Women may not be elected members. They may enter the clubhouse only after 5:30 P.M. (Delmonico's dinner hour), and even then (as at Delmonico's in 1874) they must be escorted by a man.

CHAPTER VIII

OF BLOWOUTS

ONCE THE GRIEFS of the war had subsided, Delmonico's at Four-teenth Street became the setting for a succession of banquets so ostentatious they were talked about all over the country. Some of these affairs were merely costly, gotten up with intentional extravagance; others honored events and personages of inter-national significance. Charles Ranhofer was the architect of these gala entertainments; perpetuating, at Delmonico's, after the overthrow of the Second Empire in France, those dinners and *soupers* in the grand manner which he had formerly served at the Tuileries.

The urge of the age was to spend and overspend, to dazzle ornately; taste was secondary, and some of the commissions that Delmonico and Ranhofer carried out were as gaudy as the era. It was not their taste that ruled, but the requirements of the cus-tomers, and some of these were indeed bizarre.

In a classic description of how his kitchen functioned, Charles Ranhofer said plainly: "It is a mistaken idea that everyone, willy-nilly, is compelled to take or go without the particular style of cooking that commends itself to the chef. The chef may know more about the proper cooking and serving of dishes than the customer, but should the latter have any particular fancies or weaknesses of his own in the eating line, he can, pro-vided his purse dances in close attendance upon his whimsical-ities of taste, have set before him dishes which fill the sensitive chef's heart with despair."

Should a man walk into Delmonico's and order kippered her-rings smothered in jam, that he would be served, and the cook would have to smother his rage. But even the complaisance of Ranhofer was stretched by the fancies and weaknesses of some of the new-rich who were flocking to Delmonico's in the Sixties and Seventies. What was reported to be the costliest dinner, until that time, ever served at the Fourteenth Street restaurant was gotten up in 1865 for a British stock promoter named Sir Morton Peto. Despite his apparent descent from one of Falstaff's pot-valiants, he was received in Wall Street with obsequiousness: Jim Fisk deferred to him as "the largest railway builder in the world," and was proud to include even his representative (since he could not inveigle Sir Morton himself) in a cozy tête-à-tête at Josie Mansfield's. Among Sir Morton's interests were large holdings in the tea and coffee trade, and the dinner he commissioned was for one hundred tea and coffee merchants of New York. It ran through nine courses, each a gastronomical sensation, with nine matching wines, from Napoleon champagne to Imperial Tokay.

Only so much money can be spent for food and drink, and it was in the accessories to this feast that Delmonico demonstrated how a really uninhibited freewheeler might disembarrass himself of cash and attract the most attention. Each of Sir Morton Peto's guests rested his haunches upon a silk cushion embroidered with his name; that was luxury to start with! The menus were lettered in gold upon satin, and the normally restrained *New York Times* reported the dining room "smothered in rarest flowers." Some of the wines cost $25 a bottle, the *Times* went on. "The cleverest musicians were engaged at fancy prices; Clara Louise Kellogg [reigning prima donna at the Academy of Music on Fourteenth Street] had $1,000 for two songs, and a present, besides, of a diamond bracelet. In all probability such a dinner had never been served in the Republic." The bill was awe-inspiring — $20,000 — and Sir Morton paid with satisfaction.

A couple of years later his well-cushioned guests were annoyed to learn that the "largest railway builder in the world" had escaped being jailed in England only by dodging through a loophole in the very law he had been breaking.

In one of his infrequent chats with reporters, Lorenzo Delmonico admitted frankly that some of the orders he took were silly. "Yes, indeed," he replied to a question. "We often give dinners that cost $100 a head. Why, sometimes the flowers cost $20 for each diner, and I have paid as high as $20 for each and every menu card. It doesn't take long to run up to $100 in that way."

Carte blanche dinners — ordered without limitation as to cost, with all details left to the inventiveness of the house — were of common occurrence, and each put Delmonico's ingenuity to the test. There were, for example, the three dinners commissioned by three of the city's foremost men-about-town and epicures — Leonard Jerome (grandfather of Sir Winston Churchill), August Belmont, and William R. Travers. In friendly rivalry, they told Lorenzo Delmonico to provide three dinners irrespective of cost, each to be better than the others. Delmonico called them the Silver, Gold, and Diamond dinners, and after the last mouthful had been eaten the verdict was that honors ran even; though Jerome had capped his competitors by serving *truffled ice cream* (a delicacy pronounced delicious by those who tasted it, despite its unprepossessing sound), and by the favors distributed to the ladies: folded in each napkin, a gold bracelet with a medallion engraved "J.P.," for Jerome Park, the fashionable racetrack Jerome had built in Fordham and inaugurated with General Grant, Jim Fisk, and Boss Tweed all in the grandstand.

Several years after Sir Morton Peto's splurge (in February 1873, to be exact), Edward Luckmeyer, a wealthy importer, received from the government a $10,000 refund on customs duties he had overpaid. This manna from heaven he could think of no better way of spending than on a dinner at Delmonico's which would be the talk of the town. He gave Lorenzo Delmonico and Charles Ranhofer an absolutely free hand, and the result was indeed talked about for years; in fact, when imitated by a Vanderbilt a generation later it would again be regarded as the acme of fantastic dining.

In Delmonico's largest room an oval table was constructed, to seat seventy-five guests. The table filled the entire floor space except for a passage just wide enough for the waiters to circulate. The center of the table was a lake thirty feet long, landscaped with exotic plants, waterfalls, violet-bordered brooks, blossoming hillocks and grassy glades. The lake was enclosed by a mesh of gold wire extending to the ceiling, and this formed a cage for several swans that glided upon the water; Tiffany had constructed the cage, and the swans were on loan from Prospect Park in Brooklyn. Around the foot of the wire screen was an embankment of flowers to protect the diners from splashing when the swans now and then fought. Over the lake were suspended golden cages containing songbirds. The entire Delmonico's staff was summoned to admire this aquatic-gastronomic masterpiece, and the "Swan Dinner" went down in legend.

It was inevitable that the first dining car put into service on an American railroad should be named "Delmonico"; and the extent of Delmonico's fame is suggested by the fact that this car was not launched upon an eastern railroad, but on the Chicago & Alton, in the Midwest. The date of the grand event was 1868, and by then the name and the adjective "Delmonican" had entered into general usage; people who had never seen and never would see a Delmonico restaurant used the word with full understanding of its meaning.

2.

The Delmonicos early lost count of the great personages who were served in their restaurants; they were not a writing family, and preserved few records of themselves or their establishments. However, they knew that every President of the United States, from Monroe down, had been their guest; and every succeeding President, up to Calvin Coolidge and Franklin D. Roosevelt, was destined to be. As for millionaires — the men of power whose mansions flanked Fifth Avenue and filled the cross streets above and below Madison Square — Delmonico was their caterer. Charles Delmonico could dispatch everything requisite for a reception, a ball, or a dinner — food, wines, linen, cutlery, glasses, with a battery of skilled cooks and waiters — to an address miles away, and serve the repast in flawless style. About these private entertainments the public knew little, but the activities staged in the four restaurants everybody heard about.

There were public banquets for General William Tecumseh Sherman, and for New York State's Governor John T. Hoffman and his military staff; a formal dinner given to the first ambassador from China; banquets by the Society of California Pioneers, and the annual reunions of the St. George's, the St. Andrew's, the St. Nicholas, and the New-York Historical Societies. The Bulls and Bears of Wall Street foregathered there. In December of 1868, when the Atlantic cable was reactivated after a hiatus of eight years, commencement of regular telegraphic communication with Europe was celebrated by a tremendous banquet given in honor of the telegraph's inventor, Professor S. F. B. Morse, who on a key installed at the speakers' table tapped out the first message, and received the reply twenty minutes later.

In 1871, when the Grand Duke Alexis visited the city, the New York Yacht Club gave him a nautical dinner at a cost of $5,000 — nothing remarkable by comparison with Peto's petard, although it did move the *New York Herald* to observe that "for $5,000 Delmonico can make fifty people gastronomically quite comfortable." The Grand Duke assured Lorenzo that never, afloat or ashore, had he been blessed by better cooking.

But gastronomic exuberance reached a peak in the extravaganza which Delmonico got up for a yachtsman (not pilloried for posterity by name in the newspapers) who managed to run his dinner bill up to $400 a head — not for food and wine, for that would be impossible even though the guests had gorged on nightingales' tongues, but on unexampled gewgaws and trimmings. According to the *New York Sun*, a paper little given to astonishment, beside each guest's plate was "a cut-glass basin about twenty inches in diameter and four inches deep . . . filled with water perfumed with attar of roses, on the surface of which floated half-open pond lilies." In this little lake swung at anchor a model of one of the host's yachts, carved in red cedar and furnished with "chain, rail, wheel for steering, brass work such as belaying pins and binnacle, ropes trimmed with sailor knots, scraped pine masts and booms, rigging of silk and sails of satin." This miniature ship's chandlery (it also included a golden oar and various deep-water adjuncts) the diners were able to devour with their eyes only; but the feast was almost as ornate and terminated in a pousse-café composed of *eleven liqueurs*. Delmonico's itself never topped that.

The *carte blanche* dinners commanded by a new president of the Pacific Mail Steamship Company were almost as pretentious, if not as conducive to biliousness. A day-long *"déjeuner-goûter-diner-souper"* served to three hundred guests aboard the line's *City of Peking* (for purposes of currying favor) ran through sixteen separate courses — from early morning *oeufs au jambon* (ham and eggs to such of the partakers as were unlettered, and many of them were) to midnight lobster salad and Neapolitan ice cream.

The great dinners served at Delmonico's during the Sixties and Seventies form a chapter in the social history of New York and the era. It was said that no man or woman who had attained any measure of notoriety and came within a hundred miles of New York City failed to enter one of the Delmonico shrines of good cheer sooner or later. The main burden of supervising the ever-expanding organization was carried by Lorenzo, with his brother Siro and his nephew Charles Delmonico as his principal aides. Constant, who had managed the Beaver Street house, succumbed to overwork (it was said) in 1873 and was buried at St. Patrick's. He left a son and two granddaughters, whose care Lorenzo assumed.

Lorenzo's insistence upon exactitude in every detail of the business was a source of amazement to his friends. One told of seeing the restaurateur watch a page boy who was wrapping a roll to go out. The boy used a whole sheet of paper. The head of Delmonico's made him unwrap the bun, and start again by cutting the paper in half, then cutting each half in two. Taking one of the quarter-sheets, Lorenzo wrapped the roll in a neat, compact package, pointing out to the apprentice that not only was the appearance of the parcel improved, but enough paper had been saved to wrap three more rolls.

Contrasting with this care for details was the magnitude of Lorenzo Delmonico's dealings as a wine importer. Nearly all the wines and cigars sold in the restaurants were imported directly, at a cost which no local merchant could match. As many as three hundred cases of fine vintages would be ordered at a time, and three large cellars were maintained downtown to store current stocks. These rarely dipped below $200,000 in value.

The sum total of capital invested in the combined enterprises was large for that period: Lorenzo estimated the cash investment at half a million, and his expenses at more than a million dollars a year. Rents accounted for more than $100,000. In 1861 the rent of the Chambers Street place was raised from $25,000 to $30,000; and in 1869 Moses Grinnell whacked up the rent for the Fourteenth Street house from $7,500 to $26,000. Already Lorenzo had purchased the building next door, the Suarez mansion, for $115,000, and had extended the restaurant into it. An old devotee, Winfield Scott, grown so corpulent he could no longer navigate a staircase, established a beachhead in two rooms on the ground floor of the Suarez house in order to be near his commissariat.

The weekly payroll of the four restaurants came to $13,000,

notwithstanding that the wages paid to the waiters — the most numerous group of employees — were not large; these relied on their tips, which at times were munificent. John Klages, who started as a waiter at Fourteenth Street and remained with Delmonico's almost half a century, would amuse patrons by reciting from a prodigious memory the tips he had received and the date on which he got each one, with the attendant circumstances. The biggest tip he ever got, he said, was not from a customer at all, but from Charles Delmonico, left on the table after a round of drinks with friends in the cafe — five $20 gold pieces. Charles was lavish with his money, unlike his uncle Lorenzo.

Outside business, Lorenzo Delmonico had become one of New York's foremost citizens. He lived in a retired manner and courted no public honors, although in December, 1870, he was elected to the New-York Historical Society. Charles Francis Adams, John Bigelow, George William Curtis, and Mrs. Martha J. Lamb, historian of New York City, were admitted during the same period to this blueblood organization, which would itself celebrate its one hundredth birthday by a grand banquet in the Delmonico's of 1904. Lorenzo's support of church and charities was liberal. He gave generously to his parish church, St. Ann's, on East Twelfth Street, and to the church in Mairengo where his ancestors were buried.

His position, both personal and professional, was hardly shaken when the nation rocked in the commercial collapse of 1873. Amid the crashing of banks and businesses, the income of the restaurants was reduced, but not vitally. Of more concern to Lorenzo was the suffering caused by unemployment. The winter of 1873-74 was bitter, and soup kitchens were set up to feed the destitute. Contrary to some critics, New York City has always been quick to respond to human needs, within the limitations of the social and political patterns of successive periods. Repeatedly, New York led in humanitarian endeavors — in establishing hospitals, asylums, foundling homes, and free schools, and in public benevolence. It was a New Yorker who aroused the conscience of the century against the cruelties practiced upon helpless animals and children; both societies to eradicate these abuses were founded in New York by New Yorkers. The relief measures taken to ease the misery of the unemployed in 1873 were typical of the city's social awareness, and Lorenzo Delmonico was placed in charge of the project.

In the spring of 1874 he relinquished his stewardship of the "system of soup houses assigned to my care during the recent season of unusual and severe distress" in an open letter addressed to the editors of the city's press. Between February 18 and April 7, he reported, seventy-one thousand eight hundred and ninety-two persons had been fed in one ward alone, so massive had been the operation. "I visited frequently the kitchens and the houses for the supply of soup," he stated, "and I saw few, if any, of those who were . . . asking relief who did not seem really needy and deserving."

The way the business depression cut into the revenue of the Delmonico restaurants was noticeable chiefly in the reduced call for wine. Charles Delmonico told a newsman that a short while previously he could have walked through the dining rooms and observed one, two, or three bottles of wine on every table; "but now, if we hear a cork pop, we turn to see where it is, and it is generally a bottle of Bass."

The "Swan Dinner" had occurred just before the crash, as had another banquet, almost as sumptuous, given in honor of President Grant. At this affair the President stood upon a dais while receiving guests, and some newspapers sneered that the setting was really too regal. Even when stock prices cascaded to dismal lows, the bears of Wall Street were reaping a harvest, and the gleanings from each "good thing" they maneuvered to a profit they dispensed liberally at places like Delmonico's. Thus in spite of the commercial prostration, there was still money in circulation, and Delmonico's struggled along not too uncomfortably.

But it became clear to Lorenzo that the collapse of 1873 marked the end of another era, and the dawn of a better one. The tide of fashion was pushing farther uptown. Madison Square was the hub of a new center of handsome residences, and the finest hotels and theaters were congregating there. Above Fourteenth, in the stretch of Broadway between Union Square and Twenty-third Street, were situated the smart shops; Fourteenth Street was beginning to look seedy.

In 1876, therefore, Lorenzo decided to move. The year was one of celebrations, and throngs of travelers were passing through New York on their way to or from the great Centennial Exposition in Philadelphia, where the nation was marking one hundred years of phenomenal growth since proclaiming its independence. More than half a century had passed since John Delmonico had tacked up the first signboard bearing the family name in New York City. Dynamic changes had occurred in the interval, and through them all, Delmonico's had maintained its steady progress. In 1876 Lorenzo made one move more: bidding farewell to fifteen years of fragrant memories at Fourteenth Street and Fifth Avenue, he transferred the uptown restaurant to Twenty-sixth Street and Fifth Avenue, facing Madison Square. Time would show this to be the most fruitful transplanting in the long career of the institution.

CHAPTER IX

MADISON SQUARE

THE HOUSE AND FAMILY OF DELMONICO, a newspaper man once said, were no more meant to keep still "than a green pea on a hot shovel." Unlike the dancing pea, however, their bouncings were not erratic; on the contrary, they were so systematic, calculated with such clarity of foresight, and so neatly timed, that they aroused an often-expressed admiration. In 1876 this sagacity in regard to favorable locations for their enterprises was displayed at both ends of the long line of their activity — uptown and downtown. At the same time that Fourteenth Street was deserted for Twenty-sixth, the restaurant at Chambers Street and Broadway was closed, in favor of a more commodious and modern establishment at 112-114 Broadway, near Pine Street, next door to the recently completed skyscraper Equitable Building. So brisk had business in the downtown area grown, the 22 Broad Street restaurant and the "Citadel" at Beaver and South William Streets could not accommodate the demand. New facilities were required, while the two older establishments continued to serve their regular clientele.

Any change in the location of a Delmonico's was of interest in New York; a proposal to move the City Hall could hardly have provoked livelier debate and speculation than the restaurant's change of base. A typical comment was that made by the *Herald* in an editorial headed "Philosophical Catering":

"As good wine is said to need no bush, so wherever Delmonico puts up a kitchen with eating rooms attached people are sure of a good dinner if they can pay for it, and there is no necessity of covering the city with posters to assure our citizens of the fact . . . When the Nestors of the restaurant business of New York open a new house, it is as much an event as the opening of a royal bottle of Johannisberg or of Chateau d'Yquem, hoary with the cobwebs of a quarter of a century, at the little dinner of a pair of veteran gourmands . . . *O rare Delmonico!* we would say of the great king of cuisine, as it was said of Ben Jonson, did it not strike us that a captious world might think that the perfect chef of chefs was in the habit of presenting his viands underdone. Let us rather say *sagacious Delmonico,* for it is the live tradition of nearly a century in Gotham that 'as Delmonico goes, so goes the dining.' "

To this a later generation would add, "and so goes the city."

The newspapers did their best to satisfy public curiosity about the new Delmonico premises, reporting the dimensions, interiors, exteriors, advantages, and prospects of the new establishments both uptown and downtown.

The uptown building — leased for ten years at an annual rental of $35,000 — was known as the Dodsworth Studios. It occupied the entire south side of Twenty-sixth Street between Fifth Avenue and Broadway, and had been used popularly for assembly balls and other social gatherings. The frontage on Fifth Avenue, the public was told in relentless detail, was sixty-five feet; the windows on that side overlooked a miniature lawn, and beyond that, across Fifth Avenue, the trees and flower beds of Madison Square. The main dining room was to be on that side, enjoying the view. At the other end of the building, fronting sixty-one feet on Broadway, would be the men's cafe; while in the center of the Twenty-sixth Street side (one hundred and fifty feet long) would be the entrance giving access to the dining and ball rooms on the upper floors.

The location had not been Delmonico's first choice. Early in 1875 Charles Delmonico had attempted to acquire a corner site farther up Fifth Avenue at Thirty-seventh Street, occupied by the home of former Governor Edwin D. Morgan. At one point Charles had offered to invest $700,000, paying $400,000 for the ground (all to remain on mortgage at 6%) and "I to build a house to cost about $300,000." The property took in eight lots, priced separately by Charles at $125,000 for the corner, $100,000 for the lot adjoining it on Fifth Avenue, and $25,000 for each of the six lots on Thirty-seventh Street, the entire area measuring seventy-five feet by two hundred and ten. As an alternative, Mrs. Paran Stevens, whose home stood on the opposite corner, was willing to erect a restaurant building there and lease land and building for $85,000 a year on a twelve or fifteen year agreement — $50,000 for the ground and $35,000 annually for the building. Both these proposals fell through, partly because of suspected double-dealing by an agent and partly because Lorenzo Delmonico perceived the greater advantages of the location on Madison Square.

The situation, just above where Broadway and Fifth Avenue crossed, commanded streams of traffic converging from three directions — from the shopping district below the Square — from the hotels and theaters along Broadway — and from the homes of wealth on Fifth Avenue. This meant that a wide cross section of the city's inhabitants would be passing the restaurant's doors continually. At the corner of Twenty-third Street and Broadway was the resplendent Fifth Avenue Hotel, home of politicians and businessmen ever since the Prince of Wales had given it a sendoff by staying there in 1860. Lincoln had spoken from the balcony overlooking Broadway, and Charlotte Cushman had received the plaudits of throngs there. Since it enjoyed all but official standing as Republican headquarters in the city, the strategists of that party might be seen any day at its substantial table d'hôte, digesting political schemes with the heavy fare.

Next above the Fifth Avenue Hotel, on the west side of Broadway, between Twenty-fourth and Twenty-fifth Streets, were the Albermarle and Hoffman Hotels — the Albermarle small, select, discreet, and the Hoffman House, next door, boasting the biggest bar in America, so large that eighteen bartenders were kept busy slaking the thirst of its customers. The sporting element and well-heeled playboys favored the Hoffman House, as well as connoisseurs of the type of art that stretched from end to end of the space behind the block-long mahogany bar, a Bouguereau offering for appraisal acres of nudity in the guise of nymphs disporting with satyrs. That painting, and other art treasures with which the house was liberally furnished, were a tourist sight of the city. From the Hoffman House to Delmonico's was only a step across Broadway.

Directly opposite the cafe entrance of the new Delmonico's was the St. James Hotel, a gathering place of the prosperous figures of the theater, stage stars and managers, while further up Broadway was another theatrical rendezvous, the Gilsey House. Delmonico's at Twenty-sixth Street was within smelling distance of both these centers of notoriously hungry customers.

The atmosphere on the Fifth Avenue side of the new premises was different — breathing gentility, conservatism, richness, style. The broughams and daumonts and victorias of the Avenue's residents passed Delmonico's door incessantly, and the doll-house lawn bordering the restaurant entrance was a permanent temptation for the carriage trade to stop and enter. Diagonally across Fifth Avenue stood the Hotel Brunswick, a stronghold of society with a cuisine almost rivaling Delmonico's. The Coaching Club met at the Brunswick; from its doors tooled away the brilliantly turned-out four-in-hands, guided by "sports" vain of their touch on the "ribbons," the tops of the coaches crowded with men in gray toppers and pretty girls in billowing skirts, who twirled bright parasols and were as coquettish as the bouquets that bobbed at the horses' throat latches. The coach horns tootled merrily on the way back to "Del's," where all who took part in the showy and expensive pastime were devotees of Ranhofer.

2.

The interior of the building so pleasantly and profitably situated was described by reporters after a preview inspection as the ultimate in luxury and refined good taste. The structure had

been made over completely for its new use, and one writer of
society notes for the *Herald* went on record, without equivoca-
tion, that the "appointments in every respect are the finest, com-
bining a due regard for the enjoyment of the *otium cum digni-
tate*, and totally disregarding that excess which sometimes char-
acterizes the surroundings of wealth." The restaurant, sixty by
sixty-two feet, was lined with mirrors to enhance its air of spa-
ciousness. The furniture was mahogany, and the room was
lighted by silver chandeliers under a frescoed ceiling. In the
center plashed a fountain bordered by flowers. In the cafe, the
furniture was ash inlaid with marquetry.

On the second floor were four dining rooms in contrasting
hues of satin — blue, crimson, olive, drab — and here four separate dinners could be served simultaneously without the least
derangement or inconvenience. Also on the second floor, extending along the Broadway side, was the ballroom, fifty feet
square, finished in regal red and gold. Adjacent supper and retiring rooms gave every facility for graceful entertaining.
There were more dining rooms on the third floor, and a banquet
hall that could be divided into three separate rooms if desired,
each (according to the press) "decorated in a different hue and
richly furnished."

The fourth floor was given over to quarters for a few confirmed bachelors who, as permanent residents, were being evac-
uated from their Fourteenth Street lodgings. One of the press
concluded that bachelorhood could "nowhere be more thoroughly enjoyed" than in these suites supplied "with every device to make them appreciate the comforts of life . . . upholstered in colors pleasing to the eye and furnished in magnificent
style."

The top floor housed servants' and storage rooms, and the
indispensable laundry.

Of course there were doubters who predicted that the stream
of custom would never follow Delmonico up the Avenue from
Fourteenth Street, where so many triumphs had been scored;

and Lorenzo, Siro, and Charles were perhaps not unmindful of these gloomy forecasts when they took their stations at the doors of the restaurant for the opening on September 11, 1876. For a while the outlook was foreboding: the morning patronage was thin, and there were empty tables at luncheon. But with the cocktail hour, patrons began to crowd in, until both restaurant and cafe were filled, and the verdict was — a complete success.

The rich, the prominent, and the high-livers of New York rejoiced in this fresh triumph of "Delmonico, the prince of restaurateurs, the sound of whose very name has an appetizer in it." The *Herald* expressed the general sentiment that "the new quarters and the magnificence of the surroundings will atone for the loss of the old." Moreover, Lorenzo Delmonico had shown consummate shrewdness in evaluating the advantages of the location. Now, instead of proceeding along Fourteenth Street to Fifth Avenue, and thence uptown, as Delmonico's clientele formerly had done, "the tide of promenaders of a bright afternoon — or in fact, on any day at any hour — as it emerges into Union Square nowadays keeps right along Broadway to Madison Square," the *Herald* noted, "where it is a matter of choice whether the route further along is along Broadway or up the Avenue. Go whichever way they will, they now find Delmonico's doors standing invitingly open — on the Avenue as well as on Broadway. A more central location could not have been selected."

After all, the change was not so great — merely one of "new scenes with old faces. Drop into the cafe any evening, and the same familiar faces are around the tables, and the crowd in the restaurant after the theater . . . is greater than before. Go where Delmonico will, the old admirers will follow."

Every omen, as read by the *Herald*, was fortunate. In Delmonico's "new palatial house of the roasted bird and the fragrant wine success has crowned his brow as naturally as good humor crowns good cheer . . . Here, nearly vis-à-vis that other haunt of the gourmand, the Cafe Brunswick, and facing lovely Madison Square, shall we have another rallying place for the epicure, the belle, the 'good-liver' . . . another spot consecrated to the art of cookery, where the sound of merriment and revelry will not cease from morn to night. Here the great, formal, pompous dinner parties of the associations of the rich; the political dinners, which are only disguises for speech-making; the happy and cozy family reunions; the tender gastronomical tête-à-têtes of a pair of hungry lovers just come from a feast of grand opera; and the quiet jolly suppers of convivial friends — all these will find here another gay and bright center, another happy hunting ground."

A bright forecast, that would be amply fulfilled.

3.

No less pleased were businessmen with the downtown move of Delmonico, from Chambers to Pine Street. Six weeks after the brilliant opening of the Madison Square house, the new restaurant on lower Broadway was opened, and it prospered from the first day. Descriptions of its commodious interior also filled the newspapers, and all its features were carefully catalogued — from the storerooms in the subcellar and the bakery in the basement, to the "open, airy, pleasant" kitchens on the top floor, whence the food was carried on "five dumb waiters" to the dining rooms below. On the ground floor was the quick-service counter, with a side dining room, and the restaurant proper was one flight up — Axminster-carpeted, with lace-curtained windows overlooking Broadway. On the floor above, private dining rooms, and on the fourth floor a large dining hall for workers in the Equitable Building, to which doorways cut in the dividing wall gave direct access; more than a thousand persons a day were accommodated here. Nothing like this palace of good eating had been seen in downtown New York, and on October 26, 1876 — the opening day — Siro Delmonico lent the authentic touch with his beaming countenance and blackest cigar.

"The lucky house," said one report, "was baptized in all kinds of desirable and stimulating liquids, and on its altar every edible bird and beast (in season) was offered up, not indeed in whole burnt offering, but 'done to a turn.' "

The instantaneous success of the double expansion, in the face of warnings by the supposedly wise, provided a moral which the press was prepared to drive home. The *Herald* again went to the quick of the matter when it commented:

"The business movements of so sagacious a caterer are a matter of significance to the student of our city's growth . . . The abandonment of the Fourteenth Street and Chambers Street houses, for houses respectively half a mile higher uptown, and half a mile lower downtown, is suggestive of a dual movement of our classes for business and pleasure worth noting."

Lorenzo had gauged this pull in opposite directions accurately, and at the right moment entrusted his fortunes to it. No Delmonico ever lingered overlong in a neighborhood that had seen its best days; and which was the determinative factor — the movement of population and business, or Delmonico's ability to foreshadow it — was becoming more and more a moot question.

CHAPTER X

WHEN THE KING DIES...

THE TWO DECADES that spanned the career of Delmonico's at Madison Square were to mark the golden age of the house, as they marked what in many ways were the golden years for New York. And this in spite of setbacks which might have sent an enterprise less solidly grounded in civic respect and affection spinning into a decline.

A few days before the Madison Square restaurant was opened for business, Lorenzo's mother, Rosa Longhi Del-Monico, died in Mairengo. She was in her ninety-third year, and to the last retained an interest in the progress of her sons in America. Over the years all of them had visited her periodically.

Lorenzo was sixty-three, and years of unremitting toil had begun to take their toll. He still held himself accountable for every department of the four restaurants, and in company with Siro supervised the daily marketing. The number of his employees had increased to more than four hundred. Siro and Charles were his field commanders downtown and uptown, while John Longhi maintained the high standards at 22 Broad Street, and managers trained in the firm superintended the Beaver Street "Citadel."

By now, everything about the famous restaurants was of public concern, and in spite of his natural bent towards taciturnity, Lorenzo now and then was induced to reveal glimpses of the backstage workings. In 1876 he told an interviewer something about the salaries he paid. The headwaiter at Madison Square got $1,500 a year, with board and lodging, he said, and his tips were his own. Table waiters were paid $30 a month and averaged $60 in tips.

"I wanted to transfer one man from the restaurant to the cafe, raising him from $30 to $60," Lorenzo added, "but he wouldn't go; he was making $90 in tips where he was."

The *chef de cuisine* topped the salary list by a wide margin. How much did the chef command? The way Lorenzo expressed it: "I pay my present chef $4,000 a year; his predecessor got $6,000." This "predecessor" was Charles Ranhofer.

The master cook had not joined the pilgrimage to Twenty-sixth Street. Several months before the Fourteenth Street house closed he had retired and gone back to France, where for three years he would run the Hôtel Américain at Enghien-les-Bains. The Delmonicos conceded that nobody could quite replace the greatest of their kitchen field marshals. According to perceptive judges, Charles Ranhofer might have succeeded as a general, a diplomat, or an artist, had he entered any of those professions; in his chosen work he combined the capacities of them all. No demand seemed to exceed his capacity, and his talent for organization was extraordinary. Stories were told of the exigency of Leonard Jerome, who had built, adjoining his great residence across the Square from the new Delmonico's, a theater, where he staged plays and operas for invited audiences. Jerome thought nothing of sending an order at eight o'clock in the evening for a supper of sumptuous proportions to be served to a hundred guests two hours later. And Ranhofer would serve it, with not an item missing, down to the last fork and last forkful. He disliked receiving detailed instructions. Ward McAllister would say, "Tell Ranhofer the number of your guests and nothing more, and you will have perfection." It was not unusual for him to supervise the preparation of half a dozen dinners to be served in private houses in different parts of the city, dispatch refreshments for two or three hundred spectators at a horse or yacht race, and watch over the regular restaurant service, all in one day.

The loss of such a man was felt keenly by Lorenzo Delmonico, but the blow was not crippling; for by 1876 there were many European-trained master cooks in the country, and a connection with Delmonico's kitchen was coveted because it opened the door to lucrative employment anywhere. Every rich man, every social climber, was on the prowl to obtain the services of an illustrious cook, and a chef from Delmonico's carried the greatest luster of all. So well was this recognized, that some of Ranhofer's successors signed their menus. One of the last great banquets given at Fourteenth Street was a dinner in honor of Governor Tilden, in July 1876, the year in which, many still hold, he was robbed of the Presidency. The menu bore at its foot, coupled with "Delmonico," the signature "Charles Lallouette, Chef." During the early years at Madison Square, "Eug. Laperruque, Chef," appeared on the menus of dinners of high importance presented there.

Ranhofer found himself temperamentally in exile in France; he missed the vitality of New York; and in 1879 he returned and resumed his place at the head of Delmonico's kitchens. Thereafter as long as the restaurant overlooked Madison Square, Ranhofer was in absolute command.

2.

Involuntarily Lorenzo Delmonico became involved in a "temperance" battle in 1876-77. The trouble stemmed from the irreconcilable viewpoints of New York City dwellers and upstate legislators, who, reared in a rural environment, enacted laws that ran counter to the sentiment of the city and consequently were non-enforceable. Certain zealots who believed the saloon to be the breeding ground of big-city wickedness succeeded in passing a law prohibiting the sale of alcoholic beverages on Sundays; it was a step, the backers of the measure hoped, towards closing the "dens of depravity" entirely.

The saloons of Manhattan operated under licenses issued by the Excise Board. They were willing to give token compliance to the new law, and resorted to the tactic of shutting their front doors and drawing their shades on Sunday, but leaving their back doors open; in this way business could go on as usual, while appearances were preserved. The maneuver raised a howl among "temperance" fanatics, who charged that the police were breaking the law by winking at this palpable fraud, which was true enough. But when two captains were charged with dereliction and haled before the commissioners, their fellow captains retaliated by barging into every back door they found ajar on the following Sunday, and making five hundred arrests. Their intention was to show that the law could be enforced, if the town would stand for it, which the town would not. In fact, the Board of Aldermen was so outraged that by solemn resolution it upbraided the suddenly zealous police for making the Sabbath "hideous" by their "rude and unlawful intrusion."

Delmonico's cafe was among the places rudely intruded upon, and Lorenzo Delmonico, the owner, was arrested. After march and countermarch by opposing lawyers, he was arraigned in a police magistrate's court; his appearance, it was well understood, while technically in his own behalf, was meant to carry weight by reason of his irreproachable respectability; he was the most conspicuous and esteemed dealer in wines and spirits in the city.

The *Herald*'s reporter compiled a gusty account of the hearing:

"The first person called was Lorenzo Delmonico, and here it may be added, to relieve the anxiety of nervous saloon-keepers, that none of the arrested dealers were confined in the prisoners' pen. They were all allowed to sit in the courtroom proper."

An informer, Amos J. Bleecker, swore that he had bought whisky in the defendant's establishment on the Sabbath, contrary to the law. Delmonico presented no defense, merely stating that he held a license to sell liquor issued by the Excise Board. Then his attorney brought out that Bleecker, an unpardoned ex-convict, was incompetent to testify in a court of law and his testimony was stricken. The nervous magistrate did not dare to dismiss the case out of hand, and temporized, telling the dignified accused, "I must hold you in $100 bail."

"Very well," responded Lorenzo cheerfully. "My bondsman is here."

The bondsman stepped forward, bail was posted, and the case never went further.

Eventually a higher court did rule that licenses issued by the Excise Board entitled saloons to sell only beer and ale; and that wines and liquors could be sold only by hotels or taverns which maintained at least three beds for lodgers. Delmonico's, of course, with its permanent boarders, met this requirement. But the self-styled "temperance" advocates kept agitating, and two generations later produced consequences dreadful for Delmonico's.

3.

The gawky Seventies were America's Gilded Age, when the only real criterion of success was dollars and their amassing. There was talk about the desirability of refinement, and here and there some could be found; but the tone of the times was crass and materialistic. Entertainment tastes may be gauged by the theatrical advertisements in New York newspapers on the day Lorenzo Delmonico opened his restaurant at Madison Square. At Booth's Theater, the most fashionable in town, the play was "Sardanapalus" — a name suggestive of anything but moderation and refinement. The Fifth Avenue Theater was presenting "Money"; Wallack's, "The Almighty Dollar"; Wood's Museum, "Under the Gaslight"; and at the Brooklyn Theater was an old standby, "Dundreary." There were six variety and two minstrel shows running; the Bowery Theater (which incidentally stood at the exact population center of the city) advertised the farce, "Two Men on Sandy Bar."

That there was an almost sub-surface trend away from the raucous and giddy appeared in minor news items: for example, the newspapers carrying these entertainment notices also reported (as a novelty) that an agent for the Society for the Prevention of Cruelty to Children, acting under "the new law," had arrested a circus manager and an acrobat for using children in a tumbling act. But such indications were faint and on the borders of the main stream; all over the city culture was elbowed and crushed by crudity and grossness, as the mansions of the rich often were hemmed in between vacant lots where goats browsed before squatters' shanties.

This mixture of vice and virtue, of bulging wealth and moral poverty, was pointed up by a police order that was issued in 1876 and added a word to the language of the town. The order was the famous one transferring Captain Alexander S. Williams from the Gas House District on the far East Side to the Twenty-ninth Precinct on the West Side. This precinct was bounded by Fourth Avenue on the east, Seventh Avenue on the west, Fourteenth Street on the south, and Forty-second Street on the north, and was so rich in graft that the "pickings" available to an alert police officer were said to exceed those in any other precinct. Along garish Sixth Avenue were brothels and gambling dens that gave the area the name of "Satan's Circus"; while one block east stood Fifth Avenue mansions, and that eminently respectable establishment, Delmonico's.

Captain Williams was a policeman of the old school (meaning the school of the nightstick, the fist, and the short answer) and he glorified in his nickname, "Clubber" Williams. Yet so adaptable was he to the mixed character of his new command, that when off duty and out of uniform he devoured steak with the genteel at Delmonico's, serenely looking out upon placid Madison Square. This fulfilled the prophecy that had escaped him when he was notified of his transfer: "I've been living off chuck steak for a long time. Now I'm going to get a bit of the tenderloin!" The Tenderloin thus was named — and Delmonico's was in it — though never in the sense that posterity has attached to that word.

*

4.

Shortly after the launching of the Twenty-sixth Street establishment, it became apparent that Lorenzo Delmonico's health was deteriorating. Increasingly he was obliged to shift the burden of administrative responsibility to others, especially to his nephew Charles. The business functioned smoothly, and the outlook for continued prosperity seemed bright. Gout was Lorenzo's principal ailment, but there were complicating factors, including (the medical men believed) nicotine poisoning as a result of his inordinate consumption of black cigars.

During the summer of 1881 he remained away from the city, avoiding its heat and seeking to recuperate at Sharon Springs, a resort in the upper Catskills; a friend operated a summer hotel there and Lorenzo occupied a cottage on the grounds. But his condition grew worse, and word came to friends that he was failing fast. The city generally, however, knew nothing of his illness, and the headlines on the front pages of the newspapers on the morning of September 4, 1881, were a shock: Lorenzo Delmonico had died the day before, at sixty-eight. Charles Delmonico had been with him at the close.

Tributes to the man and his accomplishments were carried prominently in the New York press. The debt which the metropolis and the nation owed to Lorenzo Delmonico was acknowledged, and the *Sun* said flatly: "The influence which Delmonico has exerted upon life in New York can scarcely be overestimated."

The restaurateur, this summary continued, "did more than build up a great business and accumulate a large fortune. He gave an impulse to good cookery throughout the country, and raised the standards of hotel and restaurant kitchens. By his success he excited emulation, and the result has been a great and general improvement in our cookery . . . This change has taken place not only in New York, but throughout the Union also. We can trace it even in little country hotels or inns, though frequently we get there the form rather than the thing . . . Instead of a very few restaurants of high class, where a well cooked, well served dinner could be procured, within ten or fifteen years they have so multiplied that they may be found in all parts of the country. Next to Paris, New York is now undoubtedly the best provisioned city, so far as restaurants go, in the world . . . For all this credit must be given to the late Mr. Delmonico, and we render honor to his memory in consequence. It was an important work to do, for our country has suffered from bad cookery, and still in some regions, particularly at the South, the kitchen is an enemy to the health of the people."

Other newspapers enlarged upon the character and services to the community rendered by the Delmonico family. Said the *Times*:

"The public dinners given at Delmonico's are part of the city's history. For many years the name of Delmonico had been everywhere received as the synonym for perfection in gastronomy. Delmonico dinners are famous the world over. Without a peer in popular estimation, Lorenzo Delmonico strove hard to deserve the honors bestowed upon him. He gave entertainments to more notables than any half-dozen other hosts."

It was the Delmonicos, oldtimers recalled, who had induced Americans to make use of a profusion of foodstuffs, available at their very doors, which had been neglected or despised before. And to Delmonico, more than anyone else, was credited the impulse that had established restaurants as a feature of American life. Throughout it all, it was said, Lorenzo Delmonico's personality and character had been "so unassuming and so averse to notoriety" that to the general public he had remained little known, although many old New Yorkers counted him a friend. "Honorable, agreeable, and energetic," the *Sun* described him, he was "never careless, and by his thrift he thrived. In matters of Swiss or French charities he was ready and generous, and in the care of the numerous children he watched over with affection, he was always liberal."

The new owner of the *New York Herald*, the younger Bennett, had grown up in the atmosphere of the restaurants, and that paper was peculiarly equipped to measure not only the culinary, but the social, role of the Delmonicos, above all of Lorenzo:

"During his long and great activity, Lorenzo Delmonico made hosts of friends and no enemies. He was the soul of honor in dealing with rich customers or poor employees . . . No business house affords a better index of the progress of New York City than the house of which he was the head . . . Delmonico moved with New York, and was a truthful exponent of the spirit of New York. Though an adopted citizen, he was as genuine an American as there is to be found, for his brilliant successes showed him to have been in perfect sympathy with American wants; and while he made a great deal of money for himself, the legitimate result of extraordinary ability and enterprise, there are few more beneficent institutions of any kind in the metropolis than the quartet of houses of which he was the head.

"Mr. Delmonico was simple in his tastes, modest in his bearing, generous to those in need, strict in fidelity to duty, a good man, a valued citizen, and devoted to all the social amenities of home. His life was useful and honorable; his death will be widely and sincerely regretted."

5.

The funeral was conducted on the morning of September 7 in St. Ann's Church, East Twelfth Street. Everything was plain, by his expressed wish. Reporters commented upon the number of men prominent in business who attended, and the family turned out in force — Charles and Siro, now at the head of the clan; Rosa, Charles's sister; Peter Delmonico's granddaughters, "the Misses Delmonico of Brooklyn"; John's daughter, Josephine Otard, and her husband; John Napoleon Longhi, and more distant relatives. Forty children were brought by Sisters of Charity from the French orphan asylum, to which Lorenzo Delmonico had been a donor. The United Waiters Benevolent Society

Columbia attended in a body; their clubhouse at 52 Lexington Avenue, provided by Lorenzo's liberality, was draped in mourning. The largest floral piece was sent by the Societé Culinaire Philanthropique, of which Charles Ranhofer was a founder and president, and Lorenzo had been a member.

The Reverend Thomas J. Ducey, who had known Lorenzo since his own boyhood, spoke a brief eulogy; Father Ducey's church, St. Leo's, on East Twenty-eighth Street, had been built largely by Lorenzo's help. Thirty-four carriages followed the hearse through the narrow streets of downtown New York to St. Patrick's, where Lorenzo was placed beside his kith and kin in the vault that had been purchased by Peter.

All the Delmonico restaurants remained closed throughout that day.

The Magna Carta
of American Dining

AN INTERPOLATION

The reader who has followed this narrative so far will have gathered that it is not a tale of sauce-pots and toss-pots, or the prattle of a vacuous gossiper. It deals with a subject as all-encompassing and important as life, if life be important, namely, the nutriment of man. Life depends on food: a banal statement; but at certain stages of his evolution from the brute, man has done without clothing; he has survived without artificial shelter; and, despite the mountainous documentation sustaining the contrary, he has made shift to get along without *l'amour*. But man has never been able to dispense with his daily dependency on food and drink. And by examining what men, in successive periods, have eaten and drunk, their rise, or decline, in the scale of civilization can be accurately charted.

This book deals with a nation's diet, and specifically with a revolution that transformed the diet of Americans from one of colonial simplicity and provincial limitations to the most copious, varied, and flexible in the world.

During the course of the last century and a half, the American diet has been enriched by graftings from many national sources. Most of these additions have come with the successive waves of immigration, each group of newcomers bringing with them the gastronomic specialities of their homeland. But these importations have been, in the main, isolated dishes, unique foods, regional flavors; only one foreign source has given to America a complete system of cookery, from the making of an omelet to the ordering of a state banquet comprising twenty sophisticated courses. That source is France, and it is the distinction of the Delmonicos to have introduced into America the incomparable French cuisine — not haphazardly, or in any modified, simplified, or abbreviated form, but the *haute cuisine* in all its ramifications, profundity, and range. Among benefactors of a people, few have contributed more effectively to improving a nation's health and spreading happiness than the Delmonicos. To this day the results of their activities can be seen, for among all the alien elements that leaven modern American cooking, the French influence is still dominant. No cookbooks are more popular than those which profess to teach the neophyte how to turn out meals like a French chef.

The debt owed by Americans to Delmonico was thoroughly comprehended in the heyday of the family. Writing in 1895, James Ford Rhodes, a scholar not given to loose overstatement, declared categorically, in the third volume of his *History of the United States 1850-1877*:

"Any person who considers the difference between the cooking and service of a dinner at a hotel or restaurant before the Civil war and now, will appreciate what a practical apostle of health and decent living has been Delmonico, who *deserves canonization in the American calendar*."

Although the italics are added here, the fervency of this tribute is unmistakable; yet a proposal to "canonize" is so extreme as to provoke skepticism regarding the rationale of the sublime suggestion. The eminent historian, like others of the host of ardent witnesses who paid lip service to Delmonico's delectable fare, may well have been misled by the eupeptic afterglow induced by some superb dinner. Documentary evidence — evidence of indisputable authority and authenticity — to justify Rhodes' apparent excess of enthusiasm has heretofore been lacking, such records as survived being too fragmentary, disjointed, and incomplete to be thoroughly convincing.

Now, however, the missing proof to sustain the eulogiums lavished upon Delmonico and Delmonico's is at length available, and the preeminence of that institution, as well as the revolutionary scope of its innovations, can be confirmed.

This proof is contained in a menu card dating from 1838, one used in the Delmonico restaurant at Beaver and South William Streets, just a year after that establishment was opened. The card is the only one thus far discovered surviving from that early period. It dispels every doubt regarding Delmonico's place as the torch bearer in the gradual transformation of American social and eating customs. It also demonstrates in what way and to what extent Delmonico's was the progenitor of every restaurant in the United States, the seed from which the industry in this country arose.

This document contains surprises. First, as to its form. The *carte* is a pamphlet of twelve pages with cover, printed on thin paper, the pages approximately six by nine inches, lightly stitched together. It is without ostentation or ornament, the typography austerely plain, decorative type used only in the name of the house ("Restaurant Français des Frères Delmonico") and the address, on the cover and first page. (Why the name of one street in the address is left blank on the opening page is a mystery.) Apparently the menus were printed in quantity, and used as necessary.

The columns allotted to the prices of the dishes were left blank, to be filled in by hand. The prices are in shillings and pence, the shilling having remained in use long after the Revolution. By modern standards, the prices seem ridiculously small, but they were anything but low for their day; in some of New York's cheap eating houses a whole meal, we have seen, could be had for a shilling, and Delmonico's charged this for a plate of soup. Dishes that were temporarily unobtainable, or out of season, were indicated by omitting a price after them.

The divisions of the menu are arranged logically, the dishes (soups, hors d'oeuvres, meats, game, roasts, dessert), grouped together in the order in which the courses fall in a meal. This was a striking novelty in New York in 1838, for the custom was to mix everything pell mell in a bill of fare, without separation or distinction. For an example of this turn to the Astor House menu of March 21, 1838, on page 34.

Culinary nomenclature still presented a difficulty, for this 1838 menu is printed in French and English in parallel columns. The naïveté, not to say occasional grotesqueness, of the translations of French terms gives some notion of the degree of *savoir faire* prevalent among New York's upper crust in 1838. If the translator was the same linguist who, according to Samuel Ward, was paid the considerable sum of one hundred dollars to translate the Delmonicos' first menu, he can hardly be said to have earned his fee. The pages are studded with instances of either carelessness or ineptitude or downright ignorance. "Épinards au jus" is gummily served up as "spinage with gravy," while "jumble of vegetables" certainly has a less savory sound than "macédoine de legumes." The phrase "à la moderne" emerges awkwardly as "modern fashion" ("small aspicks modern fashion"), and a transparent re-spelling seems to have satisfied the translator's taste, and presumably his conscience, when a word stumped him: "salmi" is pseudo-Englished "salmee," and "fricandeau" is phoneticized to truncated "fricando." Some kitchen terms were beyond the translator's guessing, and these he left for the diner to puzzle out unassisted. "Hatelet" stayed "hatelet," while the descriptive "en crapaudine" was transmogrified into the wholly undescriptive "crapodeen." Still, for a lame man trying to walk, a crutch is better than no support; Delmonico's patrons managed to obtain what they hankered after, and in a few years were able to dispense with translations and translator.

2.

In respect of variety, the Delmonico's of 1838 could hardly be matched by any restaurant of the present time. Statistics are dull when they are not impressive; but where today exists there a restaurant which can offer a customer three hundred and seventy-one separate dishes to order a dinner from? The 1838

Delmonico *carte* is a catalogue of the kitchen's repertory, and except for a few items temporarily unobtainable (like imported artichokes), any dish on the list could be called for at any time, and it would be served promptly as a matter of routine.

The list commences with twelve soups and thirty-two hors d'oeuvres. Then come twenty-eight beef entrées; forty-six of veal; twenty of mutton and lamb; forty-seven of chicken and fowl; twenty-two varieties of game; twenty roast meats; forty-eight fish entrées; fifty-one kinds of vegetables and egg dishes; nineteen pastries and cakes; and twenty-six desserts, including fruit, cheese, and coffee. Faced with this plenitude of riches, in hundreds of tempting guises, the modern gourmet is speechless; Gargantua would shrink from tackling it all.

Of course no customer consumed any substantial part of this medley at a single sitting. From the list he would select three, four, or more dishes to make up a satisfying luncheon or dinner; but the scope over which he could range while making his selections was all but limitless.

This particular menu card appears to have been used during the autumn, if we may judge by the dishes that are not priced. Those spring delicacies, shad and salmon, apparently were out of season; so were summer fruits, like strawberries and raspberries; while the omission of oranges would seem to eliminate the winter season, that fruit being then normally brought in from the West Indies around Christmas time.

3.

Astonishing as this gastronomic array may appear to a diner of today, to the New Yorker of 1838 it opened up a vista of tantalizing new flavors. Look again at the bill of fare which the Astor House management set before their discriminating guests of March 21, 1838. Recollect that the Astor was nationally renowned for luxury, and its dining room was considered the *ne plus ultra* of high living.

The lack of classification of the dishes in this helter-skelter

Astor bill has been commented upon. The hungry diner is forced to take in everything in a gulp. This list includes one soup, against twelve at Delmonico's. Hors d'oeuvres are so literally "outside the works" they do not figure at all, and vegetables are almost equally invisible. The only separate vegetable dish is a "casserolle de pomme de terre garnie"; otherwise spinach and onions are served with the veal fricandeau and mutton fillet, and tomatoes appear twice in sauces. The Astor's guests are given a choice of four roast meats, apart from roast goose and roast turkey, while at Delmonico's selection might be made from twenty roasts. By way of compensation, it is true, the Astor offers six boiled meats, if one's tastes run to boiled.

The Astor performs wretchedly in respect to poultry, offering a mere dozen variations on this fertile theme, against Delmonico's ingenious forty-seven; and in the department of sweets the hotel's purveyors fall down completely, mustering only three tried-and-true standbys — "queen pudding," "mince pie," and "cream puffs." This feeble rear guard Delmonico overwhelms with a veritable brigade of thirty-six "entremets sucrées" and "desserts" combined, and four kinds of cheese. (The generic "dessert" appended at the foot of the Astor list stood for fruit and a slice of cheese, unspecified.)

The seafood epicure the Astor House treats cavalierly, wedging him between flatulent "boiled cod fish and oysters" and an anomalous "oyster pie." This was tantamount to cramming an unlucky victim upon a crustacean, as it were, bed of Procrustes, cruelly contrived to crush all palates into a single mold. But let the wayfarer betake himself to Delmonico's, and he might navigate a sea of forty-eight succulent marine edibles, shell and scaly.

4.

Comparison of the wine lists complementing these disparate menus reveals divergences no less fundamental. In the first half of the Nineteenth Century, foreign visitors were constantly being astonished by the capacity of Americans for spirituous liquors — whisky, rum, brandy, and gin. The Astor House catered to the prevailing taste, and its bar was celebrated. Delmonico's, however, in 1838 had no bar, only a cafe, and the restaurant never figured as a drinking resort primarily. With their Continental heritage, the Delmonicos placed reliance on the fine wines of Europe. The Astor went heavily for the American favorite, Madeira, and forty brands of Madeira were available to their guests, against Delmonico's three. Heading the Delmonico cellar book in 1838 are the four finest vintages of Bordeaux — Lafite, Latour, Margaux, and Haut Brion — dispensed at a rather steep $2.00 and $2.50 a bottle. In all, Delmonico offers a choice of twenty clarets, ranging from *vin ordinaire* to a Château Margaux 1825. The Astor lists seventeen clarets, topped by Château Margaux 1831 at $3.00 a bottle. In the matter of champagnes, real and supposed, the two houses are nearly on a par, the score being ten to seven, in favor of the Astor.

5.

In these two menus, we have striking expressions of two philosophies of taste in the selection and preparation of food. The Astor bill of fare reflects what was the dominant pattern in 1838; Delmonico's is new, still on its trial. Which school soon gained the ascendancy is not in doubt. Turn to the Astor House bill of fare dated October 11, 1849, shown on page 35. The date is eleven years after that of the hotel's 1838 menu, eleven years of direct competition between New York's two principal dining rooms. A change is apparent.

In 1838 the Astor bill of fare was hodgepodge, thrown together roughly, without carefully thought out order or sequence, in fact, almost without system. In 1849 the courses are divided and organized on the logical French plan. This change, we may be sure, has been due to the expressed preference of the Astor's customers; the educational influence of Delmonico was already bearing fruit.

And not only in regard to a more convenient arrangement of

the courses; there has been wrought a change in the diet that had become more acceptable to the average American. In 1838, we have seen, vegetables were conspicuous for their absence from the Astor bill of fare. In 1849, the same dining room lists thirteen vegetables, under their own separate heading, and even includes the comparatively exotic egg plant.

This change alone was deeply significant; the process of widening and lightening the diet of Americans was under way. And at the same time that it was promoting this basic alteration, Delmonico's was establishing the pattern of purveying food in America that would be adopted universally. For Delmonico's was the first successful *restaurant* in the country, distinguishable from the service afforded by a cook-shop, tavern, inn, or hotel. In those places the dining room was an adjunct, and the customer ate what was served by the host or proprietor. Meals were at set times, and were charged for at a flat, inclusive rate.

A restaurant, by contrast, is an establishment where a person may enter at any time, and from a list of the dishes available may order as much or as little as he pleases. Furthermore, in a restaurant the price of each dish is indicated separately, so that the customer can accommodate his appetite to his purse and know exactly what his meal will cost in advance, without either paying for something he does not want, or running the risk of unpleasant surprises when the bill is presented.

The convenience afforded by such an innovation made an immediate hit with the merchants who lunched and dined at Delmonico's in the early years. Meals could be taken at opportune moments during the hurry of the day; they could be as copious or as meager as the customer wished; and the choice was not confined to a few daily "specials," but was immense. Restaurants, on the Delmonico principle, quickly appeared in imitation, spread to other cities, and long before Delmonico's career closed they had become fixtures in American life. Delmonico's modest beginnings laid the foundation of the restaurant industry of today: every eating-house in the United States, be it good, bad, or indifferent (which most of them are), derives from the coffee shop on William Street, and the later establishment at Beaver and South William.

In the history of American restaurants, the 1838 Delmonico menu card stands as a foundation document, and its importance is no less in regard to American social history. It also furnishes tangible proof of Delmonico's uniqueness and extraordinary resources, even in an early stage of the restaurant's development. Without fancifulness, this menu might be termed the Magna Carta of sophisticated and gracious (which means healthful and civilized) dining in America.

And the blending of French sauces with American staples has been as permanent as it has been salutary. Any standard cookbook contains recipes directly descended from the cuisine introduced and domesticated by the Delmonicos, besides others that are embellished with the family's prestigious name in order to lend them an aura of delectability. Though, truth to tell, most of these attributed concoctions never graced or disgraced a Delmonican table.*

---

* A personal experience illustrates how thoroughly penetrated is American cookery with the French element. In the autumn of 1966, while flying from the east to the west coasts, the author was served dinner in flight — what the stewardess called simply "chicken." It proved to be a version of *coq au vin*, chicken cooked in a casserole with wine and minced vegetables. With it were served not plain rice but a tasty *risotto*, and tiny buttered carrots. The carrots are a French-Belgian specialty. In 1838 and for long afterwards, neither *coq au vin* nor *risotto* was known in American kitchens. Yet a century and a quarter after the date of the Delmonico menu described above, these dishes could be served quite casually in an American airliner, sky-high, traveling at five hundred miles an hour, and cause no comment, an average American girl accepting them as merely a not unusual form of chicken and rice.

Part Three

CHANGES AND
PORTENTS OF CHANGE

CHAPTER I

AS THE EIGHTIES CAME IN

THE QUESTION mooted in more than one quarter after Lorenzo Delmonico's death was what would become of the business he had brought to such renown, now that it had been deprived of his guidance and discretion. The answer came quickly: the restaurants, New Yorkers were assured, would continue in operation without change of policy, under family direction.

The *Times* confessed gratification that, the death of Lorenzo Delmonico having left to Siro and Charles "the honor of standing at the head of the establishments," there would be no departure from the old regime. "Things will go on much as before. Lorenzo's work will not end with him."

The *Sun* told its public that "the general management of the firm is in excellent hands, and epicures need not entertain any apprehension regarding the ultimate fate of Delmonico's temples of gastronomy so long as they are presided over by the present managers."

It was Charles Delmonico, however, who was given the ownership of the business, and not the older Siro. This had been arranged before Lorenzo's death; his will, which disposed of a personal fortune estimated at $2,000,000, made no mention of the firm. It was the testament of a just and generous man. To his widow, Clemence Delmonico, Lorenzo left $400,000 in cash and the house at 211 East Fifteenth Street, with everything in it — "all the furniture useful and ornamental, pictures, ornaments, articles of vertu, plate and plated ware, housekeeping articles and utensils of every description." She also received the stable and "all horses, carriages, harness, and other contents."

Charles was left $600,000 outright, with other minor legacies. Siro was bequeathed the income from a trust fund of $100,000, which upon Siro's death was to revert to Charles. John Longhi, the cousin who had conducted the restaurant at 22 Broad Street since its inception, was given $10,000.

The bequests to other members of the family were numerous and detailed. Clemence Delmonico's daughters received $100,000 each, and the two children of the married daughter also $100,000 each. Rosa, Charles's sister, was given $100,000. Leon Delmonico, a son of Lorenzo's deceased brother Constant, got $50,000, and Leon's sisters, Marie and Aimée Delmonico, $25,000 each. The three Crist orphans, Lorenzo, Charles, and Josephine, were given $20,000 apiece, and legacies in the same amount went to Lorenzo's surviving sisters in Mairengo (Marie Delmonico and Adelaide Bertina), and to the four remaining children of his deceased brother, Jacques (Giacomo) Delmonico. Significant of Lorenzo's fading connection with Switzerland was the fact that while two of these four children (a nephew, Lorenzo, and a niece, Marie Bertina) were identified in the will by name, the other two nieces were spoken of only as such, their Christian names "not being now recollected by me."

There were bequests of $10,000 each to Marie Delmonico, a daughter of Honoré, and to Josephine Delmonico Otard, John Delmonico's daughter. Lorenzo left $5,000 to his bookkeeper, Alexander Gordon, and a like sum to the Orphan Asylum of St. Vincent de Paul in New York. Gordon and Charles Delmonico were named executors and trustees.

The will had been signed on June 4, 1881, three months before Lorenzo's death, and it contained no reference to claims or debts outstanding against him personally. The explanation was that there were none: Lorenzo's books balanced at the last.

Even before he drew his will, Lorenzo had given his nephew Charles power of attorney to administer the restaurants, and this bypassing of Siro, with his superior claim to seniority and his well known competence, caused surprise. It was said that Siro was deeply offended by the slight; in fact, it was said to have broken his heart. If this was the case, his manner gave no sign of it, for he continued without interruption to do the marketing for the four restaurants and appear as the affable host of the house on Broadway. He was wealthy in his own right and had never married, and he spent his money freely. His health, however, had been undermined by excessive addiction to those strong black cigars, and he had become more and more subject to violent fits of coughing. Although he consulted doctor after doctor in search of a remedy, and received the same advice from them all, namely, to moderate his smoking, he would not. His attention to the business did not relax on this account, and he remained methodical in everything that pertained to the restaurants.

John Longhi had been deeply wounded by Lorenzo's bequest of a nominal $10,000. It had been Longhi's assumption that upon Lorenzo's death he would inherit the Broad Street place, which was virtually his creation. Failure to carry out this implied bargain came as a shock, and soon after his cousin's death Longhi began to contemplate retiring from the business altogether. He was comfortably rich, having invested in real estate in Brooklyn, where he lived with his family in a house built on the old Delmonico farm. But for the time being he continued active, for he was fond of Charles and worked well with him.

2.

Changes, great changes, had come over New York since the war, but one vexatious problem had remained constant: the city was still in need of an adequate supply of wholesome water. On the day Lorenzo Delmonico died, New Yorkers were gasping in a phenomenal heat wave, after surviving a hot, dry summer; the temperature hit 100°, schools and factories shut down, and headlines in the newspapers screamed: "WASTE NOT! WANT NOT! City's Rapidly Diminishing Supply of Croton Water — No Signs of Rain — Only Enough Water Remain-

ing for Absolute Necessities!" The city fathers groped for a
solution of their quandary; a century afterwards they would still
be groping.

The city's population had shot up and up. On the eve of the
Civil War it had stood at 1,174,000; by 1880 it was touching
2,000,000. This was the figure for Manhattan alone, because
New York then comprised only Manhattan, and for most practical purposes only that portion of the island south of Forty-
second Street. Brooklyn was a separate city, the third largest
in the United States. New Yorkers regarded it with disdain as a
place of piety and procreation much given to moralizing — disdain that was repaid with homilies from a hundred pulpits upon
the depravity of the Manhattan-Gomorrah just across the river.

The metropolis's reputation for wickedness was hardly borne
out by the reports of unprejudiced travelers. In 1879-80 George
Augustus Sala, a British journalist, spent four months in New
York and his observant eye took in no great amount of sin, although he did notice many telling details.

Sala had visited America in 1863, and at that time made himself heartily unpopular by expressing outrageous sympathy with
the cause of the Confederacy. The attitude had been largely one
of youthful bravado, he admitted in more mature years; but
even under the disadvantages of wartime he had found much to
admire in New York City. He had stayed at the Brevoort Hotel,
and had been charmed by that place of leisured gentility. A guest
there was known "by his name, not by the number of his room
alone; he has an individuality, he is recognized." This had struck
Sala as singular amid the prevailing regimentation of Americans.

"Three gastronomic temples, owned by the immortal Lorenzo Delmonico," he also had found commendable on that
earlier visit. "Let it be recorded to the honor of that urbane
restaurateur," he had written in his carefully composed report,
"that although he knew [me] to be an enemy of the United
States, he gave [me] frank and cordial credit, and could only
by vehement entreaty be persuaded to send in his bill at the
expiration of each month."

One ugly feature he did see in 1863 was wide-open gambling houses, with their "faro, euchre, poker, and old-sledge"; but he had been handsomely entertained at "palatial clubs . . . the Union, the Union League, the New York, the Manhattan, and the Athenaeum; and on certain Saturday nights, at a reunion called the Century Club," where he had met "literature, art, and science in combination with stewed oysters and hot 'whiskey-skins.' " He had heard that "across the water at Brooklyn, there was . . . a very large church where an eloquent minister, named, I think, Beecher," held forth with exhibitions of sacred sensationalism, and he had actually been taken by "my old friend Phineas T. Barnum to hear another eloquent divine, named Dr. Chapin . . ."

Sala had pronounced New York in 1863 "incurably Copper-head, and at least nine-tenths Secesh." This was a gross exaggeration, although much sympathy with the South did exist in the city. The character of his hosts Sala praised extraordinarily and upon returning to London he wrote with enthusiasm:

"The Americans are an eminently hospitable and generous people. A stingy American is a monster . . . They make their money quickly, and they spend it quickly. They have no time to be miserly, for a short life and a merry one is at least the New York motto. When a broker finds Wall Street frowns upon him, or a merchant is on the eve of bankruptcy, he proceeds to Delmonico's and has a capital dinner, with plenty of Cliquot champagne . . . nothing less than the Veuve's best brand will suit him."

The dramatic contrast of culture amidst squalor was another impression Sala carried away in 1863. "Here all that is polished is new, and what is old is simply savage," he summed up. "A marble palace, seven stories high, and beside it a livery stable . . . Go out of town, and you step at once from the Sybaritic luxury of Delmonico's to a horribly coarse mess of pork and beans, with a two-pronged fork to aid you in devouring them . . . But the civilization is all here, nevertheless. You have only to go to the great cities for it. The walls and ceilings of private houses are painted in fresco by the best German and Italian artists, in a manner which only the proprietors of palaces could afford in Europe; but the marble corridors of the hotels are the veriest Augean stables of tobacco juice. In the ladies drawing room of one of the handsomest hotels in New York I marked . . . a porcelain spittoon, royal purple, picked out in gold. I think it would be difficult to find a more striking instance of extremes meeting — a brass knocker on a pigsty door."

For expressing himself with such candor Sala had been roasted by the press of the time as "a bloated miscreant," "malignant buffoon," "fat cockney," "debased libeller," and "hired emissary of the British oligarchy." Sixteen years later he returned for a second look at New York, his curiosity as keen as ever.

3.

It was November 26, 1879, just before Thanksgiving Day, when he landed. At once he experienced the same bewilderment that Dickens had felt upon his return to New York after twenty years: the city seemed to have changed entirely. A few landmarks he found still intact. Again he put up at the Brevoort, and he did recognize Fifth Avenue as far north as Fourteenth Street, where, in 1863, he had dined at "the *uptown* Delmonico's restaurant and cafe." The hotels at Madison Square — the Fifth Avenue, Albermarle, and Hoffman House — were much the same, and so was Wall Street, although the alterations there were a bit distracting; the rest of the city he found fascinatingly new. Dickens's description of New York in the 1840's, or Mrs. Trollope's remarks on "The Domestic Manners of the Americans" in the 1830's, applied "about as closely to the usages and customs of the Pottawatamie Indians" as they did to Americans in 1880, Sala concluded.

He was struck by their greater sophistication. They were more tolerant of criticism, and would frankly admit that "voracity in eating" and uncouth behavior in public had indeed been common among them previously. In 1880 Sala was pelted with no epithets when he voiced a few criticisms. For example, he said that walking in the side streets was unpleasant because "the inhabitants of the houses are still permitted to deposit ashes and other refuse in barrels . . . along the kerbstones." The sidewalks were patched and uneven, and every notion of what was *up* and what was *down* had been turned awry. The Brevoort, "though as comfortable and as aristocratically frequented as ever," was now definitely downtown; in 1863 Twenty-third Street had been just as definitely accounted uptown, and "Fortieth Street was Ultima Thule," beyond which stretched vacant land and "boulders of living rock daubed with advertisements for 'Drake's Plantation Bitters,' 'The Balm of a Thousand Flowers,' and 'Old Dr. Jacob Thompson's Sarsaparilla.' " In 1880 all these had disappeared, and one beheld in their stead "terraces after terraces of lordly mansions of brownstone, some with marble facades, others wholly of pure white marble gleaming . . . in the clear blue sky."

Madison Square struck him as the equal of anything in Paris. From there branched off "at least half a dozen splendid counterparts of the Boulevard des Capucines, the Rue Scribe, the Avenue de l'Opéra, the Rue du Quatre Septembre, and the Chausée d'Antin"; and in the new "Palazzo Delmonico" on the Square he was impressed that the cooking had kept pace with the town when he was served a "baked Alaska" — an incredible confection, he exclaimed, consisting of ice cream in an envelope of whipped cream, the whole toasted in the oven! (The dish had been invented by Ranhofer at the time of Secretary of State Seward's purchase of Alaska for the United States.)

"How many thousands of dollars a week Mr. Delmonico is clearing I do not know," Sala marveled, "but his palatial establishment, as well as scores of other restaurants and cafes, continually overflows with guests." The furniture and hangings at Delmonico's struck him as "splendid, very quiet and refined," and the elevator that carried patrons to the ballroom he deemed symbolic of the soaring prices; although on this point he spoke from hearsay only, he stressed, because every time he dined or lunched at Delmonico's (and that was often) he had been an invited guest. For the information of travelers he did say: "You may dine, I am told, very modestly at Delmonico's for about $5, including a bottle of light, but drinkable, claret. But I may also hint (also on hearsay) that a first-rate dinner at Delmonico's is a very serious affair in the way of dollars."

The same applied to the Hotel Brunswick opposite, where "the viands and dishes are quite as *recherchés* as they are at Delmonico's. The prices also are *recherchés*."

Other eating-places which he investigated and rated "strictly first-class, but a trifle inferior to Delmonico's and the Brunswick," included the dining rooms at the Gilsey House, the St. James Hotel, and the Hoffman House. "On the lower rungs of the social ladder are the so-called 'fifteen-cent houses,' where . . . you may be served with a cut from a hot joint, with bread, butter, potatoes, and pickles."

Tiptop living in New York Sala estimated to be the costliest in the world, and he had had recent experience of Paris and St. Petersburg, both notoriously expensive. For a bedroom and a sitting room at the Brevoort he paid $7 a day, meals extra, and apologized to himself for being so extravagant. The rate for a suite at the Fifth Avenue Hotel — two bedrooms and a parlor — was $30 a day, but that included all meals, and guests could invite their friends to join them at the table d'hôte without extra charge. Sala could not buy "a Havana cigar worth smoking" for less than eighteen cents, while half a dollar was "quite a moderate price for a Regalia Britannica. There is no drinkable champagne under $3 a bottle. Claret is almost equally dear." But the necessities of life were proportionately cheap and plentiful. Good beef cost eight to ten cents a pound, and the best cuts never more than a quarter. Cheese he found "wonderfully cheap." Oysters "of every size and variety of flavor" were to be had for "next to nothing." Fish "amazingly plentiful, delicious, and inexpensive. The cod is superb. Smelts abound." Vegetables "prodigious in size." An "inexhaustible supply" of tomatoes, squash, celery. "Never saw such gigantic cabbages and cauliflower outside of Valencia, Spain, and they are cheap. No stint of salads. Venison excellent and cheap. Poultry abundant. Ducks multitudinous, but a canvasback at a restaurant costs $3, and a man with a healthy appetite cannot dine off a canvasback, seeing it is only the breast that is eaten."

On the train to Baltimore he ate in the dining car and was served an excellent dinner, well cooked and well served, for $1.50.

How did the earnings of the mass of people (who did not patronize Delmonico's) stand in ratio to this abundance of cheap, wholesome, and diversified food? Sala was told that bricklayers in New York earned $12 to $15 a week; masons and plumbers, $12 to $18; a tailor, $10 to $18; and day laborers, $6 to $9. The fact that tailors and plumbers — who catered to vanity and hygiene — topped the list he thought expressive of the spirit of the city. But the carelessness with which the rich scattered their wealth startled him. Also, he believed that New York was basically and incurably frivolous in its interests. He found people of education ready to talk about " 'H.M.S. Pinafore,' the musical genius of Mr. Arthur Sullivan, the wit and humor of Mr. W. S. Gilbert [who] are at present the choicest lions of fashionable New York society"; they would discuss Wall Street's fluctuations; they would run on freely enough about the opera and "Mr. Burne-Jones's pictures or Mr. Whistler's etchings"; but about such issues as the need for a Nicaragua canal, General Grant's hopes of a third term, Chinese cheap labor, the tariff, or the desirability of withdrawing greenbacks from circulation to restore the national credit — such topics failed to elicit "anything beyond the most languid interest."

Sala considered the American Civil War "the greatest and most momentous" episode of modern times, and he was shocked by the evident desire to avoid that subject. "People here do not

trouble themselves much about things calculated to arouse em-
bittered controversy," he wrote. "*La Bagatelle* seems for the
moment to be triumphant . . . As for the rebellion, . . . it is
never made a subject of conversation in polite society." Now
and then a Republican newspaper might print "a half-spiteful,
half-bantering paragraph about 'Confederate brigadiers,' and
'the bloody shirt.' " Occasionally a Democratic organ might
recall the "exploits of the 'carpetbaggers,' and 'revenue sneak
thieves,' and the scandals of the 'Freedmen's Bureau'; but if a
man talks too much about Antietam or the Shenandoah Valley,
about the bombardment of Charleston, and Sherman's march
to the sea, he will incur a great risk of being set down as an un-
mitigated bore . . ."

4.

Such was life in New York, as viewed by a perspicacious visitor, when Lorenzo passed on to Charles Delmonico the fortunes
of their house. The long depression of the Seventies (the most
severe and protracted the country would experience until the
1930's) had passed, like the war; society glittered restlessly. The
pressure on the social strongholds grew every year more intense,
and breaches were appearing in the walls manned by the Patriarchs. One of the last gala events held at Delmonico's on Fourteenth Street had been the celebrated "Bouncers Ball." A coterie
of young bloods, socially elite and pluming themselves on their
"fast" ways (and a witness of those ways who survived until the
1920's testified that by comparison with the Jazz Age, they were
"fast" indeed; in fact, they made the Jazz Age seem "sobriety
itself"), got up a ball to which, besides members of their proper
set, they invited numerous "outsiders" — people who were
quite respectable, but outside the patrician pale. The ball went
off so brilliantly that the newcomers thereafter were accepted,
albeit forming a separate circle of selectness that overlapped,
but did not efface, the older one.

Ward McAllister conceded the claims of this younger set and

organized his Family Circle Dancing Class, to give balls of its
own almost on a social level with the Patriarchs'. (Malice had it
that McAllister was really motivated by the difficulty of launching an ugly daughter.) Soon came the Tuesday Night Dancing
Class, the Wednesday Night, the Thursday Night, and so on
throughout the week. For the Delmonicos all these spreadings
of social groups meant more custom, more prestige, and more
impregnability in their position as *the* place to entertain, as well
as to dine. And this in spite of new shocks the family and business sustained.

A major shock was the sudden death of Siro Delmonico, on
December 19, 1881, only three months after Lorenzo's. The previous evening Siro had appeared at the Madison Square cafe
with a party of friends; he had been in excellent spirits, so noticeably that his doctor congratulated him upon a decided improvement in health. About midnight the group moved along
to another cafe, and around one o'clock they broke up, Siro
going to Charles Delmonico's home at 229 West Fourteenth
Street, where he had been living. He was not seen alive again.

In the morning, the housemaid, receiving no response to her
knock, opened the door and found Siro's body sprawled on the
floor, half undressed. Apparently while preparing for bed he
had been seized by one of his coughing fits and burst an aneur-
ism at the base of the larynx. His doctor said he had been suffering from emphysema of the lungs for a long time, and that his
whole system was saturated with nicotine. One medical man
was quoted to the effect that Siro Delmonico had been known
to smoke one hundred of his formidable cigars in a single day.
This seems hardly credible, but friends who were accustomed
to seeing him always with a cigar were inclined to believe it.

In downtown New York, where he had been like a landmark,
Siro Delmonico was sincerely mourned. The press reviewed
his career from when he was first employed as a cashier at
Beaver Street, and paid justice to his affability and professional
skill. He had few interests outside the restaurants, where he

knew hundreds of regular customers personally. His memory for names and faces was remarkable, and he had come to function as a sort of walking encyclopedia to be consulted upon people and places.

His requiem mass was celebrated in old St. Patrick's. Then he, too, was interred in the family vault, and a generation of Delmonicos was obliterated.

All the Delmonico restaurants remained closed throughout the duration of his funeral.

CHAPTER II

THE KING IS DEAD,
LONG LIVE THE KING!

ONE WHO MOURNED Siro Delmonico with special poignancy was old Sam Ward. Washington's erstwhile "King of the Lobby" and hero of escapades that had made him a celebrity now was New York's genial host to notable visitors. The passing of his old friend, marking the end of a generation of Delmonicos among whom Sam had grown up, stirred him emotionally, and when emotionally moved Sam Ward took refuge in rhyming. Siro's death inspired a tribute in meter which the author deemed worthy of including in his collected works, after publishing it in the *New York World*. The elegiacs ran:

SIRO DELMONICO

He lieth low whose constant art
    For years the daily feasts purveyed
Of wayfarers from every mart,
    The Paladins of every trade.

And yet to-night gay music stirs
    The halls he strolled through yestere'en,
And mantles high the wine that spurs
    The revellers by him unseen.

Le Roi est mort! Vive le Roi!
    One leader drops, another comes;
On flows the dance, — a stream of joy
    Staccatoed by the muffled drums.

Then soon for us shall mark the tread
    Of mourning friends and chanting priests.
Ah! there are other banquets spread
    Than Siro's memorable feasts.

Sam Ward had passed years in Delmonico's pleasant alcoves. He stood in a special relationship to the restaurants, which might be expressed in a paraphrase: *In the religion of gastronomy there was but one Delmonico's, and Sam Ward was its prophet.* Ward was more various, more ubiquitous, and more voluble than General Winfield Scott, and an infinitely better talker. His social position, wide-ranging experience, and innumerable friendships among high and low had enabled him to achieve the position he occupied as America's foremost authority upon matters of the table. Ever the apostle of good cheer, he was versed in all the elements of gastronomy, theoretical and practical; he was no mean cook himself, and a host whose dinners and table talk were, if not the best, close to the best of the century. And in all seasons, in propria persona and in absentia, he everywhere promoted the cult of Delmonico's as the summit of civilized dining.

Sam knew all the members of the Delmonico family, and had seen the business grow through all its stages. He was almost the same age as Lorenzo, and had watched the great restaurateur's progress: first as a handsome young fellow at Beaver Street and South William; then as the dignified proprietor of the establishment at Chambers Street; then in jaunty middle-age at Fourteenth Street; and finally as the mellow host of Madison Square, looking out upon a world of his creation and finding it good.

George Augustus Sala knew the Delmonicos through Sam Ward. On his 1880 visit to New York Sala was charmed to find Ward's conversation more delightful than ever, and his hospitality inexhaustible. "Whether he rolled logs, or ground axes, or was a lobbyist, or a mugwump, or bull-dozed anybody, it was no business of mine to inquire," Sala believed; "Uncle Sam" was a captivating personality, the soul of kindliness, and knew more about food and drink than any half dozen other men put together. Sala dined with Sam at "Del's" in 1880 "better than I can dine at this time of day," he recalled ruefully.

In 1882 Oscar Wilde was taken to Delmonico's by Ward,

and when Lily Langtry bestowed her beauty upon Madison Square, Sam Ward was her escort. British peers beat a path to Sam's threshold, and one English tourist, after seeing America according to Ward's prescription, pronounced the two most notable sights in the nation to be the Yosemite Valley and Delmonico's. Charles Ranhofer viewed the world in the same light as Sam Ward, and proof of Sam's distinction was the report that he was the only layman the great cook ever allowed to come into the kitchen and concoct his own sauces. Old John Klages, who had become headwaiter in the Madison Square cafe, insisted that the whole room lighted up when "Uncle Sam's" cheery countenance appeared in the doorway. Klages to the end of his days (and they were long, and passed in Delmonico's service) related how Sam Ward would foregather with cronies at a corner table, and soon his clear tenor would be rising in a song. There was one John remembered especially: "Oh, we will go hunt the wild buffalo, we will go hunt the buffalo," with "something like 'on the banks of the beautiful O-hi-o' at the end."

2.

Towards Charles Delmonico, the new head of the enterprises, Sam Ward felt avuncular, for he remembered when Charles was born, and Sam was among the first to spread reassurance that under Charles's direction the restaurants would not deteriorate.

"Charley" had everything in his favor. Socially, Delmonico's was entrenched. The Patriarchs had moved with the restaurant from Fourteenth Street and they gave the ballroom at Madison Square their imprimatur. During the season, one gala entertainment followed another at the new "Del's," and all were reported vivaciously and at length in the society news.

Charles bowed to changing tastes when he eased the rule requiring women to have male escorts at all times. Under the new dispensation, ladies unescorted were served in the restaurant up to the dinner hour, although thereafter the old rule remained in force. A good story for the newspapers was "Charley's" brush with a *grande dame* who had come to town with her daughter on a shopping tour, and late in the afternoon dropped into "Del's" for dinner. After she and her daughter had taken their seats, a much embarassed Charles informed them that they could not be served. The dowager bristled.

"What do you mean?" she exclaimed indignantly. "You know perfectly well who I am!"

"That makes it all the more difficult for me to carry out a rule which we find imperative, and which is made for the protection of just such ladies as you are," replied Charles. "I will serve you in a private room, or will send a meal to your home without extra charge, but I cannot serve you here."

To her credit, the rebuffed lady left without further fuss, and later recounted the experience as a good joke on her forty years of irreproachable marriage and maternity, and also as a compliment to Mr. Delmonico and his excellently moral establishment.

Two other women tried to break the rule with more diverting results. They were Victoria Woodhull, the so-called "terrible siren," and her sister, intriguingly named Tennie C. (a telescoped version of her baptismal names, "Tennessee Celeste") Claflin — sensational "lady stock brokers" who played the market on tips from Commodore Vanderbilt, and who advocated spiritualism, free love, and votes for women. Victoria ran for President of the United States to underline her views.

Seating themselves boldly in Delmonico's restaurant, without escort, the sisters perused the menu and Victoria ordered, "Tomato soup for two."

The waiter regretted that he could not take the order. They called for Charles Delmonico, who appeared all smiles. He liked the pair, and good-naturedly he offered to cover their retreat by strolling to the door with them, engaging in conversation, so diners might assume they had merely dropped in to speak to him.

By no means, they responded; they had come to dine, and if

the presence of a man was indispensable, they would provide that accessory. Stepping to the door, Tennie C. signaled the driver of a horse cab outside, brought him in, and seated him at their table. In a firm but ladylike voice, Victoria then ordered, "Tomato soup for *three*." They were served — and Delmonico's reaped the benefit of the laughter that swept the room.

The Sorosis had moved to Twenty-sixth Street with the restaurant, and the club's activities continued to be a regular source of newspaper copy. The annual election of officers was always good for a column, and the discussions at the monthly luncheon meetings, on such topics as "The Fine Arts," "Protection of Birds," "House and Home," "The Woman of Novelists," "Dramatic Starring," "Haste in Education," "Social Atrophy," "Personal Effort,' and "The Infelicities of Literary Women," gave reporters a chance to display their wittiness. The club and Delmonico's in this way became inseparable in the public mind.

Unlike Lorenzo, Charles Delmonico was accessible to reporters, and this marked a new phase in itself. When inflation sent food prices skyrocketing in 1882, "Charley" was interviewed as an authority on the subject. Asked whether the restaurant's raising the price of a rump steak from 50 to 60 cents, and of a sirloin from 75 cents to a dollar, had not caused a general gnashing of teeth, "Charley" protested:

"I can't help it. The other day I had one of my cooks cut up four short loins to see precisely what they would make in beef, porterhouse and rib steaks, filets and Chateaubriands; and after the most careful computations, allowing even for the trimmings given to the servants and the bones used for making soup, I found the entire yield was $46.50, while the cost to me was $40.75. Considering the butter used on steaks, and rent and other expenses, that meant a decided loss to the establishment."

Vegetables were soaring in price, too, he pointed out. Celery, once 12 cents a bunch, had gone up to 30 cents, and even at that price was hardly to be obtained in quantities, so that a portion of celery *had* to be priced at 45 cents on the menu, instead of

25 cents, "And even at that it gives us no profit, for a great deal of it has to be thrown away." *Potatoes Anna*, a popular dish, was really underpriced on the menu at 25 cents, for the cooks used "about one-third of a pound, or about 15 cents worth, of butter on one portion alone — it's frightful!" Prime cauliflowers were not to be had, and he had been advised to import them from France. "We are actually importing cabbages now; about ten thousand heads arrived by a steamer from Germany the other day." Champagnes had gone up $2 a case and were due to go up another $2 soon, and Bordeaux were just as dear.

As "Charley" said, it was frightful. Delmonico's patrons had no alternative but to chew less or pay more. Which course they pursued was reflected in the public guessing that went on about this time about Charles Delmonico's income: between $200,000 and $300,000 a year net was the usual estimate. The saying, it seemed, still held true: good times or bad, however the business pendulum swung, Delmonico's came out a winner.

3.

But while the business glided along comfortably, all was not well with Charles Delmonico himself. Stories about his untypical behavior had been circulating even before Lorenzo's death, and they increased after that event. One set of rumors had to do with his real or supposed losses in Wall Street. These were lent some countenance by an episode that came to light as early as April, 1880, when Charles Delmonico sued certain stock promoters of Colorado, contending that he had been cheated out of an interest in the "Robert E. Lee Mine"; charging false representation and trying to get his money back. He did not get it, but Wall Streeters were struck by the action, for it was not like a Delmonico to sue; the family had never sought redress for an injury or loss in court.

There was no doubt that "Charley" was gambling in stocks and losing. He plunged recklessly and scorned to accept advice from friends or experienced brokers. Money seemed to mean nothing to him. Hearing of a broker who was down on his luck, Charles went downtown to Wall Street five successive days and bought wildcat stocks, simply to give the man a commission. He was swayed by every flying rumor, and each loss merely spurred him to rasher action. He had always been an easy mark for a loan, whether the borrower was a friend or a chance acquaintance, and he began to refuse to accept repayment of loans; he would push the money away and deny that he had lent it. The sight of panhandlers outside the restaurant annoyed him, and to get them to go away he would hand out five and ten dollar bills, to their bewilderment. One cool-headed beggar came back three times in a week, in different disguises, to collect this inexplicable manna from Delmonico's.

Not a few businessmen who met reverses were told by Charles to dine at Delmonico's and "live like gentlemen" until they could get on their feet again; and if they should never be able to pay him, to think nothing of it. These acts of liberality Charles never alluded to.

About 1882 Charles's health failed visibly, and the stories about his erratic behavior took a sinister turn. Now they concerned his love affairs, real or rumored, and he was whispered to be haunting "private theatrical performances in secluded parlors," where he would "lavish money, wine, and flowers on those who amused him." What foundation there was for these whispers no one can say definitely; yet men who knew him intimately were inclined to give some credence to the gossip.

One story that was bandied about by young bucks of the New York Club had a romantic tinge. When later it was divulged publicly the *New York World* vouched for its accuracy as told by "a gentleman of the highest standing as to veracity, who had known [Charles Delmonico] since he was a boy." The man's name was not published, although *World* reporters about that time were making a habit of bringing out the facts about many murky transactions. This is how, in the verbal conventions of the time, the story appeared in the *New York World* on January 14, 1884:

"Some fifteen or sixteen years ago, [Charles] was in love

with a very beautiful woman. Her name was Lizzie. . . . He was passionately fond of her and equally jealous. She lived at number 3 West Thirteenth Street, the rent of which house he paid, while she took her meals at the Fourteenth Street restaurant with him, where he had her attended to and shown the same courtesies as if she had been his wife. One day in a fit of passion caused by jealousy of another man (who died just four months ago), he struck the woman and broke her nose. This act seemed to prey on his mind a good deal, and in extenuation thereof he purchased the house in which she lived and gave it to her; and until the day of her death, some seven years ago, granted her every desire. He buried her, and for weeks thereafter visited her grave almost daily and would cause large bouquets of flowers to be taken there which completely covered the mound."

This rumored romance seemed to bear a relationship to Charles's increasingly bizarre conduct during 1863. He had always been cheerful and companionable; now he grew morose. He developed eccentricities, like sitting for hours at the parlor window of his Fourteenth Street home, watching for doctors' carriages to pass; as each went by, he would toast it in a glass of champagne. He once drank fourteen such toasts in one hour, although he had never been a heavy consumer of wine.

His appearance changed greatly. Formerly active and energetic, he became lazy and indifferent. He was subject to fits of temper, and was overbearing to employees whom he had used to treat with consideration. He repulsed old friends, including men who had shared many a frolic with him in the dubious resorts under the gaslights of Sixth Avenue. But in his most morbid, cynical moods, he kept a strict eye upon the operation of the restaurants, and nothing that went on there escaped his notice.

By the autumn of 1883, knowledge that something was seriously amiss with the head of the house of Delmonico had become so general that the family deemed it advisable to issue a public disclaimer. Under the heading of "Personal Intelligence," a "card" appeared in newspapers of September 13, reading:

"The rumor that Mr. Charles Delmonico was ill is pronounced untrue. During the summer Mr. Delmonico was not in the best of health, but he has greatly improved and is now not sick."

Three days later, a news item in the *Herald* stated that "Mr. Delmonico, whose failing health has recently caused his friends and family much anxiety, drove downtown in a coupé yesterday morning . . . visited his establishments on Broadway and Beaver Street, talked business with the managers in charge of them . . . and appeared to be in greatly improved health and spirits. He called upon friends in the vicinity of the Stock Exchange, and was driven to the Long Branch boat."

What this ambiguous phrasing imperfectly concealed was that Charles had been "escorted" by a male nurse on that jaunt downtown, and had been virtually spirited away to undergo a "rest cure" in the seaside cottage of a wealthy friend. Nothing was said about the shock his altered appearance had given to those he had met in Wall Street. Once noted for neatness in dress and the slimness of his figure, he had grown fat and soggy, and was carelessly clothed; his eyes were sunken and lusterless; his cheek was pale; his speech halting; his whole air haggard. Charles Delmonico was a dying man.

Then in January he startled New York by disappearing.

4.

The disappearance was sudden, complete, and inexplicable. It occurred just after New Year's Day, in bitterly cold weather. The newspapers splashed the word across their main pages, although the family tried to suppress it, and a search by friends, private investigators, and amateur sleuths was inaugurated. It turned up false leads by the dozen. Charles was rumored to be aboard a ship bound for Europe, accompanied by a mysterious woman for whom he had been buying up the contents of florist shops. He was stated positively to be in a Philadelphia madhouse.

On the third day a clue turned up — almost as baffling as no clue at all. Two boys playing near the railroad tracks that cross the Jersey meadows towards Newark found some scraps of torn letters, a pair of yellow dogskin gloves, and a book of Western Union vouchers entitling the holder to send free telegrams, all identified as Charles Delmonico's property. How they had come to that desolate spot was a mystery. The best guess was that they had fallen, or had been blown, from a passing train. But what train? How long before? And were they dropped by Charles?

The next day another possible clue was found on a coal dump about a quarter of a mile farther along the tracks — a heavy gold locket, engraved with the letter "D," set with onyxes; on one side a black stone, on which was traced the initial; on the other side a red stone with a Greek intaglio of a woman's head. Inside was a "small coil of blond hair, folded in white paper."

The trinket was shown to Rosa Delmonico, Charles's sister, and to the Crists, but they could not vouch for its belonging to the missing man. Except that the lock of hair was described as "blond," the description seemed to fit the locket Lorenzo Delmonico had treasured, in which he had carried the lock of Napoleon's hair. However, no identification with this heirloom (which appeared to have been forgotten in the family tradition) was ever made publicly by Charles's relatives.

By now the family was imploring the police to widen the already extensive hunt, and a reward of $500 was posted for information. Ponds, rivers and creeks all over northern New Jersey were dragged, without avail.

Then, on January 14, a couple of boys hunting rabbits on Orange Mountain stumbled upon Charles's body, lying in a roadside ravine between the towns of Montclair and Orange, half covered with ice and frozen slime in the bed of a sluggish creek that wormed along the bottom. The road was lined with the summer places of New Yorkers who knew Charles Delmonico well. Bit by bit, the course of his wanderings, and the manner of his death, were pieced together.

For some while, the family divulged, Charles had been under partial restraint, watched over by two male nurses, who were under orders never to let him out of their sight. On the day of his disappearance he had seemed particularly well, and had asked to be taken for a walk. One of the guards accompanied him; but in the street Charles eluded the man by a ruse, and boarding an elevated train (where a friend remembered having seen him), rode downtown and crossed by ferry to the Jersey side of the Hudson. Apparently he had formed the intention of visiting an old friend, General George B. McClellan, of Civil War fame, whose home was near Montclair; Charles had been there the previous summer and had admired the location, and he had spoken recently of calling on the general again.

By devious routes he apparently rode to Montclair, and then set out to walk across the mountain to the McClellan house.

Already it was growing dusk and the weather was frigid, the thermometer hovering near zero. The climb up the mountain fatigued him, it was supposed, and near the top he sat down to rest. Confused mentally, and numbed by the cold, he apparently had been overtaken by the drowsiness that precedes freezing; and toppling over, had rolled down the steep side of the gully into the creek.

5.

The shocking fate of a man so widely known and so warmly regarded inspired a flood of testimonials to Charles Delmonico's kindliness and worth. Lorenzo, the upright captain of industry, had been admired and respected; Siro, the jolly innkeeper, had been popular; but Charles, the good companion, was loved. S. L. M. Barlow, legal friend of many Delmonicos, revealed instances of Charles's liberality that had never been spoken of before. "I know, as few men know, the full extent of his generosity," said Barlow.

Once Charles's death had been established, his physician, Dr. Thomas M. McBride, published a "correction" of "idle stories which have been circulated regarding Mr. Delmonico's condition." Charles had suffered from general paresis, Dr. McBride disclosed, exhibiting all the symptoms — alternating periods of extreme exhilaration and crushing depression, and hallucinations in which he fancied himself grown immensely rich or utterly ruined, interspersed with lucid intervals. His disease was not inherited insanity, as some rumors had it; the doctor said there was not a trace of insanity in the family. And as for scandal, "there was no vice about it; any Christian gentleman might have it. It is a very common malady among men who overwork themselves and who, while living high, as it is termed, fail to get enough sleep." There was no cure, and Charles Delmonico's case had been diagnosed as hopeless from the first.

This medical report (which modern diagnostics would scarcely support) was published to counteract scandals that were being hinted in certain sections of the press. The family resented this gossip; and at Charles's funeral, held in St. Leo's Church, Father Ducey, after celebrating the mass, advanced to the chancel rail and in a brief defense of his friend spoke scathingly of men "of supposed honor" who had "maligned him cruelly." The rites were attended by civic dignitaries headed by Mayor Franklin Edson, and in the pews were many men whose names were familiar to the nation. All the Delmonico restaurants were closed and the employees attended in a body. Burial was in the family vault at old St. Patrick's (which long since had been supplanted as the focal shrine of New York's Catholicism by its namesake on Fifth Avenue). Charles was the tenth Delmonico to be placed there.

The plate on the coffin showed how brief had been his career: "Born Nov. 1840 — Died Jan. 1884." Siro Delmonico had died at fifty-seven; Lorenzo at sixty-eight; John Delmonico, the first to succumb in this country, had lived to be fifty-four; Constant, forty-eight; François, fifty. Easy-going Peter Delmonico alone had attained old age, rounding out a generous seventy-eight years. To this family America had brought wealth and fame, but not noticeably long life.

CHAPTER III

THE LOBSTER THAT LOST ITS NAME

AGAIN THERE WAS SPECULATION as to what would happen to the restaurants. The business had suffered three blows in less than three years, and no successor to Charles Delmonico was in sight; "the last of the Delmonicos, the last of his line," the newspapers called him. Lorenzo, lacking children, had left the restaurants to a nephew who had been bred to the business, about whose competence there was no question; now there was no such candidate.

When Charles's will was opened, it was learned that he had left his entire $2,500,000 estate, including the restaurants, to his sister, Rosa Delmonico, and the three Crists, Lorenzo, Charles, and Josephine. Rosa received a half interest, and the Crists the other half divided equally among them. The management of the business fell to a nephew, Charles Delmonico Crist, who not only took over the responsibility, but by act of the Legislature changed his name to Charles Crist Delmonico. His brother and sister followed this example and became Lorenzo Crist Delmonico and Josephine Otard Delmonico. Thus the dynasty was perpetuated, in form as well as in fact.

Charles Crist Delmonico ("Charles C." or "Young Charley," as he was generally known, to differentiate him from his uncle) acquired the duties of management more or less by default. His older brother, Lorenzo, an art dealer on Fifth Avenue, had no flair for restaurant keeping, and his sister, Josephine, who had been reared virtually as Rosa's daughter, knew nothing about business affairs except the smattering she had gleaned from family discussions. Rosa Delmonico had participated little in the management, although in her young days she had worked for a while under Lorenzo.

Transfer of the ownership to new hands produced hardly a ripple in the routine of the four houses. "Young Charley" lacked experience, but the staff, from top to bottom, possessed plenty. Charles C. Delmonico had been trained for a broker's career, and already at twenty-four held a seat on the Stock Exchange. Although he had dabbled in the restaurant business for a while, managing a small place near Kingsbridge, this had been an avocation, not taken seriously. Yet in short order, by attention to business he showed that he was entirely capable of carrying the Delmonico standard.

In person Charles C. Delmonico was slight, trim, graceful, and dapper in dress; in fact, he was considered one of the best dressed young men of Manhattan. His eyes were large and prominent, his mouth sensual, and he sported a grenadier mustache and pointed beard in the style of the day. Among his friends his manner was animated, although generally in public he maintained the dignified reserve that was typical of the Delmonicos. His acquaintance in Wall Street was wide, and with men of his own age he was popular.

The firm's finances he found all shipshape and secure. The only change in property arrangements which his uncle had made had been securing the property at Beaver and South William Streets in his own name. In the settlement of Lorenzo Delmonico's estate, that land and building, which Lorenzo had owned personally, was put up for sale, and at the auction Charles Delmonico bid it in for $132,000. (His chief competitor in the mild contest of bidding was A. Mouquin, himself a celebrated downtown restaurateur.) As part of the estate it passed to the heirs without complications.

"Young Charley" established his headquarters at Madison Square. He visited the other restaurants infrequently, but kept in touch with them through their efficient managers. These had all been with Delmonico for years. At Beaver Street, James A.

Hill, an old and trusted associate, was in charge; at Broadway
was Alessandro Filippini, who had started as a cook; and at 22
Broad Street was John Longhi.

The supervising manager of operations at Madison Square
was Henry Tilghman, a well known figure in New York's social
life. Tilghman had received his training in England, and started
as a waiter at Chambers Street. He had moved to Delmonico's
Fourteenth Street establishment, and thence to Twenty-sixth
Street, where New Yorkers were accustomed to find him every
evening just inside the Fifth Avenue entrance to the restaurant,
greeting the arrivals and seeing to their comfort. Though his
duties were not those of a head waiter, he frequently seated
parties of guests, and if requested assisted them with ordering
the meal. A martinet to his staff, he brooked no laxity in the
service, and was alert to detect the least infraction of the rules of
the house. Waiters were not permitted to stand and wait, they
also must serve; they were expected to be mobile, not statuesque,
attentive but not obtrusive, and neither wool-gathering nor engaged on vague errands when summoned. None of the kind im-
paled by David McCord in his "Epitaph on a Waiter" —

> "By and by,
> God caught his eye" —

none of that ilk and kidney was tolerated at Delmonico's.

Longhi was the one key executive of the organization who
had been deeply affected by the changeover in proprietorship.
Lorenzo Delmonico's failure to leave him the 22 Broad Street
business had not ceased to rankle; and shortly after "Charles C."
took over, Longhi withdrew completely. For the next twenty
years he would devote his time to his investments in Brooklyn
property, and to horticulture. Around his home on the old
Delmonico farm he built greenhouses and laid out formal gardens that attracted landscape artists from all over the world.
He was consulted upon the designs for many city parks in this
country, Europe, and Japan. Wall Street friends urged him

time and again to open a restaurant of his own, promising unlimited backing, but he declined.

"There is but one name for a restaurant in New York,"
would be his rejoinder, "and if I can't use the name 'Delmonico'
I don't want a restaurant."

With Rosa Delmonico, who was of his generation, Longhi
remained friendly, but towards the Crists he was cool.

2.

The 1880's have come to be associated with the epithet "elegant," but there was more rigor in the decade than the adjective suggests. The Eighties were pushing years, as well as a time
of increasing leisure and amenity. They also were a period of
relative social stability, even while the city was undergoing further changes. The flood of immigrants kept up; in 1887 there
were 133,000 newcomers to New York from abroad, a gain of
40,000 over the previous year. Wealth was multiplying pro-
portionately, although it was not being evenly distributed, and
the demand was growing for more outlets where the rich
could spend their wealth lushly.

In 1881, the year of Lorenzo Delmonico's death, there appeared a portent of the new era, when an ambitious young
man from Vermont opened a small confectionery shop on Sixth
Avenue at Thirty-eighth Street. He risked his entire capital —
$1,300 — on the venture, and history was to repeat the pattern
that had been traced fifty-five years before by the brothers Delmonico. The name of this Vermonter was Louis Sherry, and although Sixth Avenue was not as impressive as Madison Square,
Sherry's sights were set upon Delmonico's: some day he hoped
to have an establishment that would equal it, although neither
then nor ever did he dream of surpassing it.

Louis Sherry was the son of a French carpenter. He had been
born in or near St. Albans, and had reached New York by way
of Montreal. For a while he worked as a waiter in the Brunswick Hotel, where he had an opportunity to study the tastes

and personalities of fashionable New York. Then for two summers he managed a hotel at Elberon, New Jersey, a popular seaside resort, and this brought him into close association with numerous well known men of wealth. When he told them about his determination to start his own business, they promised to help by giving him their patronage. Counting on these promises, Sherry opened his modest enterprise in 1881.

His policy was the same as that adopted by John and Peter Delmonico: the customer must be pleased, and the quality of the ingredients used in his products must be above reproach. As time went by, Sherry became noted for paying little heed to complaints about the steepness of his prices; but the least criticism of his goods or his service brought instant, personal attention.

There were difficult times at first. Determined to improve his methods, he visited Paris and looked into restaurant practices there. In 1883 he had his first major stroke of good luck — a contract to furnish the refreshments for a gala fair, or kermess, in the new Metropolitan Opera House at Thirty-ninth Street and Broadway. The publicity this affair received set Sherry up as a caterer. Then in 1885 he captured the Badminton Assembly — one of the smartest social events of the season — and his reputation was secured. From then on the best of society was to be seen at Sherry's and his restaurant began to be mentioned in the same breath with Delmonico's. There was custom enough for both houses.

3.

Another harbinger of coming changes arrived at about the same time. In May, 1883 — on the day before the Brooklyn Bridge was opened by President Chester A. Arthur, a longtime devotee of Delmonico's, with Governor Grover Cleveland and other dignitaries assisting — there landed at New York a young Swiss, so enterprising that before the day ended he had got a job as a busboy at the Hoffman House, and had applied for

United States citizenship. The name of this hustler was Oscar Tschirky, and all the bunting and banners that decorated the streets (in honor of the Bridge) he looked on as a personal welcome extended to him by this city where a man could make his way.

Tschirky remained a busboy only four months. Then he was promoted to waiter in the restaurant. He was impressed with the stature of the hotel when he was told that the chef, Eugene Laperruque, had once signed the menus at Delmonico's. The food and service in the restaurant across the street were the best in town, although his personal acquaintance with the place was a glimpse, as he was coming to work early in the morning, of a nattily dressed gentleman alighting from a hansom cab at Delmonico's door. He was informed that this was "Charley" Delmonico himself, returning from the marketing.

It was neither diet nor necessity that brought Delmonico's and Oscar Tschirky together, but beauty and chivalry, and the thrill of that encounter — for one of the parties — lasted a lifetime. As Oscar told the story to his biographer in the autumn of his days, it happened on an evening in 1887. He was passing Delmonico's Fifth Avenue entrance, where carriages were lined up at the curb, and just as he went by, the doorman hurried forward and called to a coachman.

"I remember his exact words." Oscar related: " 'Miss Russell's carriage, please!' At that moment the door was opened and Lillian Russell came out with a party of friends. I was captivated by this fleeting glimpse. I remember the smooth flow of her blue gown, the exotic effect of her golden hair, but most of all the banked-down fire that smouldered in her beautiful face. She was the loveliest woman I had ever seen . . . I could hear but a few snatched words, uttered in a clear, musical voice. Then her friends closed around her as she stepped into the carriage . . ."

That revelation of Lillian Russell — slim and bewitching, and already the rage of New York — opened young Tschirky's eyes to what the world of Delmonico embraced. If Lillian Russell dined there, he wanted to work there. The next day he applied for a job, and Philippe, the headwaiter, promised him the first opening. A short while afterwards a vacancy occurred, and he entered the service of the house as a waiter in the cafe. From there he was soon transferred to the restaurant. His ambition was to serve Lillian Russell, and in time he would realize it — but that is a story for later. Meanwhile, at Delmonico's Oscar Tschirky received the training that in a few years enabled him to step into his own niche in New York history as "Oscar of the Waldorf."

4.

Another luminary observed by Oscar Tschirky many times at Delmonico's was Mrs. William B. Astor, who, in the American legend, became "*the* Mrs. Astor," without qualification. Since the Astors were a numerous tribe, the distinction was telling. It had not been won without a struggle, and possibly would never have been won except for the worshipful collaboration of the "Autocrat," Ward McAllister.

Mrs. Astor (born Caroline Webster Schermerhorn) was the wife of a younger grandson of John Jacob Astor, who had founded the family fortune and died the richest man in America. An older grandson, John Jacob Astor III, was the head of the clan, and his wife, the former Charlotte Augusta Gibbs, of a proud but impecunious South Carolina family, by virtue of precedence was tacitly recognized as New York's first hostess. But their relegation to second place galled William and Caroline Astor; he sulked aboard his yachts and took to fast horses and fast women, while she set out to conquer the city. To say that she succeeded would be an understatement: she crushed dissent so drastically that as long as she could stand up to receive, she would be acknowledged the "Queen of New York Society."

Ward McAllister had sensed in Caroline Astor the ruthlessness that wins: dominate she must, and then she might be gracious,

but she would never unbend. She also possessed the fortune that
was needed to achieve the highest social flights, which McAllis
ter did not. He, however, had a flair for publicity, and was established in the public eye as the conscience of the Patriarchs.
In the cause of social elevation, therefore, he gladly linked forces
with Mrs. Astor and assumed the duties of prime minister, grand
vizier, majordomo, keeper of the rolls, and master of the revels
to the woman he coyly adored as his "Mystic Rose."

First McAllister installed Mrs. Astor as queen of the Patriarch
balls. He flattered her by elaborate dinners, and in her honor
staged Newport picnics complete with lackeys, champagne,
truffled aspics, and a flock of rented sheep in a meadow to give
the authentic rustic touch. Soon Mrs. John Jacob Astor III was
cast into the shade; and upon her death in 1887, Caroline Astor
assumed the unique designation "Mrs. Astor," short and simple.
She bullied the post office into delivering to her only letters so
addressed, and the social authority she exercised this nation will
never see the equal of again. She required the bestowal of no
patent of nobility; she was her own. By her inflexible fiat, as-
pirants to social recognition were accepted or inexorably shut
out. Invitations to her annual ball, given on the third Monday
in January, were more coveted than rubies. This annual party
she gave in her ballroom, not at Delmonico's. An invitation to
one of her weekly dinners conferred a lesser distinction upon the
recipient, and these ponderous affairs were served up in the ba-
ronial dining hall of her mansion on Fifth Avenue, where the
menu matched the conversation — stately, stilted, and, before
the end of the evening or the last course was reached, sometimes
stupefying.

Mrs. Astor approved of Delmonico's. The city did not offer
a grander sight than that of *the* Mrs. Astor lending her presence
to Madison Square, squired by Ward McAllister and evincing
her democratic proclivities by dining in the restaurant. At such
times the "Autocrat" buzzed around her like a portly humming
bird; he was her sycophant, and an effective one, intriguing,

forming cliques, and filling the press with her praise. For a while an impression even arose that Ward McAllister was the force behind Mrs. Astor, and not the other way around; time would expose the fallacy of this assumption. As long as the Eighties lasted, nothing undermined the "Autocrat's" ascendancy or the power of the "Queen": Mrs. Astor's right to make or break was neither seriously questioned nor successfully defied.

It may have been at Delmonico's on Madison Square that the combination of Mrs. Astor and Ward McAllister added a phrase to the language — the "Four Hundred." The version widely circulated was that in the process of drawing up the guest list for an Astor ball, McAllister had calculated that the ballroom would accommodate no more than four hundred persons. The press — willfully, capriciously, or ignorantly — was said to have misconstrued this purely mathematical computation into a decree that "society" — the real thing — comprised no more than four hundred people.

Another account, given by McAllister's daughter, had it that a reporter, interviewing her father about the preparations for a forthcoming ball, had asked how many guests would be invited, and McAllister had replied offhand, "Oh, about four hundred."

Still a third version was vouched for by a waiter at Delmonico's, who insisted that he had been present in the Madison Square cafe when Ward McAllister called for pen and paper, and then and there wrote out his list of four hundred names.

Whether the "Four Hundred" was a misinterpretation on the part of a newspaper reporter, or was coined in a flash of inspiration by McAllister, or was from first to last a myth and an invention, the phrase stuck, and Ward McAllister's contribution to social history was made. And whether the list existed before it was talked about, or was extemporized to confirm a fiction that was passing as a fact, the "Four Hundred" did congregate at Delmonico's. There, over and above the pleasure of ordering half a partridge for 75 cents, and washing it down with champagne at $3.50 a bottle, any customer might be gratified by catching a glimpse of *the* Mrs. Astor as pure lagniappe.

5.

"Characters" were drawn to Delmonico's as irresistibly as the world of fashion, and they came from all segments of life. When recalling the throngs that frequented the Chambers Street restaurant in its heyday, Sam Ward had listed businessmen, lawyers, politicians, editors, and society sparks, but had excepted the Church. With the revolution of years had come a revolution in this respect, and at Madison Square the cloth was liberally represented. John Klages, headwaiter in the cafe, often overheard priests debating whether canvasback duck might not be construed as a fish food on Friday, and the arguments sounded strangely one-sided.

The debate had subtlety, for the canvasback (be it explained to a generation that knows it not, at least in public restaurants) is unlike other waterfowl, in that it does not feed by preference on marine life. Its favorite food is the roots of an aquatic grass called wild celery, which grows abundantly in the Chesapeake Bay region. The flesh of the canvasback, therefore, has little or none of the fishy tang common to other wild ducks; and the theological significance of the absence of fishiness might be a point susceptible of the closest reasoning.

To "Del's" at Madison Square resorted the stars appearing at the nearby theaters. There was always a flutter when John Drew, or Richard Mansfield, or Kyrle Bellew entered the dining room and took a seat with studied insouciance, "trying to look unconscious" of the women's devouring glances; or when Pol Plançon, or Campanari, or Christine Nilsson, or Jean de Reszke dropped over from the opera house for substantial reprovisioning. The theatrical producers took their meals there — Augustin Daly, Charles and Daniel Frohman, Maurice Grau, Henry Abbey, and occasionally Tony ("Mr. Antonio") Pastor. There were "sports" and layers-of-odds like "Mattie" Corbett and "Sol" Lichtenstein. Law and politics were represented by those bowwow trenchermen — Judge Truax, Judge Gildersleeve, Bourke Cockran; while, for contrast, there was little Abie Hummel, in his black suit. He was the brainy half of the partnership of Howe & Hummel — two practitioners of legal chicanery who had been retained by more burglars, "con" men, yeggs, thieves, defaulters, blackmailers (male and female), perjurers, poisoners, and artists dealing in imaginative murder or simple mayhem than any dozen other law firms. Hummel was propriety and affability itself outside of business hours, and no one spent ill-gotten gains with a freer hand. He seldom missed an evening in Delmonico's cafe, although his ponderous partner, "Habeas Corpus" Howe, appeared there less frequently; by the 1880's Howe's florid bulk was giving way under the strain of the riotous living he carried on elsewhere.

How a man made his money was no concern of "Del's"; he was welcome so long as his behavior was correct and the "solid" element raised no objection. Hummel was well-mannered; and even the stalwarts of the Tenderloin police, unchoosey as to the sources of the incomes that were much larger than their salaries, took their ease in off hours with the dudes and the dandies, the Cuban patriots and prima donnas, the lovely women and lonely old maids, who nightly gathered there. Nor was the unction of religion withheld from the well-fed throng.

A patron of imperishable benignity was the Reverend Thomas J. Ducey. In addition to fulfilling parish duties, Father Ducey occupied the position of virtual domestic chaplain to the Delmonico family. His mother had been housekeeper for James T. Brady, the celebrated forensic orator of the mid-century whose name had been all but synonymous with the Chambers Street Delmonico's. This early association had given Ducey a tenuous connection with the world of wealth, and as a priest he had devoted himself to the spiritual welfare of that class. Men and women plentifully blessed with the goods of this earth are surely entitled to the consolations of religion as much as the poor; indeed, if Holy Writ be trustworthy, they may need those consolations more. To them Father Ducey extended the blessings of church and ceremonial in the style to which they were accustomed.

In 1880 Father Ducey was enabled to build his own church — St. Leo's, in East Twenty-eighth Street — mainly with the assistance of two intimate friends, Lorenzo and Charles Delmonico. St. Leo's was a small church and select; the congregation was drawn from the well-to-do who lived in the neighborhood. Father Ducey (like a London monsignor of the same period) was sometimes lightly termed the "apostle to the genteel," yet he was as compatible with the poorest suppliant as with the proudest millionaire. He solicited the welfare of his flock on weekdays as well as Sundays, dined where they dined (at Delmonico's), and was a constant reminder of their hopes of heaven in the banquet hall, as in the sacristy. The dinner hour was his vespers, and it was said that the text Father Ducey elucidated with the profoundest penetration came from the Gospel according to St. Matthew, chapter 11, verse 19: "The Son of man came eating and drinking." At times the diocesan authorities wondered about Father Ducey; he was considered "erratic"; they certainly looked askance at some of the jokes the good Ducey was inspiring. Example: "Why is St. Leo's like a certain theater on Fourteenth Street?" Answer: "Because it has a tony pastor."

Father Ducey pursued what is known as "the even tenor of his ways" — even while wending his way back to the rectory from Delmonico's — and might have winningly invoked the sanction of the concluding sentence of the above-cited Scriptural verse: "But wisdom is justified of her children."

6.

Of all the "characters" who passed through Delmonico's hospitable doors — at Fourteenth Street and also at Twenty-sixth — few were as odd, and none was so unlucky, as the man who just missed having his name on the tongues of millions through generations unborn. It came about apropos of a lobster.

Ben Wenberg was a sea captain engaged in the fruit trade between Cuba and New York. When on shore, he bivouacked at Delmonico's. In regard to his food and attire he was extremely fastidious: no salty pea jacket or rakish nautical cap for him; he was a dandy. His usual costume was a long Prince Albert coat of fine cloth with a diagonal weave, pantaloons tailored snug and shaped to the instep, high-heeled boots with pointed toes made of glove leather to his order by Adam Young, the fashionable bootmaker, and the latest thing in shiny toppers crowning his iron-gray, curly hair. Ben Wenberg allowed no one to come between him and the table; yet though he ate industriously, he was as thin as a rail.

One day in 1876, home from a cruise, he entered the cafe at Madison Square and announced that he had brought back a new way to cook lobster. Calling for a blazer (a chafing dish with spirit lamp), he demonstrated his discovery by cooking the dish beside his table, and invited Charles Delmonico ("Old Charley") to taste. Charles said, "Delicious!" and forthwith entered the dish on the restaurant menu, naming it in honor of its inventor, or at least its introducer to New York, *Lobster à la Wenberg*. It caught the public fancy and became a standby of the after-theater suppers that were in vogue, and Wenberg preened himself upon having perpetuated his name to the remotest posterity.

Unfortunately, he and "Charley" had a falling out. The cause is not known, but the consequence was devastating to Wenberg's expectations of gastronomic immortality. Charles erased the dish from the menu; but since patrons kept calling for it, he was forced to compromise. By typographical sleight-of-hand, he reversed the spelling of "Wen" to "New," and *Lobster à la Newberg* was born.

Such was the power of a Delmonico.

A man who witnessed Ben's initial preparation of the dish recounted the scene thirty years afterwards, and recalled particularly that at the end Wenberg took from his pocket a small flask, and shook into the pan a little of the reddish powder it contained — the inevitable "secret ingredient." Delmonico's cooks were satisfied that the stuff was only cayenne pepper, though Ben never told. This same witness of Wenberg's first demonstration maintained that the dish, when "made to perfection," should contain only "lobster, sweet cream, unsalted butter, French cognac, dry Spanish sherry, and cayenne pepper." The recipe standardized by Charles Ranhofer departed from this formula, and for those who may wonder how *Lobster à la Newberg* (or *à la Delmonico*, as it was interchangeably called) was prepared at its birthplace, here is the Delmonico recipe verbatim:

Lobster à la Newberg, or Delmonico

Cook six lobsters each weighing about two pounds in boiling salted water for twenty-five minutes. Twelve pounds of live lobster when cooked yields from two to two and a half pounds of meat with three to four ounces of coral. When cold detach the bodies from the tails and cut the latter into slices; put them into a sautoir [saucepan], each piece lying flat, and add hot clarified butter; season with salt and fry lightly on both sides without coloring; moisten to their height with good raw cream; reduce quickly to half; and then add two or three spoonfuls of Madeira wine; boil the liquid once more only, then remove and thicken with a thickening of egg yolks and raw cream. Cook without boiling, incorporating a little cayenne and butter; then arrange the pieces in a vegetable dish and pour the sauce over.

There you have it — the lobster that lost its name, and gained fame.

Part Four

"DEL'S" IN
THE NINETIES

CHAPTER I

DIANA AND
DIAMOND STOMACHERS

BY THE NINETIES, "Del's" had become so entwined in the city's life that the restaurant, and the people seen and heard there, drew almost as much public notice as did the capers of politicians at Tammany Hall. The style of newspaper reporting, like everything else, had undergone change; now it was more chatty and familiar, whereas in the Eighties it still retained a certain restraint. When Clemence Delmonico, Lorenzo's widow, died on September 13, 1887, the press announcements were dignified and concise. They mentioned that she had continued to live in the house at 211 East Fifteenth Street, and had remained active in French welfare and religious affairs; but beyond that, nothing. The funeral was held in St. Ann's Church, and was attended by the current custodians of the family's public reputation, Charles C. Delmonico and his brother Lorenzo, with a committee representing the Société Française de Bienfaisance and a delegation of children from the St. Vincent de Paul orphan asylum. Burial was at old St. Patrick's; the estate was appraised at $365,-000.*

* It is curious that Clemence Delmonico appears to have been the only foreign-born member of the Delmonico family who bothered to acquire American citizenship. The Delmonicos who came to the United States from Switzerland, under Swiss law never forfeited their native citizenship, and American practice at that period was lax. Clemence Delmonico was not Swiss but French, born in France. Her marriage to Lorenzo complicated her status, and after Lorenzo's death property interests became involved. On the advice of counsel, therefore, she took the precaution of regularizing her citizenship. A letter preserved in the S. L. M. Barlow Papers at the Huntington Library in California, dated April 19, 1883, deals with this step, unique in the Delmonico chronicle. Written in a beautifully formed script, on delicate note paper with wide mourning border and an elaborately engraved monogram, "C D," in black, this interesting communication reads:

In a tone almost as reserved, that same year, the press had reported a generous action of Charles C. Delmonico. A messenger boy picked up a counterfeit bill just outside Delmonico's cafe and was showing it to a group there when a policeman came along and arrested him. At this instance of an abuse that was rife at the time — indiscriminate harassing and arresting of boys — Charles Delmonico demanded that the policeman arrest him too, inasmuch as the bogus money had been found at his doorstep. The "cop" was understandably chary about "running in" the boss of Delmonico's, but he was compelled to by the insistence of Charles's friends. At the station a perturbed sergeant hushed up the *faux pas* by discharging everybody concerned. It would require a mayor nominated at Delmonico's to do away with this particular police abuse.

The year 1890 saw the launching of a real rival to Delmonico's when Louis Sherry opened a magnificent restaurant at Fifth Avenue and Thirty-seventh Street. One notable feature was the spacious ballroom, that outshone in splendor the somewhat tarnished red and gold of Twenty-sixth Street. Sherry's room was seventy feet square, compared with fifty feet square at Delmonico's, and it immediately captured some of the season's smartest dances. When, at length, Mrs. Astor, gowned in the simplicity of white satin and diamonds, joined the set at Sherry's, the seal of approval was affixed, attesting its social acceptability.

Delmonico's was not unduly alarmed. Its foundations were

"Cher Monsieur

"Si pour la régularité de mes affaires il faut que je me fasse naturaliser Américaine je suis prête à le faire et si Monsieur votre fils peut venir me prendre lundi pour aller au City Hall je l'attendrai à dix heures et demi.

"Veuillez agréer Monsieur l'assurance de ma parfaite considération.

"C Delmonico."

(Dear Sir

If in order to regularize my business affairs it is requisite that I be naturalized American I am ready to do so and if your son can come and pick me up Monday to go to City Hall I shall expect him at half past ten.

Please accept sir my perfect consideration.

C Delmonico)

too deep to be shaken easily, and the Patriarchs, themselves a symbol of immovability, declined to budge from their accustomed stamping ground. Charles Delmonico reciprocated their loyalty by redecorating his ballroom in a style of unmuted opulence. The transformation piqued public curiosity, and the press responded with its usual fulsome attention.

"The style is flamboyant," the *Herald*'s society reporter conceded, "but why not for New York's Four Hundred?" The musicians' balcony was upheld by demure caryatids and chubby cupids nestled above the mirrors on three walls. Everything was calculated to "enhance the effectiveness of Ward McAllister's mutton-chops," the report read. "The room where many a fairy-slippered belle has tripped with many a manly swell; where many an ambitious statesman has sounded the tocsin of his party's hyperbolical sentiments; and where 'Our Own Chauncey' [Depew, an inveterate joiner and after-dinner orator] has roasted his compatriots from England, Ireland, Scotland, France, Netherlands, Canada, and others of his native lands, with rich, ripe chestnuts — has been entirely done over in what experts avouch to be pure 'Louis Quinze.' "

2.

Concrete evidence of Delmonico's durability was given in 1890, when the building erected by John and Peter Delmonico at Beaver and South William Streets in 1836 — the old "Citadel" — was replaced by a handsomer structure on the same site. The cornerstone of this new Delmonico's was laid on July 10, 1890, by Charles C. Delmonico. He deposited a copper box, about ten inches square, containing documents commemorative of the event. These included a history of the Delmonico firm since 1836, some copper pennies that had been found under the old portico, silver and copper coins of 1890, "shin plaster" currency issued by Delmonico's during the Civil War, and a copy of the menu of the Beaver Street house on February 28, 1890, the day the old restaurant closed.

It had been proposed to immure the box under the portico, at the apex of the triangular lor; but the contractor pleaded that it be deposited at the northeast corner of the building, because the coins found under Solomon's Temple had been under that corner, and that meant good luck. Charles Delmonico was amenable, only stipulating that he deposit the box himself, which he did in the presence of a few friends.

On July 7, 1891, the new building was opened to the public, and as usual the newspapers blossomed with eulogies upon its elegance and appointments. Eight stories high, it had cost $360,-000 exclusive of the land — for which, it was said, the Delmonicos had refused $225,000. Cafe and restaurant occupied the ground floor, the dining room being rated "one of the handsomest in New York." The walls and columns were "principally of delicately colored Mycenaean marble, veined with pink; the capitals of the pillars and the dado and ceiling finished in soft ivory white, picked out with golden wreaths and graceful festoons in relief." The woodwork was stained oak, and the floors were of small white tiles. Special recognition was given to the "brilliant electric lights and many mirrors." On the second floor the ladies' dining room was finished in maroon, and there were also two private dining rooms, while the kitchen was on the top floor, the intervening floors being given over to business offices.

Oldtimers noted with satisfaction that a few reminders of the original building had been retained: a marble mantel that had lent charm to the old second-floor room Charles had placed in his private office, and the Pompeiian pillars and cornice again graced the entrance. These relics were found to have suffered damage from New York's severe climate, and to protect them against further deterioration they were installed under the overhanging roof of the semicircular porch, sheltered from the weather. Through the familiar doorway was resumed the flow of customers who had been passing (and sometimes touching, for luck) the antique columns during their half-century stay in New York.

3.

Meanwhile, Madison Square was taking on new brilliancy.
Directly across the park from Delmonico's, at the northeast corner of Madison Avenue and Twenty-sixth Street, the most picturesque hippodrome New York ever possessed — the Madison
Square Garden — had been opened to a delighted public in
June of 1890. The block had formerly been occupied by a
freight and passenger railway station; and when the railway facilities had been moved to Forty-second Street, the shed-like
building had housed Barnum's circus, and later was converted
into a resort — Gilmore's Gardens — by Patrick Gilmore, the
enterprising leader of a popular band.

The new structure, designed by that lover of night life, Stanford White, was an architectural hybrid not unsuited to the
parti-colored employments it would be put to. There were
echoes of the Doge's Palace at Venice in its facade of terra-cotta
brick; a covered loggia ran along two sides in another Venetian
touch; the Moorish tower terminated in a Spanish Renaissance
lantern that enclosed three sky-high promenades, one above the
other — the "loftiest points attainable by man on Manhattan
Island." The huge building was underwritten by a syndicate in
which J. Pierpont Morgan was the major stockholder, and its
one steady tenant each autumn was the National Horse Show.
Horse Show Week in November brought an outpouring of
fashionable people from cities all around, and during that week
Delmonico's was jammed to the doors. The boxes for the show
were auctioned off each year, and some boxholders trundled in
their own easy chairs and Persian rugs for greater comfort during their viewing of the fanciest turnouts the pride of wealth
could display.

Not until a year later, on November 2, 1891, was the Garden's most memorable feature unveiled. That was the statue of
Diana the Huntress atop the tower — a virgin-slim figure,
poised in the act of running, her bow drawn to let fly an arrow
at the youth Actaeon. The rumor had gone out that Diana
would be bare to the buff, and a fever of expectancy was

worked up among New Yorkers of all qualified ages. On the afternoon of her debut a crowd gathered in the Square to witness this defiance of prudery and glorification of art in its loftiest aspects. Some spectators (it was said) came equipped with powerful field glasses, determined not to overlook a trick or miss a twinkle.

A brisk breeze was blowing at five o'clock when a workman climbed to the top of Diana's head and loosened the robes in which she had been swaddled while being fastened in place. Along Broadway "hundreds stopped to watch," said one newspaper, while from the Fifth Avenue Hotel and the Hoffman House the politicians lumbered out, "their minds not on politics." The workman soon was astride Diana's shoulders, removing the muslin; then, descending lower and lower, he "stripped the goddess bare. As he reached the crescent at Diana's foot, the last of the scanty drapery fluttered down, and thousands," said the *Herald*, "could see the virgin in all her nudity." Whether the sound wafting upwards from the rapt multitude was a sigh of surfeited sensuality or a shout of applause deponents disagreed; in any event, the effect was electrical, literally so, for exactly at 5:15 the lights were turned on — incandescent bulbs strung around her head and outlining her bow and arrow, while giant searchlights bathed her in their glow.

"The effect was beautiful," the *Herald* attested. "As the searchlights played on the golden limbs and the golden bow of the goddess, set off by the dark background of the heavens, they made Diana more graceful, more charming, and more striking than ever. The people seemed never to tire of watching. Every man and woman who passed up or down Broadway, Fifth or Fourth Avenues, or the cross streets, turned to admire."

So began Diana's reign as the undraped patroness of Madison Square. The statue was the work of Augustus Saint-Gaudens, and was made of copper sheathing, gilded; at close range it was anything but sylph-like, standing eighteen feet tall, weighing two thousand pounds, and studded with rivets like a steamboat's hull. Turning on ball bearings, it served as a weather vane, swinging with every puff of the wind, pointing its arrow towards every quarter of the peering city. The forces of prudery denounced Diana's exposure, and Anthony Comstock tried to get somebody arrested, all in vain. Philadelphia expressed mortal offense, and deplored the morbid degeneracy of Manhattan. Diana was unperturbed, and the *New York Times* mused that the goddess's silhouette "might not suggest itself as nakedness to ordinary minds — were not Philadelphia always with us . . . Actaeon today would live in Philadelphia."

Diana continued to be displayed, luminous by night and lovely by day, and Madison Square for some time after her unveiling — the Square where baby carriages had been predominant — became the haunt of "elderly gentlemen, Delmonico elegants, Casino Johnnies, and every other variety of local dude," lingering "in listless idleness," gazing raptly upwards, yet not in prayer. True, some connoisseurs who shared the period's preference for feminine opulence grumbled that Diana was deficient in bulges fore and aft, but their carping cut no ice with the public.

Two years later the statue was replaced by a smaller replica, White and Saint-Gaudens having decided that the original was out of proportion to the tower. Thereafter, Diana stayed serenely on her perch, constant in variability, twirling with the winds to aim her never-sped arrow towards every inquisite quarter impartially. From the harbor to Harlem, she saw all, heard everything, and revealed nothing except her supple self. Manhattan adored her. During her reign Madison Square assumed an aspect palpably Parisian, especially at night, when the lamps gleamed amid the trees, the hansom cabs lined the curb, and through the darkness throbbed the rhythmic clop-clop of hooves and jangling of harness. The air uplifted one then like a swirl of champagne, as in and out of hotels and theaters the pleasure-bent surged. On the fringes of the crowd blurred forms melted into the shadows, and then cries, and laughter like sobbing, might briefly interlace the saucy, sentimental songs that tinkled from the cafes. Never again would New York produce a mood or a setting like Diana's corridor, where stood the two temples of her cult — the Garden and Delmonico's.

4.

Oscar Tschirky had found the discipline of manager Tilghman as relentless as it was reported to be, and in later years he would give his opinion that that was one of the basic factors which made Delmonico's "the greatest eating-place in New York." Oscar's competence again brought rapid promotion, and at about the time Henry Tilghman retired, worn-out by overwork, Oscar was put in charge of the private dining rooms. Tilghman's disappearance was accompanied by rumors that the "perfect steward" had been detected in some delinquency, and cashiered. Charles Delmonico was distressed by this baseless slander, and made abundantly clear that Tilghman was simply exhausted by years of devotion to the business. Far from having "fled to Paris," Tilghman, said Delmonico, was at his home in the city; and the spiteful rumors were traced to disgruntled employees who had run afoul of the martinet. Tilghman was succeeded as general manager of the Madison Square house by Eugène Garnier, a veteran of Delmonico's.

Still Oscar had not encountered Lillian Russell again. Then one day word came from the office that "Diamond Jim" Brady would give a supper to Lillian Russell that evening. Oscar served *that* supper himself. As he told it:

" 'Diamond Jim' arrived with Miss Russell and four other guests, a dinner of just the right and fashionable size. I will never forget him as he arrived at Delmonico's. Even if I had not known who he was, I would have been impressed. So would anyone else. He carried a cane with a diamond head, wore two diamond rings, a diamond stickpin in his black silk tie . . . I found him warm, friendly, and jovial."

Tales of Brady's prowess as an eater already were rife in New York, and they would grow to heroic proportions. Oscar was prepared to serve double, triple, or quintuple helpings of everything on the menu; but to his astonishment — and with what shock to his sensibilities — Lillian Russell ate more than "Diamond Jim" by far.

Which raises the question: how much did "Diamond Jim" Brady really eat? His capacity became traditional in New York: reliable witnesses testified to it, and his global paunch was plain evidence of the cavity he had to fill. Dozens of oysters, gallons of orange juice, steaks "smothered in veal chops" were said to be his normal fare. But Oscar Tschirky, whose testimony is worthy of belief, affirmed that although he served Brady many times, both at Delmonico's and at the Waldorf, he never saw him eat other than moderately. "If he was a great eater he must have done his stuffing elsewhere," was Oscar's unequivocal statement. "Every time I waited on him his order was pretty much the same . . . He would start off with a dozen raw oysters. Then he would usually have a filet mignon with one green vegetable. For dessert there would be either a slice of apple pie or a portion of watermelon if it were in season. His only beverage was orange juice . . . That was what he ordered the first night I served him at Delmonico's."

But Brady's guests — including the willowy Lillian — this was what they devoured, according to Oscar: oysters, soup, fish, entrée, roast, two vegetables, sherbert, game salad, ice cream, cake, and coffee. And though Brady never drank wine, for his guests the choicest vintages flowed without stint.

"I had the surprise and disillusionment of my life," said Oscar of that evening when he saw La Russell tuck into the grub with the determination of a stagehand.

Consider now the testimony, equally emphatic, given — in print — by George Rector, the cheerful Boniface whose restaurant at Times Square set the pace for the Great White Way in the late Nineties: In his reminiscences, which contain much levity but are not devoid of truth, Rector circumstantially described Brady's gorging as a regular, long-continued phenomenon, and George Rector also served "Diamond Jim" many times and regarded him as a friend. Still further, there is the medical evidence adduced after Brady's death, that his stomach was distended to several times normal size. Against all this stands Oscar's testimony; so that apparently how much truth underlies one of New York's most enduring gastronomic legends becomes an enigma shut up in the oyster of the past.

As for Lillian Russell, New Yorkers could never see enough of her, and as the years added to her avoirdupois, they were privileged to see more and more.

5.

Delmonico's was becoming crowded — overcrowded — as the city still expanded. As early as 1891, the *New York Herald's* society reporter bewailed the congestion: "It is wretched to stand about in the small hallway waiting for a table, yet it is an inviolable rule of the house that no table will be reserved after half-past six, no matter how important you may be, or how expensive a dinner you may order." "Young Charley" was adhering to his uncle's precedent of allowing no exception to rules. It seemed to the *Herald* that foreigners must find the situation absurd. "The Parisian has his Café Anglais, Maison Dorée, Bignon, Voisin, Maire, Café de Paris, Durand, and Joseph, not to mention half a hundred others nearly as good. But we have our one Delmonico's. You can say what you please, that other places are as good; they may be. Delmonico's is by no means superlatively excellent these days, but people won't go to other places. So there you are, standing in the hall, waiting your turn, as if at the barber's." It sounded ill-tempered; but waiting on an empty stomach is no sweetener of one's disposition.

In 1891 Sorosis severed its long connection with Delmonico's, but only because the membership had outgrown the accommodations available there. A vote was carried to transfer the club's

headquarters to Sherry's, which was delighted to get this pub-
licity-attracting patronage. The parting with Delmonico was
amicable.

Sherry's was one of the socially select ballrooms that season,
with Delmonico's and the assembly rooms of Madison Square
Garden. The newspapers lumped all three as generally "beautiful, finished in the prevailing mode of Italian Renaissance and
French Louis XVI; well adapted to show off the best points of
our pretty girls, and the *embonpoints* of our treasured matrons."

" 'Claret for boys, port for men, and brandy for heroes!' "
the *Herald* quoted. "So we say, Sherry's for girls, the Garden
for women, but Delmonico's for the heroines of many seasons!
It is plain that society has abandoned all idea of entertaining at
home, beyond the mild pleasantry of a dinner party, or the mad
revel of a tea. All dancing is to be done in public rooms. Mrs.
Whitney, Mrs. Vanderbilt, and Mrs. Astor may give small
dances, because they have a little more room than their neighbors, but they are only little spokes in a wheel that promises to
revolve more rapidly than ever this year of 1891, and of which
the hub is the public ballroom; to be hired at so much a night
— food, wine, attendance, and welcome all fixed at a certain
price, and all unsatisfactory."

No similar complaint had been heard when Delmonico's was
introducing the custom; but pressure of numbers was forcing a
dilution of standards, just as the current tendency towards slang
speech was extending the license accorded to newspaper chit-
chat.

"Apropos of 'Del's,' " the *Herald*'s chatterer digressed, "a
story is being whispered of a certain society woman whose good
looks are far in advance of her bank account. She invited a few
friends to go to the theater, and then to Delmonico's. At the
box office she asked one of the men to pay for the tickets, as she
had forgotten her purse. He did so with alacrity, but his enthusiasm waned when, at the close of her elaborate repast at
Delmonico's, she asked him to charge the amount due on his ac-

count. He did this, and now, a year after, is unkind enough to say that the next time he gives an entertainment forced upon him, he will ask the privilege of naming the guests — among whom his forgetful hostess will not be numbered!"

Times and tastes were corruptible when tales like this appeared, foreshadowing the modern gossip columnist, who would not blush to tell all — twice over.

Reverting to the prime topic — the forthcoming balls — the *Herald*'s social observer concluded that, "looking over the program, it seems that the very young buds are to blossom in Sherry's pink-and-gold room. The full-blown roses will, as usual, fill the Madison Square Garden assembly rooms with their perfume; while the wall flowers, the old timers, the patricians, will cling to their old walls at Delmonico's. It seems a fit and proper arrangement.

"Early hours are advisable for the Sherry dances," this arbiter of decorum went on. "Let the young people assemble by nine sharp, and get through with their orgies by midnight. From half-past eleven to half-past one is a good interval for the young married women who will patronize the assemblies, and from twelve to three will be the usual average for the hardened and seasoned devotees of the Patriarchs. Awful hours to keep, but then, these people always dine out, go to the opera, and show up at a ball at the last moment. It disturbs their dinners and dignity to hurry, and affronts their reason to consult a timepiece. Can you imagine Mrs. Astor, or Mrs. Paran Stevens, knowing what time it is after they have once got into their ruby velvet and diamond stomachers?"

At Delmonico's no one could.

CHAPTER II

FIRE AND
PISTOL PLAY

IN RESPONSE TO A RUMOR that the restaurant was about to be moved farther uptown, Charles Delmonico reassured the diamond-stomacher auxiliaries of the corps of customers that no such interruption of their tardy convocations was intended. The lease on the Madison Square premises had been renewed recently for eight years, at an annual rental of $62,500, he told reporters, and, *"Deo volente,* I propose to occupy them and go no farther." The persistency of rumors of an imminent displacement was annoying, and "Charley" showed his irritation. "Every time the 'scandal,' as I now call it, gets into print, I am deluged with offers of real estate on desirable Fifth Avenue corners all the way from here to Harlem," he shrugged. "But we are not moving."

All seemed serene in the best of all possible restaurants. Yet the pushing of the general crowd was continual, so that neither Sherry's nor "Del's" was other than relieved when, in 1893, a fresh facility for entertaining the ambitiously resplendent took the field. This was the Waldorf Hotel, at Fifth Avenue and Thirty-third Street. George Boldt, its operator, had in mind to "bring luxury to the masses" — or at least to the prosperous middle class, — and the building erected on the site of an Astor mansion was a fantasy of sumptuousness. Amid splendor such as only millionaires had thitherto known, any drummer from Oshkosh might luxuriate for a day and feel that his bill, steep as it might be, was not an overcharge. A restaurant in keeping with "royal suites" was part of the plan — something bigger and if possible better than any existing.

In this program Oscar Tschirky saw his opportunity and seized it. Applying to Boldt for the position of headwaiter, he was told to submit letters of recommendation. Oscar wrote a letter setting forth his qualifications, and asked his customers at Delmonico's to endorse it. Soon he had eight pages of signatures from New York's most influential citizens. Boldt was satisfied, and Tschirky thereupon became what he would always remain, "Oscar of the Waldorf."

The hotel opened on March 13, 1893, and after a slow start attained a popularity that would never decline. With its addition, the Astoria, which was opened in 1897, it was the foremost hotel of America; but in spite of Oscar's skill, acquired at Delmonico's, "Del's" remained America's foremost restaurant. This was partly because of the peculiar bond that existed between Delmonico's and many of its customers. The bond was in some cases almost one of kinship. Men whose hair was gray, who had roystered at "Del's" in their salad days, brought their sons and grandsons there to be formally introduced to the house and its staff. And these inheritors of a tradition of good living improved their welcome in ways much exceeding strict business.

An example occurred with Sam Ward's grandsons, the young Chanlers. Orphaned in early childhood, they had been reared by guardians who were grudging in the matter of pocket money. As college students, before they had come into their inheritances, the lads were often strapped. In order to acquaint them with the social life they were destined to lead, and at the same time shield them from temptations, the guardians allowed the boys unlimited credit, in lieu of cash, at certain "good" establishments, among which was Delmonico's. For Sam Ward's grandsons what would not Delmonico's do! The restaurant on Madison Square became the young Chanlers' banking house, and many the dinner that was charged to the guardians and never served.

The difference between Sherry's and Delmonico's, socially approved though both houses were, continued to be evinced in

small ways. It was Sherry's, and not Delmonico's, that figured
in a feud with residents of its neighborhood, who objected that
the yelling of the men calling customers' carriages disturbed
their slumbers. Some of those complaining were themselves
patrons of Sherry's; but they demanded quiet in the streets after
two or three o'clock in the morning. Two carried their griev-
ance to the police, and Captain Schmittberger, of the Tenderloin station, was impelled to notify Sherry that he was flirting
with a grand jury indictment for maintaining a public nuisance.
Sherry tried his best to abate the racket. He installed an electric
call-board above the entrance, but the coachmen wouldn't look
at it. He hired runners to go down the line and alert the coachmen wanted; it was no go, the drivers refused to heed a whisper.
Then Sherry hired hacks from a livery stable and parked them
at the door, but the customers insisted on using their own carriages. The bawling kept up, and arrests were made, and Sherry
appealed for sympathy, and hot words were exchanged, and
the public for a while took up the squabble.

Nobody could imagine so undignified a dispute occurring
at Delmonico's on Madison Square.

2.

Sherry caught the fancy of women with his introduction of
the five o'clock tea. At that hour the elite of New York trooped
to his dining room to consume gunpowder, green, lapsang soo-
chong, and Darjeeling, amid a stimulating babble of gossip.

Delmonico's remained the favorite of women for luncheon.
"What would the women of New York do without 'Del's,' their
home and refuge?" ruminated the *Herald*. "In fair weather
and in foul, in spring and in winter, in summer and in autumn,
they head for Delmonico's as if it were the only place left to
them on earth. The reason must be that at Delmonico's, New
York women, and their imitating sisters from out of town, can
collect, eat, drink, and regard each other, without anybody
knowing or caring particularly whether it is Mrs. Astorbilt,

of Fifth Avenue, Mrs. Snooks, of Newark, or Miss Prettyface, of the Royal Flats. In absolute security and peace they sit at adjoining tables and look so much alike you cannot tell one from the other."

Initiates, of course, had only to listen to the orders given to separate the types. For the "Mrs. Astorbilts" there seemed to be a standing order — oysters, scrambled eggs with truffles, toasted muffins, and filet Béarnaise. For "Mrs. Snooks" it was roast beef, mashed potatoes, ice cream, and green tea. For "Miss Prettyface," quail on toast, small bottle.

"On Saturday the crowd clamoring for these extremes of food is something astounding," the reporter marveled. "The green tea people, of course, get in first. The scrambled-eggs-and-truffles people, if they are wise, send their small boys or their maids to hold the fort for them until they get there. The rest of the people, who have made no provision except hunger, stand about in the hall.

"So great is the pressure at this midday meal," continued the raconteur, "that I have seen women like Miss Prettyface — and men, too — who had no acquaintance with that amiable and passive old gentleman, Mr. Frank Work, actually go into the room and with a bare apology sit down at his table, and watch and wait until he had put the last of his luncheon, which he likes to eat slowly and deliberately, into his mouth, and then beckon to their friends in the hall to come and join them at the table from which the poor old fellow has been crowded out."

Why the crowds continued to cling to Delmonico's was a conundrum that preoccupied numerous observers of social customs. During the course of these speculations, the establishment's reticent permanent lodgers were drawn into the public light, to their dismay. Their names, until then as obscure as their bank balances were sound, became familiar generally, and they acquired a notoriety which they had not sought. There was, for one, "little Mr. Pettit," whose dearest possession was a wonderful collection of poker chips; often these were heard clicking in his top-floor suite.

Peppery Mr. Pettit had been a protagonist in a serio-comic episode of the Eighties when the stammering William R. Travers inadvertently sat on Mr. Pettit's new hat in Delmonico's cafe. A few days later the excited little man sputtered to a reporter that Travers was refusing to pay for the damage, and that he (Mr. Pettit) was going to sue for redress. This threat from a Delmonico lodger Travers laughed off as "a joke," increasing the fury of Mr. Pettit. Travers then inserted a "card" in the *New York Sun*, naming four prominent New York men who would testify that he (Travers) had apologized at the time of the accident; that he had not been served with a bill for damages; and that he certainly was not being sued. "I was not aware that I had seriously injured Mr. Pettit's hat," Travers protested gravely. "If I have done so, and of course I accept his statement to that effect, I will cheerfully pay the bill when presented." But positively he had not "crushed a hat," he had "sat on a hat," and that by accident. The presumptive duel was averted; but "Mr. Pettit's hat" was kicked about for weeks in the clubs.

The popular belief was that Petit eschewed luncheon, for he was never seen at that hour in the restaurant, where he dined religiously. "For twenty years his slim little figure has been tucked under the table in the extreme southeast corner of the room, a table out of all draughts, but which gives a splendid *coup d'oeil* of the room. There he is to be found every night punctually at a quarter to seven. Nothing but fire, death, or something horrible happening to his chips upstairs will ever turn him away from his pastures. Unlike Mr. Work, who always pre-empts the northeast corner of the room for luncheon, Mr. Pettit has made this his abiding place for the dinner hour only.

"The fame of Delmonico's has traveled far beyond the seas," commented this news writer. "About the first thing distinguished visitors to our shores do, when they get their land legs on — and some of them before — is to hie them to Delmonico's. Without going back beyond the 'Del's' of today, one can run over a long list of famous men who have made constant play with knife and fork there, and ogled *les jolies Américaines* over their glasses of Château Lafite." Names sprang to the writer's pen: the Comte de Paris and the Duc d'Orleans; the Duc d'Uzès and Comte d'Hausonville; the Marquis de Lasteyrie, Lafayette's grandson, and the Duke of Marlborough and Lord Mandeville, afterwards the Duke of Manchester. It was said that "a dish of terrapin and a red-head duck cooked by a Delmonico chef gave the Hon. Alan Johnstone the pluck to propose to Miss Pinchot." The blue-chip list marched on and on.

This same recorder of celebrities to be seen at Delmonico's noted that "the gentleman who is responsible for all the crowding and jostling is quite the least observed of anyone. Charles Delmonico — with the assistance and cooperation of the old employees of the establishment, and the advice and influence of many of the old patrons — above all by close attention to business, coupled with a rare faculty for always saying and doing the right thing — has admirably succeeded in carrying forward the obvious mission of his family in America — to provide the very best service for good livers in the world."

Yet the puzzle remained: why, after all, should one stand and wait for one's dinner? The riddle teased the deductive faculties of the *Herald*'s society expert. That "New York society, which has been brought up practically on Delmonico's methods, has expanded greatly since the Fourteenth Street house was closed and the move uptown was made," was an obvious fact. And so was the fact that "New York today has outgrown Delmonico's. In perhaps any other city in the world the crowds would rush on and beyond 'Del's.' A few do go, but they come back the next day and ask again the question they asked before — 'Why should I stand and wait at the door for my food?' No one knows why. But here in New York we all crowd around the door of Delmonico's and wait for our turn the way Englishmen would wait for the only bathtub in Bucharest!

"Well, why not?" was the philosophical conclusion. "The proof of the pudding is in the eating, isn't it? Yes, but not only that. The delights of the pudding rest also in the company in which it is eaten."

3.

Pudding and delights came near going up in smoke, one wintry morning in 1893. An early cook upset a pan of grease; a blaze flared up instantaneously, created a cloud of smoke, and brought firemen on the run. They flooded the basement and the fire was put out before it could cause much damage. Nevertheless, a shiver ran through many a New Yorker; for what would happen should the institution so anchored in the city's unconscious be, some fateful night, extinguished?

Charles Delmonico took the episode in a light vein, at least outwardly, and described with relish the panic flight of his lodgers on the top floor. "Little Mr. Pettit, our roommate from time immemorial, came flying down, three steps at a time, as though possessed by a devil," "Charley" told reporters. "Joe Mora [a respected broker] skinned down the winding banister like streak lightning. Steady-going, handsome old Jim Paulding, when he felt the hot air forcing its way into his chamber, wheezed: 'Another Turkish bath? Why so early in the morning? My hour is from four to seven in the afternoon.'" Fred Hoey, an Adams Express executive whose hobby was trap-shooting, had the worst fright, because he had five hundred cartridges in his room. "It was manifestly his duty to get out of there," chuckled "Charley." "On the other hand, Harry Prince, the last to be aroused, came down the stairs slowly and languidly, as if bored by the tumult raised around his bedstead."

Assembled in the lower hall, and satisfied that they were out of danger, the refugees inspected each other with mutual curiosity. "Joe Mora wore the Castilian pajamas of old Spain," said Charles. "Jim Paulding, like the solid Down-Easter he is, wore a long, white cotton nightshirt split up the sides, revealing the length of his athletic limb. Little Mr. Pettit shivered in a gossamer dressing gown evidently bought for looks and not for warmth; and Freddie Hoey had on his fore-and-aft great coat — it fitted him as well before as behind."

For weeks customers were uneasy, and the horrid question

was pressed home remorselessly by the press: "What if, instead of a little flurry in the kitchen, the establishment had burned down?"

In the opinion of the *Herald*, "the whole social machinery of entertaining would have come to a standstill. Do hungry and thirsty people appreciate what Delmonico's is to them? Suppose we all marched out of a theater some night and were greeted with a ruin? Where would McAllister's patrons be then? Where would the assemblies, dancing classes, cotillions be held? What would become of those little supper parties, poker parties, and private functions held in the suites of rooms on the second and third floors? What would become of the little servant maids, who block the desk in the front office every day with orders for bouillion, pastries, croquettes, and other luxuries which they carry away to private apartments? Where could Frank Work possibly go for his midday meals? Where could Oliver Sumner Teall make so large an impression with a white chrysanthemum? And where else could Monsignor Ducey obtain such inspiration for his Sunday discourses — above all, to a flock unfed?"

The questions were facetious, but the intimation of imminent doom acquired serious point shortly after the fire, when Charles Delmonico announced that the restaurant at 22 Broad Street would close. So Delmonico's, at least in all its members, was not immortal. Management of the Broad Street place had been transferred to two oldtime employees four years previously, and now the owners of the property wished to sell it, and Charles felt that the rent of $18,000 a year was not justified by the diminishing trade. So it was good-bye to the haunt where "fun-making fellows from the Stock Exchange" had been ordering "another bottle" for a quarter of a century. The grizzly-gray sign "Delmonico" came down for the last time on Broad Street, and on the closing day old-stagers gathered to swap stories. One white-haired banker, as he lifted his glass, sighed that he had bought the first cocktail at the bar on opening day, in 1866, and was determined to buy the last.

4.

Destructive forces seemed at work to upset many settled ways and familiar customs; but nothing quite so unsettling had ever happened at Delmonico's as the event that made headlines in November, 1893: "PISTOL BULLETS AT DELMONICO'S!" The crossheads told the appalling story: "Crying 'Down With the Rich!' Crank fires Through the Windows" — "Waiters and Richly Dressed Diners Rush Pell-Mell for Safety" — "One Small Man's Bravery" — "Confusion Reigns Supreme."

At five-thirty in the afternoon, a man described as "well built, sharp-featured, with glaring light blue eyes," halted in front of the Fifth Avenue entrance of the brilliantly lighted restaurant. Although ordinarily at that hour the room would be half empty, this was during Horse Show Week, and every table was taken.

This week, and this week only, Delmonico's was serving its annual salute to the horsey-social set who had taken over both sides of the Square — the celebrated Horse Show dinner, which comprised, among other stable pleasantries, "bay oysters," "purée à la rein," "saddle of two-year-old with horseradish sauce," and "bridle cakes with roan sauce," topped off with "pony of brandy."

This Nag's Head feast was just getting under way when "suddenly," ran the account, "outside the entrance the stranger drew a revolver, brandished it over his head, and yelled: 'Curse the rich! Curse them now and for all time!' Then he fired through the window, the bullet striking the ceiling."

Pandemonium ensued. A second shot barely missed a waiter, and the stranger charged through the door, firing at random and hitting nobody. As a reporter put it temperately, this "brought the meal to a panic-stricken close." Waiters and customers ran for the exits or dove under the tables — under one of which manager Garnier was crouched, screaming "Murder! Murder!" One diner ("a little man") who clearly resented the intrusion, jumped up and grappled the gunman, and a fireman

who happened to be passing dashed in and helped. By this time
a policeman had arrived, and the assailant was disarmed and
marched off to the lockup, "followed by an enormous crowd."
The prisoner was in high fettle, sang German student songs and
joked with the turnkey.

In the morning, visibly deflated, he identified himself as a
stonecutter by trade and a Socialist by faith, and said that he had
been "drinking heavily" and had decided "to give the Delmonico crowd a fright." Purchasing a brand new revolver for the
occasion, he had set out to "frighten the rich into a change of
heart."

The diners at Delmonico's, however, experienced neither a
change of heart nor any alteration in their diet. "Cracked as a
crab" was the consensus regarding the deluded youth, and two
hours after the uproar the waiters were flitting about their recondite tasks as noiselessly as ever.

Cranks and troublemakers, like other afflictions, seldom come
singly, and a few days after the shooting a woman strode into
Delmonico's and requested the bullets left by "that fellow who
shot into the dining room." She had "a great idea how money
could be made out of them," she explained. "You see, everyone
who was here at the time would like to have one as a souvenir,
and I could raffle them off at $2 a ticket."

Charles Delmonico told her that he already had converted
them into souvenirs and distributed them among his friends.
Whereat she upbraided him for taking the bread out of her
mouth, until a hall boy was sent to fetch a policeman. Then she
decided it was time to go, and went.

The restaurant at Beaver and South William Streets, built in 1838, after fire had destroyed the original restaurant on William Street.

New-York Historical Society

Delmonico's at Fourteenth Street and Fifth Avenue. It flourished from 1862 until 1876.

The Delmonico restaurant at Broadway and Chambers Street, 1856. The restaurant was the corner building, next to the Irving Hotel with the awnings.

Delmonico's at Fifth Avenue and Twenty-sixth Street — Madison
Square; 1876 to 1897.

New-York Historical Society

The second restaurant at Beaver and South William Streets, opened in 1891. The Pompeiian columns from the earlier building were preserved. This building is still standing (1967).

The Last Stand. Delmonico's at Fifth Avenue and Forty-fourth Street, opened in 1897. This photograph was made after the closing of the restaurant when changes had been made, but something of its original style remained.

New-York Historical Society

A Private Dinner at the Forty-fourth Street restaurant in 1898.

Mayor William Jay Gaynor.

Ward McAllister — "the Autocrat."

CHAPTER III

THE EXPLOIT OF
LITTLE PHILIPPE

PHILIPPE, THE HEADWAITER, was a little man, but he was a man of great resources. Never in any crisis had he been known to lose his head or withhold his hand from a tip. No obstacle cooled his courage, no deterrent (barring bullets) could deflect him from the performance of his duties, no mischance could cause him to flinch or falter. Blandly beaming, he appeased standees kept waiting an hour in the hall, unsnarled congestion with the aplomb of a traffic policeman, waved parties to tables which they might or might not have selected themselves with a suavity that melted objections, and soothed ruffled customers with the oil-and-honey of perfect empathy. In exchange for a gratuity, there was no favor he would not grant, short of compromising the honor of the house. With Philippe, Delmonico's always came first.

The headwaiter of a restaurant is its grand tactician. On him rests the responsibility of carrying out the battle orders issued by the strategist-in-chief, the general manager. The chef may command the supplies, the wine steward the ammunition train, but the man who must bring all the forces of food, drink, and service to bear upon the objective, and win or lose the engagement, is the headwaiter. His is a post requiring resources, and as we said, Philippe had them. Philippe, in fact, was a pearl among the oysters of his profession.

But in the career of every great campaigner there comes a time when to win seems impossible, when the sheer weight of opposition, the obstinacy of the enemy, nullify every stratagem hitherto known to warfare, and only an inspiration of blinding brilliancy can snatch the palm of victory from the mire of defeat. Such a moment arrived for little Philippe one frosty, clear night in January 1893. The occasion was a Patriarchs ball.

Nothing in the preparations portended a crisis. For the dancing, the ballroom and the red room had been assigned, with the customary two orchestras — the Hungarian band, very *chic*, in the red room, and Lander's orchestra in the ballroom gallery. Supper to be served downstairs in the restaurant, the buffet to be spread in the cafe. Decorations sparse, almost austere, potted plants and flowers in the corridors, everything luxuriously simple; departure from the established pattern would have gravely affronted the traditionalists who were staging the ball. Menu in keeping: the food, not Spartan, yet exempt from all showiness. This was not an occasion requiring a gastronomic display; the buffet was provided merely to recruit the energies of the guests in preparation for the cotillion. Philippe perused the card quickly:

CHAUD

Bouillon
Huîtres Viennoise
Croquettes de chapons, d'Orsay
Bouchées de riz-de-veaux aux champignons
Filet de boeuf aux fons d'artichauts, Macédoine
Terrapene à la Maryland
Thé et café

FROID

Galantine de poulardes aux pistaches
Aspics de foie-gras decoré
Paté de gibier aux truffes
Mayonnaise de volaille
Salade de homard
Cailles farcies
Sandwiches
Rilettes
Canapés

Entremets de douceur

Gelée aux abricots	Charlotte aux bananes
Gateaux noisettes	Meringues Bavaroises

Pièces montées

Glaces fantaisies

Bisquits glacées	Merveilleuses
Nesselrode	Parfait nougat
Bonbons	Mottoes
Fruits	Petits fours

Dessert

VINS

Moët blanc   Apollinaris

Nothing to present any difficulty there, absolutely a routine refreshment. Philippe turned his attention to the early arrivals coming from the theaters. Then perversity took a hand.

It was an evening (a witness of the memorable action set down) "bright and cheery, when the millionaires were out and Broadway was full of people hastening for that bite of supper always prompted by frost and festivity in the air. A good proportion of the crowd turned in at 'Del's,' until the restaurant and cafe were packed with animation and orders.

"Now it happened," went on this raconteur, "that a social function of great importance was in progress upstairs — one of those swagger balls that demand the entire and exclusive use of Delmonico's after midnight. It also happened to be one of those nights when ordinary people like to linger over the delights of the table and the bottle. Orders were filled with astonishing promptitude, bills were presented with unheard of dispatch, and for once an air of 'your room is better than your company' was adopted by the usually Chesterfieldian Garnier and the urbane Philippe.

"Twelve o'clock struck and still the crowd lingered in the restaurant. As soon as a table was vacated, waiters seized it, stripped it, picked up the chairs, and swept the floor underneath it. Then a window at the back was opened, and then another, until finally the women were frozen out. They departed good-naturedly, recognizing the high importance of the event upstairs that was causing their eviction.

"Not so in the cafe. The Old Guard was out in force this night and refused to be dislodged, cost what it might."

At one table Nat Goodwin, "Johnnie Drew," and other stage stars were "discussing Ada Rehan and the Theater of Arts and Letters." At another Richard Harding Davis, Reginald de Koven and friends were talking books and music with profundity. At another, several bookmakers headed by "Sol" Lichtenstein were figuring the hypothetical odds on a hypothetical sparring match — not that they believed the two fighters named would ever come to blows, but figuring odds was their vocation, and good workmen keep their tools sharp. There was a clutch of pigeon shooters, deep in technical discourse about nitro powders and bursting guns; while across the room "Worthy Whitehouse and a lot of dandies" were bemoaning the inevitability of their joining the doings upstairs, and vowing they would hold off until the last possible moment. To resume the eyewitness relation:

"Mr. Meyer Jonasson, Mr. Harry Rothschild, and lawyer Abe Hummel sat at a table pontificating on politics; in a corner sat Charley Delmonico with friends. But Charley knew what was coming and slipped away early.

"The strains of the waltz came down through the ceiling, combined with the stamping of feet on the part of those very fresh young gentlemen who consider it the proper caper to pound out the time of a polka on the floor. Little Philippe surveyed the scene with regret and apprehension. To him had been entrusted the duty of clearing this room by one o'clock at the very latest, and it was now half-past twelve. His generalissimo, Monsieur Charley, had deserted him. He must fight the fight alone.

"The Old Guard sat close to their bottles, conscious of their danger.

"Suddenly the swinging doors leading to the bowels of Delmonico's were flung open and six stalwart Alsatians barged in, carrying a huge screen which they threw up as a breastwork, fencing off the end of the cafe. Immediately in their rear came a supporting column, armed with sections of an immense table, which they put together with astonishing rapidity. These were followed by a skirmishing force with cloths, napkins, knives, forks, and other paraphernalia of table service. They had evidently been ordered to make all the noise possible, and they obeyed to a man. The din was hideous.

"The Old Guard received this attack in a manner worthy of its traditions, sending a sharp fusillade of orders into the bar by the few waiters who were neutral and had not yet received their tips. The clatter of dishes and forks and knives only caused the Old Guard to talk the louder.

"Then the device that had worked so well in the restaurant was employed. A current of cold air was turned on the hardy veterans of a hundred encounters, but it was a lamentable failure. Equipped with their heavy fur great coats, the Old Guard simply wrapped these more closely around them and sat steady.

"In a moment the odor of delicately prepared food arose behind the screen. One of the bookmaking fraternity stealthily got up from his chair and peeped over the top of the screen. In a stage whisper he announced, 'They're going to bombard us with cold quail and lobster salad!' "

But the buffet was for another purpose. Nevertheless, the aromas made Richard Harding Davis and his party "so frightfully ravenous they surrendered at discretion and marched off with colors flying to tackle Welsh rarebits elsewhere.

"By now Edgar Murphy, one of the pigeon sharps, was telling a story. Everyone had heard it many times before, but it served as an excuse to sit still and pretend to listen. The group was so intent they did not notice little Philippe's reconnaissance around one end of the screen. His face was distorted. He had tried every device ever used to clear the room, and it was now a quarter past one. He couldn't absolutely order some of the best patrons off the premises; his authority did not extend that far.

"The silence was broken only by Murphy's voice as he droned on, 'And the man said to the little boy, "Have you seen a yaller dog here with a tail an inch and a half long?"' Philippe was in agony; he, too, had heard the story and he knew that it took half an hour to tell. At any moment Lander upstairs might strike up the supper march, and the dudes and dandies would come pouring into the cafe from the ballroom. The place was still full of smoke. What could Philippe do?

"Suddenly he struck his hand to his forehead as an idea struck him. He disappeared. The Old Guard, having ordered drinks ahead, were not dismayed by the fact that the bar had closed at one o'clock, and they were still deep in Murphy's story and other Christmas novelties when something awful happened.

"A knock was heard at the Broadway entrance. Jimmy Wade, in charge there, opened it, although it is never opened after one o'clock. All eyes were turned to see who the intruders might be.

"Three of the dearest, sweetest, darlingest little dudes in New York minced in. They were gotten up to kill. Gently assisting each other to remove their Inverness capes, and smoothing the down on their upper lips, they smiled, and one lisped:

" 'Beastly cold night. Are you going to the dawnce?'

" 'Mein Gott!' exclaimed Sol Lichtenstein. 'Ve vas attagged in der rear!'

"The Old Guard sprang to its feet. Every man recognized his peril. They could stand every outrage, endure every affront put upon them, but an incursion of dudes completely unnerved and conquered them. Grimly and gingerly, keeping as far away from the newcomers as possible, the actors, the sportsmen, and the pigeon sharps folded their great coats about them and stalked out. Philippe's stratagem had succeeded. He had simply asked the man at the door admitting to the ball to send three of the most pronounced dudes in town around to the cafe entrance.

"Bravo Philippe!"

When the audacious maneuver was relayed to the Patriarchs, they concurred in a "bravo Philippe." The victory confirmed what they had always felt — that upon Delmonico's they could rely; at Delmonico's they would be secure; they hoped secure forever.

CHAPTER IV

THE END OF
THE "AUTOCRAT"

THE 1920'S HAVE BEEN TAGGED "The Era of Wonderful Nonsense," but in New York City the 1890's would have fit that phrase better. Between the two decades there was a wide difference, which was typified even in what they drank: it was the difference between vintage champagne and bootleg gin. The Nineties were ingenuously giddy, and their world was secure; the Twenties would be harshly hysterical, in a world that had been jarred by great social upheavals. Just before World War I, during a period that formed merely an extension of the Nineties, a successful operetta could be called "Naughty Marietta"; such a title on a theater marquee in the Twenties would be inconceivable. The Nineties understood what it was to be nice, while they were being naughty; the Twenties would rush beyond comprehension of naughtiness, or concern with things nice.

In 1895, dwellers in what had begun as Nieuw Amsterdam were taking stock of the swollen contours of their metropolis produced by the absorption of the outlying counties — Kings, Queens, Richmond, and the Bronx — with Manhattan, to create Greater New York. The gain in all aspects that could be counted, weighed, or measured was incontestable; but with the altering of the city's shape, something was leeched out of the onetime proud designation, a "New Yorker." Who would care to refer to himself as a "Greater New Yorker?"

At Delmonico's the metamorphosis was hardly noticeable, for few of its patrons hailed from either paterfamilial Brooklyn or the bucolic Bronx; its purview was still Madison Square and the adjacent neighborhoods. So at "Del's," the year that hatched out Greater New York produced only the customary annual register of events, some of them important, and others of curious interest only. Among these (a sign of the changing times) was a carefully staged testing of New York State's recently enacted civil rights law.

What was commonly called the Maltby Act, "to protect all citizens in their civil and legal rights" without regard to race, creed, or color, was signed by Governor Levi P. Morton on June 15, 1895, and the next day — a Sunday — three Negro gentlemen set out to determine its effectiveness. They were Charles W. Anderson, private secretary to State Treasurer Colin; H.T. Burleigh, composer and teacher at the National Conservatory of Music; and Richard E. Stovall, president of a political club. Anderson had helped to frame the law and had worked for its passage, so he felt a special responsibility for its enforcement. He explained the purpose of the test in advance, saying, "The colored citizens of this city and State do not intend to abuse their privileges, but we propose to stand jealously by our rights." Expressing confidence that "every fair-minded white man" would lend support, he invited reporters to come along.

Unexceptional in dress, speech, and deportment, the party of three first entered O'Neill's restaurant, at Sixth Avenue and Twenty-second Street, and took a center table amid a buzz of excitement. Waiters, manager, and cashier whispered together; then a quiet order was flashed around the room, and instantly (as one newspaper reported the phenomenon) "every waiter became deaf and dumb." Anderson called out orders, and tried to clutch passing waiters, but they remained oblivious of his existence. It was a palpable freezeout, and at length the group went to the cashier's desk, exhibited a copy of the law, and explained that the refusal to serve them constituted a violation.

"Let us understand each other," said Anderson. "You refuse to serve us, knowing that by such refusal you violate this law?"

The cashier gazed into vacancy and spoke not a word.

The three then tried Shanley's, on Sixth Avenue at the corner of Twenty-third street. There the manager consented to serve them — if they would sit behind a screen. Promising him a prosecution, they moved over to Bartholdi's hotel nearby, where they ordered steaks. After hectic conferences among the waiters and clerk, in which several angry guests joined, the steaks were produced — burned to cinders. Making a show of eating them, they paid the bill, and sallied forth to the Brunswick Hotel, on Fifth Avenue opposite Delmonico's. There the headwaiter politely informed them that the dining room was open only to hotel residents on Sundays.

The crowning test remained. Crossing the Avenue, the three men entered Delmonico's, and were served without a murmur. True, little Philippe wrung his hands in silent misery, and his staff "posed about the room like living statues of offended dignity"; but the fashionable habitués of the restaurant seemed to enjoy the novelty, and when, after a first-rate dinner, the visitors pushed back their chairs and (to quote a caustic reporter) "insulted their waiter with a tip, which he pocketed," good-natured smiles rippled through the room.

Shortly after this episode (headlined by the *Herald* "A Comedy in Color"), Delmonico's by contrast became the scene of one of the stateliest banquets ever staged in New York, as three hundred representatives of every great commercial interest in the United States celebrated the centennial of Jay's Treaty. This famous treaty, negotiated by John Jay in settlement of differences with Great Britain, gave American merchants "the same rights at sea that the Revolutionary War had given American citizens on their own soil" — freedom to come and go, to barter and to buy at will — thereby laying the foundation for the maritime prosperity to which New York owed its first growth.

Dinners of state were regular occurrences at the Square; for despite the competition of Sherry's and the resplendent new Waldorf, no place commanded quite the same prestige. The Ohio Society, the Friendly Sons of St. Patrick, the St. Andrews

Society, the Chamber of Commerce of the State of New York, the "Superintendent, Inspectors, and Captains of the New York Police," the Hotel Men's Association, the First Panel and the Second Panel of the Sheriff's Jury — these met on common ground at Delmonico's for their annual dinners. At the eighteenth banquet of the New York Jewelers' Association, three hundred guests ate Delmonican fare off a service of gold comprising more than one thousand pieces, lent by the leading jewelry firms of the city.

This golden splash of Mammon worshippers may have moved a street-corner exhorter, Maxwell F. Johnston, soon afterward, to try his counter influence at Fifth Avenue and Twenty-sixth Street. With his wife he opened by a nasal singing of hymns until a crowd collected, then he launched his harangue, inveighing against sinners who were sunk in gluttony and wine-bibbing. As the time was a quarter past nine in the evening, diners in the restaurant were annoyed by the racket, and manager Garnier asked a policeman to remove the nuisance. But the preacher produced a permit to preach in the streets signed by the mayor, and continued his vociferous call to righteousness, and Delmonico's customers were obliged to swallow verbal hell-fire with each forkful of terrapin. The preacher, possibly concluding that he was casting seed upon barren ground, finally departed, and did not appear there again.

2.

An event of significance — marking the close of one period and the beginning of another as sharply as the inauguration of Greater New York — was the death, on the last day of January, 1895, of Ward McAllister. Born in the year when Delmonico's was founded, he was sixty-seven. So great had been the changes in New York's habits and tempo, however, that his disappearance caused hardly a stir. For some time the once potent "Autocrat" and his "Mystic Rose" had been fighting a rear guard action against the horde of new claimants to a place in the gilded

sunlight of society. Mrs. Astor had succeeded rather better in
the struggle than McAllister, although the bastions of her for-
tress were being overrun one by one. Between her and McAllister a coolness had fallen, that amounted to indifference on her
side: having no more need of him, she turned him off like a discharged upper servant. The awe his pronouncements had once
inspired had been dissipated, and the press had made his affectations to look progressively sillier. Even the Patriarchs tolerated
rather than respected him. At one of the last balls he attended,
he was dilating to a Philadelphia visitor upon the excellence of
the arrangements — his own, of course — and commiserated in
his hesitant, explosive way:

"In Philadelphia you have no one like me to arrange your
balls and parties."

"Oh, yes, we have," came the bland reply, "but they are
hired."

Such cruel banter measured the depth of McAllister's descent.

It was a wintry day when his hearse, followed by a cortège
of carriages, their coachmen and footmen in livery, wound all
but unnoticed down snow-flecked Fifth Avenue; past Mrs. Astor's mansion, where the shades were drawn but not in mourning; through Washington Square and east to Grace Church on
Broadway, the church of ultra-fashion in Ward's salad days.
His pew was banked with flowers, and the floral pieces upon
the altar resembled those adorning one of his banquet tables.
Lander's orchestra, to which he had given so much employment,
served him in death, playing the "Dead March" from *Saul*; and
although Mrs. Astor did not deign to attend, two of the Patriarchs were present, with a scattering of other fashionable
mourners.

In his book, *Society As I Have Found It*, among the oddments
of cherished trivialities which he passed along to posterity, Mc-
Allister had written: "If you want to be fashionable, be always
in the company of fashionable people." At his funeral the crowd
was made up mainly of women shoppers, who blocked the en-

trance during the service and afterwards snatched souvenir roses from the pews and altar. Few remembered on that day that for all his coxcomb strutting, Ward McAllister had been at base kindly and inoffensive; vapid, but possessed of some taste; a snob, but not a cutting one; a man who divined his unique vocation and fulfilled it with a fidelity which few dedicated exponents of a cause could match. For two decades he gave elegance, a sense of form, and a *panache* to society in the metropolis, and his precepts had been bred into a generation. Although society had already dispensed with him, the results of his labors were apparent on all sides.

An example of this was given during the last Horse Show Week Ward McAllister lived to enjoy. The reporter of social doings for the *New York Herald* — a journal especially perceptive in that field — was remarking upon the orders for food one heard fashionable women give casually at Delmonico's: "raw oysters, stuffed lobster or crab, a small steak." And the chronicler went out of the way to stress that this simplicity of taste was a matter of preference, and not due to inability to thread the labyrinth of the restaurant's menu card, for the youngest of the women could give "a good criticism as to the brand of wine, or tell you just why the sauce is, or is not, right." A generation that had been trained to take the nuances of cookery and the graces of the table as matters of course owed much of its education to that indefatigable mentor, Ward McAllister.

The passing of the doyen caused no interruption in the Patriarchs' annual rites. He would not have countenanced a hiatus, for the sanctity of social engagements he believed could only be abridged by death; and if one died after accepting an invitation to a social function, then, in his opinion, *one's executor should appear at the appointed time as a substitute.*

To supervise the Christmas Eve ball that ushered in the Patriarchs' twenty-third season, a committee of four was appointed to serve in McAllister's place. The arrangements strictly followed precedent: Lander's orchestra in the ballroom balcony,

the Hungarian band in the side room, holly and mistletoe decorations supplied by Tiffany. The cream-and-gold, mirror-
lined ballroom glittered under four chandeliers ("quite the
most becoming room in town for women in ball gowns"), just
as in previous years. There was the usual crowding, and oldtimers complained that the crush was becoming quite insupport-
able. Sauntering invisibly through the corridors, hovering
above the cotillion, inspecting the buffet of thirty dishes, the
paunchy wraith of the "Autocrat" would have had reason to
puff with pride on that first Christmas Eve of his immortality.
His spirit was there.

3.

Eighteen ninety-five was the year when New York (and
gradually the eastern and midwestern sections of the country)
first became acquainted with the "alligator pear," or avocado,
and if reliable witnesses do not err, the introduction took place
at Delmonico's. Richard Harding Davis was co-sponsor of the
delicacy. That Gallahadian idol of the popular press toured
Central and South America in 1895, and at Caracas he was served
avocados. So intrigued was he with their buttery, musky flavor
that he brought a basketful back to New York. He carried them
to Delmonico's, where "Charley" peeled one, tasted, and approved. Thereafter a supply was shipped regularly to the restaurant, and the avocado's popularity began.

Richard Harding Davis's opinion of Delmonico's had changed
radically since his impecunious reporter days, when he had
called it enviously a place "where you can get a very good
breakfast for $17." During the Nineties, Davis might be seen at
"Del's," squiring a glamor girl or two, whenever he was not
chasing a war or revolution.

Avocados had been known to Charles Ranhofer (who seemed
to know everything that could be known about edibles common
or exotic) long before they graced the tables of Delmonico's.
He mentioned them in the monumental kitchen guide and cook-

book which he published in 1894, entitled *The Epicurean*. In
size and weight this volume resembled an unabridged dictionary,
and besides four thousand recipes it contained the essence of all
the wisdom and skill Ranhofer had distilled in a lifetime of
single-minded application to his subject. The book was designed for professional cooks, not for the housewife, and it
ranged through a maze of topics, such as the sources, seasons,
and purchasing of supplies of all kinds, menus, table settings,
and "useful and important hints to those about entering the profession." Its aim, the author made plain, was to explain "the best
and most effective manner of preparing healthy and nutritious
food." The work was dedicated to "the memory of Messrs.
Delmonico, as a token of my gratitude and sincere esteem."
Charles C. Delmonico accepted the dedication in a letter concluding, "A perusal will I think give one an appetite."

Ranhofer had been preceded in Delmonican authorship by
Alessandro Filippini, who from Delmonico's kitchen had progressed to management of the lower Broadway restaurant.
When that branch was discontinued, in the late Eighties (to be
succeeded by the Café Savarin), Filippini embarked upon a
successful career as a compiler of cookbooks and food consult-
ant to railway and steamship lines. His initial work, issued under the terse and comprehensive title *The Table*, appeared in
1889, and was reprinted several times. His aim, as he explained,
was to bring the ideals of Delmonico to "the family table," and
his *was* a household handbook, intended to be used by the "average family of means."

This work also was feelingly dedicated to the Delmonicos.
"Having been with 'Delmonico's' for nearly a quarter of a century," he wrote to Charles C. Delmonico, "and as a mark of
reverence for those departed and of respect and esteem to those
living, I should feel honored by your permission to dedicate the
book to *The Delmonico Family*." Permission was granted and
thus the Delmonico influence was extended to household kitchens.

Filippini was far from an impractical man, and the counsel he believed would be most helpful to the "average family of means" in the Nineties may be gauged by his enumeration of the steps that should be taken to ensure the success of a dinner party. First, the table must be laid "with studied attention." Flowers and side decorations should be lavishly provided, otherwise the effect will be that of "a boardinghouse table." The temperature of the room must be carefully regulated — never above sixty degrees! The dinner must be served hot; and "noises with plates and glasses" were to be avoided. The servants ought to be drilled to fill the wine glasses no more than three-fourths full, since otherwise "the guests are in danger of soiling their dresses, and, again, it is not considered good form."

What Filippini considered "a fair menu for a New Year's dinner" started with oysters, and then serpentined through two soups, hors d'oeuvres, bass, filet of beef, saddle of mutton, sweetbreads, terrapin, canvasback duck, celery salad, artichoke hearts, French peas, string beans, plum pudding, and vanilla and pistachio ice cream, with fruits and coffee to close. The wines suggested for this simple home spread were Haut Sauterne, Amontillado, Rauenthaler-berg, Pommery Sec, Château Latour, and Chambertin, plus cordials at the end. Since Filippini's book enjoyed popularity, evidently this example of a holiday dinner for an "average family of means" was not exceptional.

4.

Ranhofer's book brought about a rash of press interest in gastronomy, and the city's celebrated chefs were sedulously interviewed. Pascal Grand at Sherry's, Ranhofer at Delmonico's, and others contributed views and recipes, and described how their kitchens operated. The details fascinated a generation that had been reared in the cult of elaborate dining. They were impressed by Pascal Grand's proud statement that "from vegetable boy to chef in the kitchen of a Sherry or a Delmonico is a journey of some twenty years duration." And Ranhofer wrote in the *Metropolitan Magazine* for December, 1896:

"No man who desires to possess perfect health and long life should be without a devoted physician and a wise cook."

With a vocabulary reminiscent of the prandial style of old Sam Ward, Ranhofer described his field of operations. Soups he made himself, so vital did he consider its soups to be to a restaurant's reputation, and he personally tasted and seasoned every dish. Timing the courses of a dinner was difficult, he stressed, for the chef had to calculate "with the precision of a mathematician . . . in order that the most delicate entremets will be served smoking hot, and therein lies the essential point of his ability as a scientific cook." The waiter must collaborate exactly. Should a customer order two mutton chops, one to follow the other, the waiter must know how long it takes to cook a mutton chop, and hand in his order for the second so that it could be brought to the table sizzling hot, just as the diner was polishing off the first. Delmonico's waiters were trained in such skills.

Ranhofer echoed Sam Ward in laying down the rule that "something more is necessary than a well cooked dinner; it must be equally well displayed." The table should be set "with taste and elegance," the plates warmed, the meats well carved, the cold hors d'oeuvres and salads perfect. There must also be an appreciative audience for a chef's complete success, and in this regard Delmonico's was ideal; its customers, Ranhofer said, were "by taste and breeding Epicureans."

The most expensive foods are not always the best, Ranhofer held, and the cost of a dinner will always be relative. At Delmonico's, he could vouch for it, one might obtain "a very good dinner, with an excellent *vin ordinaire*, for six persons for $12."

This was true: by the standards of the day, Delmonico's was not prohibitively expensive. Furthermore, two could dine at the price for one at "Del's," because the portions were large and an extra cover would be laid without charge. An entire bunch of celery, for example, was served as one portion, and a serving of soup, price 60 cents, was enough for two. A small steak cost 60 cents, and one that would satisfy two hearty appetites only

$1.50. Oysters were 25 cents a portion. Canvasback duck, the most expensive entrée on the bill of fare, remained pegged for years at $3.50, and a redhead duck cost a dollar less.

The wine prices were comparable, although there were vintages in the cellar that only a Maecenas could afford. The "Delmonico" brand of champagne, incidentally, was not produced by the family; Lorenzo Delmonico gave a winemaker permission to use the name, and the brand never sold as popularly as Pommery Sec or "The Widow" (Veuve Cliquot).

An occasional splurge at Delmonico's was within the means of a prosperous middle-class householder, if his palate drew him that way and if he avoided those "extras" which could send the cost skyrocketing.

5.

Reporters found hotel and restaurant kitchens a fruitful source of copy for their Sunday articles. One newspaper filled an entire page with its reporter's tour of two noted kitchens — at the Waldorf, and at Delmonico's. Although their standards were equally high, the contrast between them was interesting.

At the Waldorf, which had been opened less than a year, everything was spic and span, fixtures gleaming, rooms spacious, light and airy, walls spotless with fresh paint, equipment up-to-the-minute. The kitchen over which Charles Ranhofer presided was more picturesque. Plunging down a flight of shabby stairs, the reporter was taken along a narrow, dimly lighted passage into "a big low-ceilinged underground room, so divided by partitions and so blocked off by innumerable tables and refrigerators and storage closets as to be a veritable labyrinth to the stranger."

When the kitchen had been laid out, in the Seventies, it had been scaled generously; but the increase of business had necessitated irregular additions. There were cooks on hand who had worked for Lorenzo Delmonico thirty years before, and a few even predated Ranhofer. The description ran on:

"The ranges extend the length of the room, and opposite them are stoves for the vegetables, leaving an aisle sacred to the use of the forty-five cooks in caps and aprons, upon whose final efforts depends Delmonico's fame. Well do they know their importance, and they show it. The waiter does not live who can move the least of them from his imperturbability. Nor can anyone else, except alone the veteran Ranhofer, the most influential cook in America.

"When this gloomy, crowded, busy kitchen, dark with smoke and brilliant with polished copper pots hanging from every rafter, is assailed by a swarm of eager waiters, wonderful indeed is the clash of tongues and orders and the clash of dishes . . . The pen into which the waiters are allowed to come is necessarily very small, and is accessible to the kitchen proper only through two openings in the wire gratings that separate. In this the hubbub of waiters is appalling. They crowd, push, and jostle each other, in a mighty scramble for the best attention of the cooks. Here and there rush the chef's assistants, giving orders; and the chef himself, with his thoughtful, kindly face, emerging from the tiny closet office where he concocts his menus and invents his masterpieces of cookery, walks up and down, and keeps all moving smoothly."

Food prepared in such a kitchen, concluded this observer as he stumbled up the rickety stairs to the restaurant, "*ought* to taste better than things cooked in any other kitchen in town."

The general sentiment seemed to be that it did.

CHAPTER V

"HOME IS WHERE
THE HEART IS"

ALREADY THE AIR was surcharged with *fin de siècle* fantasies when in 1896 Charles Delmonico announced that "Del's" was preparing to move uptown to keep pace with the city's changing social center. In the light of Delmonico history, this decision should hardly have provoked surprise, although again (as had occurred in the past) the abandonment of an old Delmonico site brought out the croakers, who disapproved the new location, and gloomily reprehended the whole scheme. Certainly a change was disagreeable for oldtimers to contemplate.

The new restaurant was to be on the northeast corner of Fifth Avenue and Forty-fourth Street. On April 20, 1896, Charles signed a fifteen-year lease, at an annual rental slightly less than the $62,500 he was paying at Twenty-sixth Street, and the owner of the property, Theodore A. Havemeyer, undertook to erect a building for Delmonico's occupancy. Already the plans were being drawn by James Brown Lord, the architect who had designed the recently completed Delmonico building at Beaver and South William Streets.

Negotiations had been going on covertly for months, but not so secretly that Louis Sherry failed to learn about the project. His own announcement followed shortly, saying that he would move into a "splendid structure" to be built to Stanford White's designs on the southwest corner of Fifth Avenue and Forty-fourth Street, diagonally facing the new "Del's." This confrontation of the rivals promised to be worth watching.

Both the night life and the high life of the city had been moving northward for some time, and the district around Herald

Square, at Broadway and Thirty-fourth Street, now was dotted with clubs and theaters. Even above Forty-second Street, along Broadway and Seventh Avenue, there were oases for the hungry like Rector's, which was attracting crowds by its gaiety and such innovations as New York's first revolving door.

Tastes were changing, and institutions like Delmonico's must alter with them. It was a shock, however, to many a Delmonico regular when "Charley" made it known that in the new restaurant smoking would be permitted in the restaurant. This was a scrapping of the by-laws that had governed New York for sixty years. Furthermore, an orchestra would play during luncheon and dinner at the new "Del's." Rector's had introduced the novelty, and gourmets frequenting that dining room had learned that a melody dispensed discreetly might not ruin a main course.

Smoking had been confined to the men's cafe at Delmonico's, and the press gave "Charley" credit for submitting to new customs gracefully. "Fashion Now Decrees That There Are Necessary Concomitants to the Feast of Reason," read one complacent headline. And what seemed even more remarkable: "Women Raise No Objection." Indeed, it was "Del's" women patrons who had persuaded "Charley" to lift the ban. They were tired of seeing their husbands, sons, and lovers disappear into the bar for a smoke. In Europe, smoking in dining rooms was the rule: at the Berkeley, Prince's, Savoy, Bristol, or Criterion in London, or at Voisin's, Pailliard's, Les Ambassadeurs, or Joseph's in Paris, men smoked in the presence of ladies. So really Delmonico's was only falling into line.

2.

While the new uptown building was taking shape, there was no indication that Delmonico's would desert Madison Square. "Charley" held out hope that the Twenty-sixth Street house would be kept; the location was convenient for shoppers especially, and the lease had two years to run. Madison Square itself was still smart, although it has lost some of its after-dark attractiveness. A close-of-the-century guidebook described the crossing at Broadway, Fifth Avenue, and Twenty-third Street "really the heart of the metropolis, one of the most frequented spots in the city." Because it was the main shopping center, it drew crowds not only of New Yorkers, but of visitors from all parts of the world.

"One can see things at their best here in the daytime, during the spring and fall of the year," the animated description ran. "Fashion is queen, and marshals armies of her votaries, whose chariots dash over the smooth, white, wide, asphalted roadway bordered by Madison Square Park. The sidewalks teem with throngs little less attractive than the costly gowned maids and matrons who go shopping in their carriages. Richly liveried coachmen and footmen, prancing steeds and crested panels, equine trappings that keep a rhythmic accompaniment to the roll of the wheels, fleeting glimpses of fair faces, millinery that entrances feminine eyes and confuses those of the other sex with its manifold modes and miraculous combinations of colors — the attractions are countless and their succession never-ending."

The future of "Del's" on the Square seemed unaffected, when, in November, 1897, the new Forty-fourth Street building was opened. That was a gala month in a gala year. Two weeks before the opening, the Astoria Hotel, built alongside the Waldorf at Thirty-fourth Street and the Avenue, had received its first guests. Nothing like its luxury had ever been seen before, even the Waldorf was quite outshone. There was "Peacock Alley," there were the Rose Room, the Palm Garden, and other dining rooms, presided over by "Oscar." New Yorkers were bewildered by the grandeur of the place, and at once took the Waldorf-Astoria into their affection.

That same month, the thirteenth annual Horse Show, more brilliant than any predecessor, opened at the Garden, and on the same day — November 15 — a thousand guests roamed through the new Delmonico's, inspecting everything. The building, the atmosphere, the furnishings, the setting, all bespoke solidity; "Del's" was at its apogee. Everywhere the best taste prevailed. Along the Fifth Avenue side was a miniature flower garden, like the one at Madison Square. The main entrance was on Forty-fourth Street, and the ladies' restaurant overlooked the Avenue. This room was "daintily finished in oak and upholstered in blue." Next to it, on the ground floor, was the Palm Garden, separated from the office by "plate glass windows reaching from the floor to the ceiling." The cafe was finished in Elizabethan oak, and the dining rooms on the second floor were decorated in rich, muted tones. Each had its own anteroom, and all could be thrown together to accommodate large parties. The ballroom was on the third floor, "lighted by electroliers, screened by a mass of small glass beads;" the walls were covered with rose-tinted silk, and the woodwork was green. On the same floor were two small reception rooms, one the "bride's room," reserved for the use of the bride at weddings. There was a roof conservatory above the ballroom, and Delmonico's lodgers were not overlooked; their apartments were ranged along the Fifth Avenue end of the two top floors, while at the other end were servants' rooms and the laundry. The kitchens were in the basement, and pumps and machinery occupied a subcellar.

Society was sure it could function in this expanded headquarters, where rose-silk walls shut out the rumblings of coming events.

At the start of the month when Delmonico opened its new uptown quarters, and when the Astoria Hotel and the Horse Show were the high points on the current social calendar, New Yorkers voted in a municipal election. Pitted against the candidate handpicked by Tammany (Robert S. Van Wyck, of an old New York family); were an independent, Seth Low; a Republican, General Benjamin P. Tracy; and Henry George, the single-tax advocate who was leading a popular uprising under the banner of "Jeffersonian Democracy." On the eve of the election, Henry George died. His funeral was held on election day. It drew throngs of idolizers, more than fifty thousand persons filing past his coffin in the Grand Central Palace. As the cortège moved slowly towards Brooklyn and Greenwood Cem-

etery, men knelt in the streets and wept for the loss of the one
man they believed capable of delivering them from long-stand-
ing inequities.

With George eliminated, the contest became a pushover for
Tammany's disciplined forces, and when General Tracy conceded defeat, Tammany's boss, Richard Croker, merely grunted:
"What's he got to concede? I knew he was licked before the
vote was counted."

Upon the national scene new winds were blowing, also, and
eddies from those currents swept into Delmonico's. On November 12, of that eventful year, the aggressive Assistant Secretary
of the Navy, Theodore Roosevelt (a New Yorker well acquainted with "Del's"), addressed a dinner of the Society of
Naval Architects and Maritime Engineers in Delmonico's Madison Square banquet room, taking as his theme the need of the
Navy for "more docks, power, and men." The United States
"cannot evade the responsibilities imposed by the Monroe Doctrine and the question of Hawaii," the speaker pounded home.
The buildup of the Navy must go forward. "Whereas fifteen
years ago we were contemptible among naval powers, our flag
has now begun to take the place it should upon the high seas. If
we have a proper Navy, it will not tend towards war, but towards peace. In our past history we have once been forced
into war chiefly because we had no powerful Navy, and two
or three times from the same cause we have been brought to the
verge of war. But never has peace been so much as threatened
by the fact of our having a Navy . . .

"We cannot evade our responsibilities. We have announced
time and again our adherence to the Monroe Doctrine. Unless
we are willing to be put into the contemptible attitude of those
who bluster without being able to back up their words by deeds,
we must prove that our attitude is not a sham."

As for Hawaii, an issue much agitated just then, the speaker
put the case squarely:

"If we annex Hawaii, as every consideration of interest and
honor bids, we shall need an adequate Navy to enforce our posi-

tion on the Pacific. If we do not annex Hawaii, we shall need a much larger Navy, because, as Hawaii cannot stand alone, some other power must necessarily take it, and from that moment menace our whole Pacific coast."

It was not recorded that the hundred and fifty naval architects who listened to these sentiments demurred. The *fin de siècle* was a time of muscle-flexing.

3.

Few people in New York could hark back to a time when no Delmonico's existed; permanency and "Del's" seemed inseparable. Therefore the jolt to habitués arriving at Madison Square for luncheon in April, 1899, was severe as they read the neatly lettered cards that were scattered upon the tables. On the eighteenth of that month, the cards announced, the establishment of that location would be closed for good. The lease had run out, and Charles Delmonico believed the declining volume of business would not warrant keeping the place going. That luncheon was eaten amid gloom.

To many, desertion of Madison Square for any reason was a profanation. An old and respected employee, Leopold Rimmer, was moved to pen his dissent. Rimmer had been hired by "Old Charley" Delmonico on a snowy St. Patrick's Day in 1866, and he believed the current representatives of the family were making a profound mistake. "Look back at the genius of old Mr. Lorenzo Delmonico (the noblest, best-hearted, and most generous man that ever lived), who built the Twenty-sixth Street house," he urged in a memoir composed in quaint Austrian-English and printed at his own expense. "Situated upon the finest piece of land in New York . . . in front of a fine park . . . There is Admiral Farragut's statue right in front of Delmonico's . . . The park itself is a sight, with its big trees, its wonderful fountain and flower beds. There is not such a piece of land in any city, not in Paris, nor in London, or Berlin, or Vienna."

Grizzled patrons nodded in agreement. To give up that site —to leave Diana's court, while she remained, as lithe and airy as on the day she was hoisted to her pinnacle — seemed a travesty of good sense. Yet though veterans like Rimmer might lament, Charles Delmonico was firm, and the faithful gathered themselves to bid farewell to a landmark, and to mark the passing of their day.

The final evening came, and not a chair was vacant. Every table had been reserved, many people coming down from the new uptown "Del's." By two's and three's they arrived in their carriages, alighted at the familiar portal, and passed into the well-known room overlooking the park. Handshakes and nods of recognition were exchanged, and here and there tables were pulled together for groups of six or eight, who had known "Del's" for a lifetime. Names that were household words were called back and forth. Abe Hummel and stiff-collared Richard Harding Davis were on hand, with others forgotten today — "José Mora, John Habershaw, Mr. and Mrs. James H. Eaken, Nikola Tesla, Mr. and Mrs. Kalish" — the list was long.

As the hours wore on, the laughter died down, and the room became almost silent. Men smoked the last perfecto, and stared meditatively at the last rare vintage in the glass. In that room they had learned to drink champagne *brut*, to judge a *pâté de foie-gras*, to tell when a canvasback duck was done to perfection, just as they could tell when a coat was properly cut, a play well acted, a song well sung. Merchants, bankers, actors, authors, bookmakers, lawyers, men of affairs, sportsmen, divines, rounders, and dilettantes — they had grown gray there. Memories went back to "Old Charley," to Siro, and Lorenzo; some few recalled Peter Delmonico. Vanished days, to which they were bidding good-bye. *Ridet argento domus* . . . tags from Horace drifted hazily through the minds of some who were thinking about Sam Ward and the other kings of gastronomy, whose feats had been celebrated in that room. Now this "Del's," the best of "Del's," was vanishing, too.

Somebody murmured about its being time to go. With the open connivance of the waiters, salt shakers, matchbox holders, and other objects were pocketed for keepsakes; the waiters even made parcels of such mementos. In a corner ruminated an old New Yorker, one for whom all roads had led to Madison Square and "Del's." How often had Diana espied him entering Delmonico's door! He sat at his table — not *a* table but *his* table, where he had dined for years. At length with a sigh he pushed away the empty demitasse, laid the napkin down in front of him, and slowly drew back his chair. Henri the headwaiter ("he of the sweeping side-whisker," who had succeeded Philippe, translated uptown) stood by respectfully.

"It seems like saying good-bye to home," sighed the old New Yorker, and suddenly the sense of betrayal welled up in him.

"Oh, Lord!" he groaned. "It was the saddest day in the lives of the Delmonicos when they decided to give up this lovely corner — flooded by sunshine from the park in the day, surrounded by theaters and clubs by night! Bah! Delmonico is no Pierpont Morgan or Goelet to jump uptown and build a club without some slight feeling of regret or remorse! He should have stopped by the park and taken his chances!"

The old New Yorker eyed Henri ferociously.

"New York has always followed Delmonico's, more than Delmonico's has followed New York!" he snapped.

Rising stiffly, he swept the room with a glance and stumped out.

At midnight Delmonico's on the square ceased to exist.

The old New Yorker's resentment the *Herald* put down to "an old-fashioned man's regret at losing an old-fashioned resort." Yet the *Herald* confessed that the Madison Square location was "one of the most central and agreeable in town," and there had been an atmosphere about Delmonico's there that had made it different. "No one seemed ever at a loss for an acquaintance or a gay nod at 'Del's.' Of the history of the house," the commentator concluded — "is it not writ in every page of the social life of New York?

"No, there can never be just such another place as this Delmonico's was. Because many of the men who made it are gone, and times have changed, and we have changed with them."

Part Five

"SUNSET AND EVENING STAR"

CHAPTER I

NEW TIMES,
NEW TREMORS

IT WAS THE TWENTIETH CENTURY, and Delmonico's entered it solid and assured. The year the establishment moved to Forty-fourth Street and Fifth Avenue was the year of Queen Victoria's Diamond Jubilee: she had ascended the throne in the year John and Peter Delmonico opened their Beaver Street house, when they already had been in business ten years. Few people could recall when Victoria had not been England's queen, and in New York hardly a soul remembered when there was no Delmonico's. The institution which had survived so many upheavals, such changes in tastes and custom, was the pride of New Yorkers, and amid the fond and frequent allusions to its longevity no uncertainty was expressed about its continuing to flourish indefinitely.

"As our grandfathers used to hobnob over their ices and sherbets away downtown on Beaver Street (New York being just as hot in summer then), and our fathers feasted on canvasback duck and burgundy at Fourteenth Street . . ."

The phrases recurred like a refrain in an accumulation of memoirs.

"Great-grandmothers danced in the Beaver Street place whose great-granddaughters will make their debut in the new building on Fifth Avenue . . ."

The prospect, whether one gazed backward or forward, was smooth and reassuring.

The restaurant's new home certainly outshone in splendor any Delmonico's of before. Oldtimers might grow lyrical over the fabled restaurant of the Sixties, down on Fourteenth Street

— its Blue Room upholstered in satin, its Chinese Room, its Library Room, where the cream of New York aristocracy wined and dined in regal state — but the Palm Garden, the banquet rooms, the restaurant and cafe of the new establishment eclipsed all former glories.

A few sharp eyes did detect flaws in the arrangements. Loyal, plain-speaking Leopold Rimmer was one of the few not comfortable amid the new surroundings. To him the Forty-fourth Street building, while impressive on the outside, was clumsily laid out. The entrance he felt should have been on Fifth Avenue, not on a side street. The kitchen was unnecessarily spacious and high-ceilinged, whereas the restaurant was cramped, with its low ceiling; the dining room he dismissed as "small and low and black, with three windows looking at a stable." The whole interior seemed to him "a big mistake . . . [The architects] did not know what hotel service was, and never asked anybody who knew something about it."

There was a basis for the criticism, for this new "Del's" did differ from the establishments that had gone before, and the difference was not always an improvement. The restaurant, from one point of view, did overlook a stable. When Delmonico's invaded the area, Fifth Avenue north of Forty-second Street was still conglomerate, with smart new buildings and run-down houses dating from a rustic past side by side. Directly across Forty-fourth Street from Delmonico's canopied entrance stood Tyson's Meat Market. Next to it was the Willow Tree Inn, an ancient frame house deriving its name from an anemic willow tree that arose from the sidewalk at that point. Behind the inn was a livery stable, redolent of odors and flies. These unprepossessing appurtenances would change soon and handsome buildings would replace the shabby houses; but the incongruous spectacle of the elegance of Delmonico's and Sherry's (opened a year afterward, on October 10, 1898), alongside vestiges of the city's shanty past, lasted into the new century. Leopold Rimmer's grumbling had a reason behind it; it was more than an old man's resistance to change.

Rimmer felt that he had another error to lay to the account of Charles Crist Delmonico. This was the publication, with Delmonico's blessing, of Charles Ranhofer's compendium of cookery, *The Epicurean*. This, said Rimmer, had been "the greatest mistake ever made against the interest of the Delmonicos' business," because that book "gave away all secrets of the house, and every Tom, Dick, and Harry who calls himself a cook, and has learned his trade in Delmonico's kitchen, can make up the finest dinners with that book, which tells him everything he doesn't know. There is hardly one hotel in New York today whose chef did not learn his cooking at Delmonico's, every one of them. The book gave all the secrets to the world — the market, what is in season, where to get it, and what is the correct thing to eat every day and all the year round. This is the error that was made by Mr. Charles Crist Delmonico."

If error it was, "Charley" did not recant. It was true that half the first-rate hotels and restaurants in New York (of which there were now many) were staffed with graduates of Ranhofer's system of cuisine and Tilghman's perfection of service. Ranhofer for a while had conducted a regular academy of cookery, and possession of a certificate of proficiency from him insured professional success. Ranhofer himself had supervised the transfer of the restaurant's kitchen to Forty-fourth Street; but in 1898 he retired, to die a year later in his home on West End Avenue, and be mourned as the "pioneer who introduced to Knickerbockers new dishes and new methods of cookery . . . who enjoyed the confidence of princes and millionaires, and was known to Epicureans the world over." At Delmonico's, the Ranhofer dispensation was perpetuated by his successor, M. Grevillet.

2.

Charles Delmonico professed to feel no concern over the competition offered by Sherry's, across the Avenue; he was confident that Delmonico's would retain its fashionable patronage. Actually, the pendulum of popularity swung back and forth between the rivals: one season Sherry's would be the rage, the next, Delmonico's would be *the thing,* and nobody could tell why. Sherry was fertile in devising novelties. The five o'clock tea remained his specialty, and for a while his "table de luxe" brought in crowds. How a "table de luxe," which was simply a dinner at the fixed price of $3, without wine, differed from a "table d'hôte" was not explained, except that it cost more; but ordinary folk marveled that $3 could be spent on a fixed-price dinner, and many tried it.

There were happenings at Sherry's that somehow never occurred at Delmonico's. Even before moving to Forty-fourth Street, Sherry's had aroused the resentment of that venerated fixture, the Sorosis. Luncheon was served at the club's monthly meetings, and in January of 1895 the fare that Sherry's provided caused an outburst that echoed in the press. Rebelling against slovenly service and parsimonious menus, Mrs. Jennie Lozier, a former president of Sorosis, blurted:

"We paid $155 for our last luncheon and I could have done the whole thing for $20! Why, when one lady told the waiter who was pouring the consommé to fill up her cup, I thought he would drop dead!"

Another member scornfully suggested that the menu should have read:

> Bouillion in half-cups
> Croquette à la Mystery, with peas
> Salad à la What-is-it?
> Rolls
> Ice Cream
> Coffee (?)   Tea (?)

The beverages were so ambiguous, that when a waiter handed one lady a cup of some murky liquid, she said: "If this is coffee, bring me tea. If this is tea, bring me coffee."

Another asked a waiter to identify the reddish strings in the salad, and when told it was "smoked beef," handed back her plate with a "not for me."

"Those mysterious affairs supposed to be timbales were terrible," snapped still another outraged luncher. "We pay Mr. Sherry $900 for this use of his room a few hours each month, and besides that, he is paid $1 for every person who takes luncheon. But we are like old tenants; no effort is made to please us!"

Many of the club's members were women of means who knew perfectly well the difference between a carelessly cooked, badly served luncheon and one prepared and served with style. In spite of their facetiously ascribed ability to sustain life on "candied violets and frappéd rose leaves," the women of Sorosis expected substantial, palatable food in exchange for their money, and although Sherry tried to allay the storm, the club voted to transfer its meetings to the Waldorf. In all the long association of Sorosis and Delmonico's, no such breach of harmony had occurred.

The season after this uproar, Sherry's was caught again in scandalous notoriety, this time emanating from a bachelor party in a private room. That event culminated in a police raid, charges of indecency or intended indecency on the one side, and of roughhouse police behavior on the other, leading to a hearing before the board of police commissioners. The testimony adduced that the lasciviously headlined "Little Egypt" had enlivened the party with her "danse du ventre," the host's taste in entertainment (he was a grandson of Phineas T. Barnum) being decidedly earthy. The presiding police commissioner, Theodore Roosevelt, seemed bored by all the talk about chorus girls and exposure; and when it came out that the host had intended to stage his frolic at Delmonico's, and had been given a frosty refusal, Sherry was upset, for this seemed to put his house in the second rank. No one could imagine "Little Egypt" dancing at Delmonico's.

The theatrical and night-life sets had, it is true, forsaken "Del's" for gayer settings along Broadway. The area soon to be christened Times Square blossomed with late-hours resorts that specialized in midnight lobster and champagne, and in some of these eating places the cuisine was first-rate; Rector's and the Knickerbocker Grill were second to none. But the social world stuck loyally by Delmonico, despite its rather dowager air.

3.

Charles Delmonico supervised the Forty-fourth Street place as he had the restaurant on Madison Square. Every evening he might be observed, just inside the entrance, noting with his quick glance every arrival, as Henry Tilghman once had done, and in touch with all that was going on in the house. Regular customers would nod, though strangers usually overlooked the proprietor; if they were introduced they expressed surprise that the master of Delmonico's should be so unobtrusive. "Charley" dressed in quiet good taste and had an unmistakable air of distinction, despite his self-effacement.

His health, unfortunately, was not good. The summer before the move was made to Forty-fourth Street, he had been disturbed by the publication in New York newspapers of a rumor that he was suffering from mental illness and was under treatment in Europe. How the story originated nobody knew (it had been cabled to New York from London), and at the restaurant it was indignantly repudiated. Charles Delmonico was in France on one of his periodic business trips, it was stated, and had taken the waters at Aix-les-Bains, that was all; certainly he was not ill, mentally or otherwise. His return to New York in genial spirits confirmed this. But the incident distressed the Delmonico family because it revived memories of the late Charles Delmonico's death.

Nevertheless, "Charley's" health was not good. He suffered from rheumatism, and in the spring of 1900 visited Virginia Hot Springs in search of relief. Unexpectedly, he there found instead romance, and a telegram informed the restaurant's startled staff that "Mister Charles" had become engaged to marry a Brooklyn girl, Jeanne Edwards, the daughter of a wealthy shoe manufacturer. Miss Edwards was reported to be his junior in age; Charles was forty, and had been thought to be settled in bachelorhood. His fiancee was described as tall, charming, and athletic, excelling in riding, driving, and golf, and she was said to be fond of dancing.

The wedding was held in the bride's home at 119 St. Mark's Avenue, on October 10, 1900. Father Ducey officiated. After a honeymoon trip, Charles reappeared at the restaurant, where the staff moved with a lighter step, now that it appeared that the Delmonico line would be perpetuated.

4.

So newsworthy had everything about Delmonico's become, the most trivial incidents involving the restaurant were given almost religious attention by the press. Let a cook upset a kettle of grease, and the alarm would be good for a column, although the damage would be trifling. When Maggie Clancy, a Delmonico laundress, had a hand accidentally crushed in an elevator, the newspapers became quite agog over the fact that during her stay in Bellevue Hospital she received her lunch every day from Delmonico's, delivered by a uniformed attendant in a Delmonico truck. She was the first (and so far as memory could reach) the only Bellevue patient to have meals sent in from Delmonico's.

When a $250,000 mortgage was negotiated on the Beaver Street property, the transaction received widespread notice, although the newspapers were not told the reason for the loan. Actually, the cash was needed in part to defray the cost of opening the new Fifth Avenue quarters, and in part to allow Lorenzo Crist Delmonico, who was becoming more and more restive over his involvement in the business, to realize on his share by selling it to his aunt Rosa. This transaction was not divulged by the family at the time.

One news item that read strangely to oldtimers was an account, shortly before Charles Delmonico's marriage, of a law suit to recover $181.70, the cost of a dinner that had been served to a Nassau Street lawyer in 1898. No defense was entered and the Delmonicos received judgment in full. But this abandonment of a basic policy of the house was considered significant. Louis Sherry had not hesitated to go to law to collect debts, but Delmonico's had never done so. Leopold Rimmer claimed, perhaps with exaggeration, that Lorenzo Delmonico at his death held "dead-beat" chits amounting to half a million dollars, but had forborne to sue to collect them. He believed that the loss of prestige would have overbalanced any money gains. That such had ceased to be the policy of the house spoke volumes for those who could read the signs, for it gave an inkling of the fact which was being concealed from the public — that despite its animated appearance, Delmonico's was financially in trouble.

Just at this time, a fresh shock was dealt to its stability. In May, 1901, Charles Delmonico, more and more plagued by rheumatism, went to Colorado Springs for a long vacation, leaving the business in the charge of his manager, Eugène Garnier. Charles's wife went with him, and there had been no advance warning when a telegram startled New York on September 20, 1901, announcing that Charles Delmonico had died suddenly.

The funeral was held in New York, at St. Leo's Church. Father Ducey celebrated a requiem mass for his friend, whose nuptials he had blessed less than one year before. The church was filled to the doors. Interment was in Woodlawn Cemetery. The masses of flowers were sent to St. Vincent's and the French Benevolent Society Hospitals; and that day the two Delmonico restaurants, at Beaver and Forty-fourth Street, remained closed until 5 P.M.

CHAPTER II

"AUNT ROSA"

EXCEPT FOR THAT MOMENTARY SHUTDOWN, the activities of Delmonico's, uptown and downtown, continued without noticeable change after Charles Crist Delmonico's death. Eugene Garnier, as executive manager, had stated that there would be no change of policy, and the press had again commented upon the role which inheritance had played in the house's three-quarters of a century of success. As the business had descended from uncle to nephew in the head office, so it was in the departments below stairs, one generation succeeding another. Old servants were retired on pensions, and there were openings for the youngsters as they came along. The organization developed by the elder Delmonicos hummed smoothly for each group of heirs, among whom nearly every employee counted himself.

The public was interested, of course, in learning what disposition of the ownership Charles had made. His will revealed that his entire interest in the firm (a minority interest) had been left to his aunt, Rosa Delmonico, who already owned most of the stock. Now she became almost sole proprietor, her niece, Josephine Crist Delmonico, retaining a one-sixth interest. The will, executed in 1885 shortly after the death of Charles's uncle, had not been revised, and made no mention of the widow. This occasioned surprise, especially when the residuary estate (which was believed not to be large) was divided equally between Charles's brother, Lorenzo, and sister, Josephine. Jeanne Edwards Delmonico was wealthy in her own right, however, and no contest was expected, nor did any develop. A close intimacy had grown up between Jeanne and Josephine Delmonico, and they would remain companions for years.

"Aunt Rosa," as the new head of the firm was known to the staff and old patrons, once she emerged into the limelight, was credited by the press with having been more influential in the management of the business since Lorenzo's death than had been supposed. An unassuming woman in her early sixties, Rosa looked younger. In newspaper articles she was depicted as having been "the power behind the throne" at Twenty-sixth Street especially. Although she had appeared at that restaurant and at Forty-fourth Street intermittently during her nephew's superintendency, only a few customers knew her by sight; if she espied one of these in the dining room, she would stop and chat as with a family friend.

As directress of the business, "Aunt Rosa" set up a routine of her own, from which she seldom varied. At the time of her nephew's death, her home was at 11 West Fifty-sixth Street; but she shortly moved into a brownstone at 144 West Seventy-fifth Street, where Josephine Delmonico kept her company. From there she discharged most of the responsibilities of her position. Every week, on Saturday, promptly at one o'clock, she would arrive at Forty-fourth Street to receive reports from Garnier and the department heads. She would discuss problems of administration with them, and resolve questions of finance or policy. An inspection of the entire premises followed, with special attention to the kitchen. When satisfied that all was shipshape, she would withdraw until the next Saturday, keeping in touch during the week by telephone and messenger. The weekly financial report she required from Garnier she checked meticulously. Under her guidance, the destinies of the house of Delmonico were assumed to be secure.

2.

"Aunt Rosa" — perhaps fortunately for her peace of mind — was not in the restaurant on the evening of Monday, December 1, 1902, when a train of events started which was to engross New York for months. Not that Delmonico's really was involved at all, but its association with the principals in the drama caused it to be spoken of publicly as at least a passive accessory.

When Delmonico's stood at Madison Square — in the Tenderloin, that district of mixed fortunes — a gambler named Richard Canfield maintained a luxurious resort at 22 West Twenty-sixth Street, barely a few paces from "Del's." At this Madison Square Club, as it was called, men of wealth could relax at faro, roulette, cards, or dice, in the "comfort and dignity" to which they were inclined; for Richard Canfield was an art connoisseur of sensitivity. He observed, as did Charles Delmonico, the drift of society farther uptown, and since his patronage was the same as Delmonico's, he moved in that direction, too.

Shortly after Delmonico opened at Forty-fourth Street, Canfield bought the building next door, number 5 West Forty-fourth. He paid $75,000 for the place, and then engaged an architect to refurbish it. The architect spent $400,000 on the remodeling, while the furniture — the Chippendale chairs, the rare porcelains, the paintings, including a room full of Whistlers, the Oriental rugs and bibelots — cost $500,000 or more. Canfield's, known as "the house next door to Delmonico's," became the most sumptuous establishment of its kind ever to be seen in America.

The service was on a par with the setting. Dollar cigars were free, and at eleven o'clock a cold buffet was served by Canfield's own chef, with wines of the choicest years and vintages. Should a patron fancy more substantial fare, it would be brought in from Delmonico's next door. The play was high, and stories of enormous losses — and winnings — became a staple of New York gossip.

All this irritated the guardians of civic righteousness. The energetic, ambitious district attorney of New York was William Travers Jerome, and between him and Canfield there existed a mutual dislike. Jerome had promised publicly to close down every "gambling hell" in town, and had succeeded in putting many minor operators out of business. But Canfield seemed immune; in fact, he was quoted as having boasted ("profanely and in his cups," according to Jerome) that the district attorney would never get inside the fortified door of "the house next to 'Del's.'" This challenge Jerome could not ignore; and whatever his other qualities, Jerome was as tenacious and scrappy as a terrier.

Both men were often seen at Delmonico's. Jerome's father and uncle, Lawrence and Leonard Jerome, had been among the gayest of the wits and sportsmen who had held forth on Fourteenth Street in the Sixties, and Canfield was as discriminating in his culinary tastes as he was in paintings. He had been known to get extremely high, on occasion, at "Del's," and once regaled a dinner of college lads with the oration he had delivered at his school graduation exercises forty years before — Josiah Quincy's "Our Obligations to the Fathers of New England." This masterpiece Canfield had spouted from memory, with elocutionary gestures, to great applause.

The annual dinner of the St. Andrew's Society, a grand affair, held in the banquet room of Delmonico's on December 1, 1902, numbered among the four hundred guests District Attorney Jerome and a lieutenant of police. As midnight approached these paid little heed to the speech of Mayor Seth Low, the evening's principal speaker, for that afternoon Jerome had obtained a warrant to raid "the house next door."

A detective appeared in the doorway and signaled the two waiting men. Quietly they collected their overcoats and joined a group of men outside who had just arrived in a police wagon. Walking along Forty-fourth Street to number 5, they saw the house lighted and evidently occupied. A policeman ran a ladder up to a front window, smashed the glass, and stepped inside. Jerome followed, and encountered Canfield himself, protesting that not a card had been turned in that house for more than a year. This happened to be the truth; but the raiders discovered a secret closet full of gambling equipment, and Jerome arrested Canfield's resident manager.

The raid made a sensation. Other gambling resorts were invaded on the same night (including the famous "House with the Bronze Door" on West Thirty-third Street, designed by Stanford White and filled with art treasures), but Canfield's downfall was the most discussed. His customers were said to include many of the nation's millionaires, and the interlocking of Canfield's and Delmonico's patronage was commented upon. Of course, not all, or even many, of Delmonico's customers had frequented "the house next door." Few were eligible; but for the elect, the transition from dinner at Delmonico's to a game next door had been easy and natural.

3.

The smirks and innuendoes about this accidental relationship were obnoxious to "Aunt Rosa"; but they were not to concern her long, for in 1904, after three years of active proprietorship, she died in her home. The date was March 24, and she was in her sixty-fifth year.

Again it became the mournful duty of Father Ducey to celebrate a funeral mass for another Delmonico. The services were at St. Leo's, and the pew "Aunt Rosa" had occupied for years was filled with lilies. At the head of the bier stood a large cross of lilies and violets, the tribute of Delmonico employees, many of whom attended in a body. Father Ducey spoke of the deceased as the friend of his young priesthood and one of his oldest parishioners. Delmonico's flag drooped at half mast, and the newspapers spoke about the "last of the Delmonicos, the last of her line."

Almost at the hour when Rosa Delmonico expired, John Napoleon Longhi died in Brooklyn, in his eighty-fifth year. Born in Ticino, he had been the last link with the homeland and the founders of the restaurants. To Rosa Delmonico he had been deeply attached, although he found the Crists uncongenial. During his final illness he expressed a wish to see Rosa once more, but her death supervened, and his own almost coincided.

Again the question arose: what of the restaurants? The answer was contained in Rosa Delmonico's will. This thoroughly businesslike document had been executed a year previously, and by it control of the firm passed to Rosa's niece — the sister of Charles C. and Lorenzo C. Delmonico — Josephine Otard Crist Delmonico. Rosa left to Josephine the half-interest she had inherited from her own brother Charles, together with the additional share bequeathed by "Young Charley," making in all a two-thirds interest. Lorenzo Delmonico received a one-third interest, which later was reduced to one-quarter.

The clause placing unrestricted control in Josephine's hands was unequivocal:

"It is my express wish and desire, and I hereby direct, that my niece, the said Josephine Crist Delmonico, shall have and exercise a controlling interest in the management, conduct, and direction of said business, and that she shall control and dispose of the same as and when she shall see fit, absolutely free from any control or dictation of any person or persons whatsoever."

Named as co-executors of the will were Josephine herself, and Albert Thieriot, a close friend of Rosa. Neither was required to post bond, and together they were given unlimited authority to perform any act necessary, to conduct the business how and as long as they might deem proper, and to sell any portion of the estate if they should so wish. For any loss that might be incurred, which was not the direct result of "willful negligence or misconduct, arising or growing out of the conduct of the business," the executors were not to be held responsible "or in any wise to be held accountable, but such loss shall be borne by the business." Should the receipts of the business be insufficient to meet losses, they were to be paid out of the residuary estate.

This provision against possible losses sounded odd, in view of the crowds filling the restaurants every day; but on the other hand, the delegation of power to Josephine could not have been made more explicit. That Josephine and her brother Lorenzo did not see eye to eye "Aunt Rosa" was aware; she herself had had differences with Lorenzo.

Rosa's considerable personal estate went to Josephine, and her portfolio of gilt-edged stocks and bonds was divided impartially between her niece and nephew.

So, the newspapers observed, Delmonico's would continue to be headed by a woman. Eugene Garnier was to remain as manager, and inasmuch as he had been with the restaurants thirty-two years, he could be relied upon to maintain the standards for which they were famous; so far as the public was concerned, there need be no apprehension. Said Garnier:

"Delmonico's for so many years has run along so smoothly in the old grooves that the coming of one or the going of another Delmonico in the ownership will not have any noticeable effect on the conduct of the business."

CHAPTER III

BEARDS IN THE SOUP

EUGENE GARNIER had every justification for making predictions of this sort, for he knew that Delmonico's preeminence was due to more than the subtle conjurations of its cooks, or the seemingly effortless service, or the splendid setting; it lay in the tyranny of habit. For hundreds of Delmonico's regulars, the restaurant had become less a convenience than a convention, a social form and custom. It was the citadel of conservatism, and like its patrons was growing more conservative. Delmonico's had achieved its position by a long evolvement, truly a feat of continuity, and this position was not to be easily undermined by younger rivals.

This was illustrated by a sudden agitation about beards in proximity to soup plates, that had been stirred up by George Boldt, the autocratic manager of the Waldorf-Astoria. Boldt was a consummate *hôtelier*, and he was also Prussian. He believed that bearded waiters were unsightly and unsanitary, and forthwith every male Waldorf-Astoria employee was ordered to shave. Boldt wore a beard himself, but then he was not a waiter, and his own facial adornment remained the Waldorf's lone exception.

This trampling upon personal privilege set off a rattle of controversy between those hirsute and those clean-shaven. Partisans took sides, everyone was expected to, and diligent reporters consulted the heads of leading restaurants to ascertain their views.

Louis Sherry took the matter lightly. There had been no complaints about the bearded waiters and cooks at his place, he

shrugged, and a man's preference for going whiskered or whisk-
erless would seem to be his own affair.

At Delmonico's, both staff and customers went bearded or
beardless as their fancies ran. John Klages's mutton-chops had
graced the cafe from time immemorial, and never had given
offense. Eugene Garnier was nonplussed by the question, and
suggested that a full beard or flowing Dundrearies might confer
a dignity upon the wearer which no smooth-faced youth could
inspire. At Delmonico's, beards would continue to wave in the
savory steam of Delmonican dishes, Garnier ruled.

At the Waldorf, manager Boldt tried to apply his no-beards
edict to the hack drivers outside the hotel, but there he met resistance. The whiskered drivers deserted the stand, and after
the hotel's guests had spent several days hailing oblivious han-
soms, Boldt capitulated. The hackies came back, but the hotel
staff remained clean-shaven.

2.

So steadily did the volume of Delmonico's business increase,
by 1905 there was talk of taking over Canfield's house, and the
house next beyond that, for more space. Garnier squelched that
rumor as premature. Unguessed by the public, Delmonico's
was not functioning as smoothly as the amount of patronage
would seem to indicate, and despite the rising income, financial
difficulties were appearing. But these were so well concealed
from outsiders that the city was startled when Albert Thieriot,
one of the co-executors of Rosa Delmonico's estate, filed a petition on November 14, 1906, for the courts to appoint a receiver.

This brought into the open the long smouldering dissatisfac-
tion of Thieriot and Lorenzo Delmonico with Josephine's management of the business. In Thieriot's action, Josephine was the
defendant, and her brother also signed the petition as an heir of
Rosa Delmonico. Although the application explicitly stated
that Delmonico's was not insolvent, it charged that unless the
operating methods were changed, bankruptcy must result.

There had been premonitions of the catastrophe, to which neither press nor public hitherto had paid much attention. In the previous July, a final appraisal of "Aunt Rosa's" estate had revealed that though she had left personal property worth $360,718, her interest in the business (including the Beaver Street plant) was valued at only $174,554. Meanwhile, the rental of the Fifth Avenue premises was $56,000 a year, and there were contingent liabilities which the estate would have to pay if the business did not. Among these was one bank loan of $196,000, and two others aggregating $450,000, secured by mortgages on the Beaver Street land and building. The Beaver Street mortgages, it appeared, had nearly doubled during Rosa's tenure; and the reason for this was indicated when the appraisal of Charles C. Delmonico's estate showed that he had borrowed heavily from the firm, which at the time of his death was in fact losing money. His gross personal estate was appraised at $91,597, and his one-sixth interest in the restaurants at a mere $10,248. The conclusion to be drawn was that the value of Delmonico's, as a going concern, had shrunk to about $60,000 from the million or more placed on it at the death of the elder Charles Delmonico in 1884.

Thieriot's application for a receiver to conserve the remaining assets was well documented. The friction between Josephine and Lorenzo C. Delmonico had been of long standing: her inclinations were social, she liked to travel, and the real management of the restaurants had been left to Garnier and his subordinates. Matters had reached such a pitch, Thieriot stated, that in February, 1905, he had engaged a firm of accountants to investigate the conduct of the restaurants for the years 1902, 1903, and 1904 — the years when "Aunt Rosa" had held control.

The report submitted by these accountants read like a hotel man's nightmare. The books, they said, had given "no information as to the actual earnings of the business. We were unable to arrive at the cost, return, or profit of any one of the departments because the books do not show the information. Both restaurants seem to be run entirely by employees without any responsible head, the consequence being a lack of system and check, and opportunities for waste, extravagance, and theft are apparent on all sides. Of the annual turnover of a million dollars the books do not show what portions of this came from wines and liquors, what portions from eatables, cigars, borrowed money, or any other source; neither do they show any divisions of the purchases of these articles, but are all put in one general account."

Large sums had been paid out without any apparent explanation, the report went on, and "as a consequence of conducting the business on these lines the profit and loss accounts made up from the books of the firm for 1902, 1903, and 1904 show very poor results. . . . The foregoing figures show positively that if the business continues to be conducted on the same lines as have been pursued for the past few years, the losses will accumulate and necessarily bring about disaster."

This report so alarmed Thieriot, he said, that he had insisted upon a change, and by agreement with Josephine Delmonico supervision of the firm's accounts had been turned over to the accounting firm. As a result, Thieriot's application set forth, whereas on March 1, 1905, the accountants had found a debit balance of $85,243.45, between that time and June 30, 1906, the profits were $124,464.72, derived from practically the same gross income. This was deemed proof positive that "the bad system in operation was responsible for the losses."

On March 1, 1905, the firm's indebtedness, some of it of long standing, was $184,477.19, the report stated, and by June, 1906, under the new supervision and control, this had been reduced to $56,898.90, "practically one month's current bills." The credit of the business, it was said, had been restored by this professional control.

However, in October, 1906, one month before the application was filed, Josephine Delmonico had given notice that she was resuming control, and had dismissed the accountants. Whereupon Thieriot felt that his duty as co-executor required him to ask for a receiver, since Josephine was "not a business woman and never had the slightest business experience."

A pot shot was taken at Josephine's executive manager:

"For some years prior to the death of Rosa Delmonico, the business of the firm was managed by one Eugene Garnier, who was entitled 'manager,' and in whom was vested by her, and after her death by said defendant, the sole control of said firm, and under whose administration the business had nearly reached a condition of insolvency when the said plaintiff, Thieriot, intervened."

3.

To all this Josephine Delmonico and Eugène Garnier entered denials. It was she, and not Thieriot, who had proposed installing the accounting firm to control of the books, she contended; and since under her aunt's will she had been given the sole control of the restaurants, she intended to exercise it.

Garnier indignantly retorted that "previous mismanagement" had piled up debts, so that by the time he took over there were claims totaling $336,000 against the business, exclusive of bank loans. This he had succeeded in reducing to $184,000 when the accountants stepped in, he insisted. Furthermore, except for the bookkeeping, he had conducted the business in such a manner that income had picked up every year under his management, and the money the accountants claimed to have saved for the firm during the previous year had really been earned by him.

Thieriot indicated how high were the stakes in this struggle for control of a rich patrimony, informing the court that the firm's assets included the Beaver Street property, worth $800,000 or more, with fixtures valued at $100,000; the Fifth Avenue lease, worth, with the fixtures there, not less than $280,000; a stable worth $30,000; and livestock worth $3,000; plus the good will of the name, which could not be valued exactly but certainly was "very great."

A series of legal maneuvers followed. Two weeks after applying for a receiver, Thieriot withdrew the application, by mutual consent, and three days later he petitioned the surrogate's court to revoke the letters testamentary issued to Josephine Delmonico as co-executor under her aunt's will; contending that she could not legally be at the same time a surviving partner in the business and executor of the estate, and also asserting that her management had been improvident and extravagant.

The surrogate deliberated for a week, and then removed her as executor, both on the legal technicality and because of her statement that she did not intend to "submit to be guided or in any way controlled or influenced by the judgment of her co-executor or co-trustee, or by any person interested in the estate," and also that she intended to retain Eugene Garnier as manager.

"Upon all the conceded facts," the surrogate ruled, "I am of the opinion that the respondent (Josephine Delmonico) is guilty of misconduct in the co-execution of her office as co-executrix, which warrants the revocation of her letters and her removal as trustee."

Josephine's response was to appeal this decision, and on February 25, 1907, the appellate division reversed the surrogate and restored her as co-executor. This gave her again complete control over the restaurants. Garnier was confirmed in his place as general manager, and the system of operation was not changed.

4.

Delmonico's had been shaken by the dispute, although its external operations bowled along as usual. Josephine Delmonico meanwhile absented herself for longer and longer periods, traveling much with her brother's widow, Jeanne Edwards Delmonico. For Josephine, the prestige of heading Delmonico's was a sufficient satisfaction.

Among factors that were changing life in New York City, costs were going up everywhere; yet Delmonico's prices did not rise with them. George Rector, whose restaurant at Times Square was enjoying a blaze of prosperity as the haunt of Broadway's big spenders, recalled that in 1906 one could get a first-rate dinner for four at his place with two bottles of champagne for $20; and if the host treated his guests to the theater afterward, that would cost him $7.50 more. It was much the same at Sherry's or Delmonico's; to spend thirty or forty dollars of an evening required a stretching of one's ingenuity.

By the standards of the time, these were not low prices, but they were not high enough to offset Delmonico's mounting expenses. The drain of loans, which were being negotiated at frequent intervals, was a burden. In November, 1908, Josephine Delmonico resolved the business into a stock company, Delmonico's, Inc. It was capitalized at $500,000, and Josephine was elected president, Jeanne Edwards Delmonico vice-president, and Eugene Garnier treasurer. This opened the way to seek an infusion of needed capital, and rumors of a projected sale again became rife. Each rumor, as it arose, Josephine, after some hesitation, repudiated. But she *was* looking for support: Garnier was about to retire, and would finally leave in 1910.

James B. Reagan, operator of the highly successful Knickerbocker Hotel, provided a behind-the-scenes glimpse by the disclosure that he had turned down a proposal to take over "Del's" under a stock-and-salary arrangement that would have guaranteed him $75,000 a year; but, as he explained, the Knickerbocker and Delmonico's both were "full-time jobs, and I couldn't cut myself in two." However, he felt and fervently said that he had been complimented by the offer, since Delmonico's occupied a place "which no other restaurant has ever been able to reach, and it would be an honor to be associated with it."

Thus, though outwardly still a monument of solidity, and as glamorous as ever, something was basically wrong with Delmonico's. Its vitality was ebbing. Yet vitality there was in the old organization still.

CHAPTER IV

GENTILITY'S LAST STAND

THE NAME WAS STILL STERLING. During the bickering, New Yorkers did not the less enjoy the amenities of "Del's," and although now there were numerous other centers of social resort, Delmonico's remained preeminent. The gap that separated the more recent entries from the "one and only" was amusingly demonstrated by the newcomers themselves, albeit unwittingly. The intrepid Boldt, boss of the Waldorf-Astoria, precipitated a fresh crisis of good taste when he decreed that no gentleman would be admitted to the Waldorf's dining rooms at the dinner hour unless he was wearing evening dress. It chanced that two of the first victims to run afoul of this sumptuary ukase were men prominent in society, noted for their nice observance of etiquette, as etiquette had been construed in New York before the usurpations of Boldt. These gentlemen, turned away at the door of Boldt's restaurant because they were in business suits, repaired in the same suits and a high dudgeon to their lawyers with demands for reparations to their dignity.

Reporters made a beeline to Sherry's and Delmonico's. How those exemplars of social acceptability proposed to meet this issue, was the question. Sherry felt that Boldt's action was "most undemocratic"; any gentleman would always be welcome at *his* establishment. Eugene Garnier was baffled. Instruct a customer of Delmonico how he should dress? It was unthinkable! "No such rule exists at Delmonico's, and never will," said he firmly. "There is no occasion for it. The question of dress is one that settles itself. Suppose," he ventured a hypothesis, "a patron who has been coming here for years should arrive on a train and go for dinner in the main dining room. Shall we exclude him because he is not in evening dress?" The pain stamped upon Eugène's face showed how preposterous he considered the idea. "No, as long as a man is decently dressed, we cannot refuse to serve him; and even to suggest to him what he should wear would be — well, very rude."

Boldt stuck by his rule — no swallow-tail, no soup — and snide observers intimated that he might be justified. Was it to be expected that among the thousands flocking to the Waldorf-Astoria from every point of the compass, all should be either to the manor born or to the manner bred?

As a bastion of conservatism, Delmonico's went its genteel way. During the first two decades of this century, the names that were familiarly heard there took on a faintly antiquarian flavor: old New York was disappearing, submerged by the new New York that so little resembled its progenitor. The Patriarchs had disbanded, their mission fulfilled; gout and hardening arteries were not conducive to ballroom capers. Yet there was sap in the old family trees. In December, 1906, the first of two subscription dances in the grand ballroom at "Del's" was sponsored by Mrs. Frederick J. De Peyster, and society news writers voted the affair not only "extremely elegant" but also "very spirited." The guest list was studded with old New York names. After the cotillion a buffet supper was served under the attentive eye of little Philippe, and then (in keeping with new times and new tempos) there was "informal dancing." The favors were as restrained as secured position could wish: for the ladies, little Christmas trees trimmed with tinsel and a red candle; for the gentlemen, "a handsome and useful Mission candlestick with a red candle trimmed with a red ribbon bow."

The first Junior Cotillion of that season ("for the rosebud element in society") was held at Sherry's at the same time — an early dance, starting just after ten o'clock — and the favors there, too, were "simple and attractive," befitting the ingenue tone of the evening.

Outside the walls of these strongholds of tradition, the city was strident and fast-moving. Taxicabs were supplanting hansom cabs, although as late as 1909 a seventy-mile-an-hour gale, which toppled the Archangel Gabriel off the roof of the Cathedral of St. John the Divine, blew a small boy under the hooves of horses in the street, and the accident could be reported as a common traffic hazard. Along Fifth Avenue the sidewalks became so congested that an ancient ordinance was dug out which allowed the city to revoke permission to householders to utilize the sidewalks out to the "stoop line," and down came the high steps that had been a feature of Manhattan for generations. Sherry's and Delmonico's lost their pretty flower borders, to the grief of Arthur Nies, assistant manager of Delmonico's. For half a century there had always been a little lawn and flowers at the door of Delmonico restaurants, he said, and "green spots are all too few in this busy, unsentimental metropolis of ours." Besides, there was a practical reason for the flower beds: "Lorenzo Delmonico did not relish the idea of having dust blown into his carefully prepared sauces."

Nies felt that individuality was being pressed out of New York and New Yorkers. "What has become of the old New York diner of twenty and thirty years ago?" he asked. Where were men like Captain Ben Wenberg, for example, who could wear varnished boots and a high hat in a sea breeze, and who did not entirely trust even a Delmonico cook? "The cafes and hotels of the Seventies and Eighties had many regular diners who were distinctly different from each other," Nies insisted. "Nowadays all seem to be very much alike, do the same thing, dress in a similar manner, and even talk alike."

The trend towards uniformity had made it all but impossible to distinguish a gentleman from a bounder, Nies lamented. An individual (who *was* individual) had stalked into the office and identified himself as "Captain E. T. Butler, 21st United States Cavalry," stationed at Governors Island. The officers there, he said, were planning a surprise party for Major F. D. Grant, and "we want you to submit estimates for the banquet. Also, send these cigars to the post at once."

The stranger tossed down a list, and reached for his check book. Nies noted that he was wearing a fur-lined overcoat and a pearl scarfpin — *prima facie* evidence of a bank account, in more settled days — and accepted the proffered check for $50. The cigars came to $40, and the visitor pocketed $10 in change and stalked out, puffing a complimentary panatella.

The check bounced; Delmonico's learned that there was no "Captain E. T. Butler" in the Army, and the 21st Cavalry was in the Philippines. The officers at Governors Island were mystified by the arrival of $40 worth of cigars, but being gentlemen, they returned the lot to Delmonico's. Two days later, according to the irreverent *Herald*, the police were "performing that miracle of zeal and discretion known to them as 'working on the case.'" And there the episode ended, except for strengthening Nies's disgust with modern changes.

Of greater significance than the impudence of a rogue was the fact that the contretemps was aired in the newspapers. In Lorenzo Delmonico's day, such a swindle would hardly have succeeded; and if it had, the fact would have been consigned to the deepest Delmonico wine vault, never to come to light.

CHAPTER V

A MAYOR FROM DELMONICO'S

NIES'S LAMENT for the passing of individuality among Delmonico's customers was, of course, premature; old men generally consider their times as moribund before they become so themselves. In 1910 there occurred an instance of individualism run wild, which sufficiently refuted the old manager. This was the bursting upon the New York scene of never-to-be-equaled individualist William Jay Gaynor, the city's most picturesque mayor. The chapter had for background Delmonico's.

In midsummer of 1909 the political situation in the city was violently agitated. An election was coming up in November, and Tammany Hall was faced with a three-front opposition — from the inchoate but belligerent Fusion forces, from the equally tumultuous Republicans, and from top-of-the-lungs publisher William Randolph Hearst, who was trying to carry off the acrobatic feat of planting his feet simultaneously in all camps and belonging exclusively to none. In this emergency, Charles F. Murphy, Tammany's taciturn boss, hit upon Gaynor as a candidate for mayor under the Democratic banner. Gaynor was then a justice of the New York Supreme Court, entering upon his second fourteen-year term.

Judge Gaynor had built a reputation for nonconformity by the conscientious effort of a lifetime devoted to going his own way. He fitted into no category in heaven or on earth. Born poor, of an English mother and an Irish father, he had been reared on a hardscrabble farm in upstate New York. He attended a one-room schoolhouse, decided to enter the priesthood, became a lay student of the teaching order of Christian

Brothers, journeyed to San Francisco with the order, gave that up, abjured Catholicism, returned east, taught school, studied law, practiced successfully, engaged in politics in Brooklyn, where he made his home, with furious independence, happily sending several political sharks to jail, was elected a judge, and had established himself as the possessor of a hot temper, extensive learning, and unrivaled powers of pungent expression. A master of the plain Anglo-Saxon vocabulary ("the short words are the best," was his rule), he was fearless in stating his views without deference to time, place, or the listener. He was not averse to treading upon any corn that was placed in his path; and with all his explosiveness was so transparently honest and ruggedly well-intentioned that he won friends at the very time he infuriated them.

He knew more law than most lawyers who appeared before him, and let them know it. He told the American Bankers Association, "your reputation was bad before the time of Cato the Elder"; and when a startled reporter ejaculated "Who?" turned to the representatives of the press and snapped, "Cato! Cato! Have you ever heard of him?" Without a pause, he then favored the bankers — J. Pierpont Morgan sitting at his elbow — with a free translation of the passage in Cato's *De Rustica* showing that in ancient Rome money-lenders were classed lower than thieves.

Although nominally a Democrat, Judge Gaynor was a thoroughgoing maverick whom no fence could hold within bounds. Consistently unpredictable, he had committed the party heresies of supporting Henry George, the single-taxer, and William Jennings Bryan, in the latter's crusade for free silver. Above all abominations he hated peculating politicians, and said so on every available occasion. Joseph Pulitzer, who disliked but feared him, rightly called Gaynor "nobody's pocket judge"; he was nobody's pocket anything. In private life he was erudite, read the classics for recreation (Epictetus and Cervantes were his favorites), took pride in operating a farm at his Long Island summer home (often quoting in court lessons inculcated by his geese), and domestically and among friends was affectionate, kindly, and generally good-humored. He had married, divorced, and married again, and had a numerous family of children.

All in all, no less likely a man for Tammany to hit upon as its candidate for mayor of the city of New York could have been found; and when he was nominated, probably half of New York believed Tammany could not have found a worse candidate. The press was universally hostile when his nomination was made known, and Tammany's potent district leaders had frankly blenched when Murphy first proposed Gaynor: they were afraid of the man. But Murphy insisted that with Gaynor the Democrats could win against the Hydra-headed opposition; without him, probably not. In a private dining room at Delmonico's the issue was threshed out, Murphy carried his point, and with a groan the party announced that Judge Gaynor would be their man in the forthcoming contest.

2.

The place where the nomination had taken place (for the subsequent party convention in Carnegie Hall was only a clambake to keep the rank and file happy) indicated changing times. Charles F. Murphy, a ponderous man once described as "personally very pious and socially very dull," was a former saloon-keeper from the East Side. He had succeeded Richard Croker as the master of Tammany, and since his rise to influence and coincidental affluence he had spent most of his working days as regularly as a clock. Every morning he was to be found at Tammany Hall on Fourteenth Street, carrying out the multifarious duties of his position; but as the afternoon wore on, he would gather up his bulk (for he was a man of great dignity of person) and betake himself northward to Fifth Avenue and Forty-fourth Street for a drink and a dinner at Delmonico's.

This partiality for exotic food in surroundings alien to most of Tammany's braves was regarded with repugnance at the Hall; daily association with "uptown swells," it was feared, would rot the boss's moral fiber, and the practice was to be discouraged. But Murphy was unmoved by the criticism of his underlings: he was not a boss for nothing. Thus it was that Judge Gaynor was nominated in a cloud of fragrant cigar smoke at Delmonico's after a most persuasive dinner.

When the word was carried back to them, the braves trembled for their sustenance. The man who made the nominating speech at the window-dressing convention held shortly afterwards put the case with candor and clarity when he exclaimed of the candidate he was offering to the party and the city, "There is, I fancy, not a man who he had not offended, myself included, many, many times." Everybody present remembered when the speaker, running unsuccessfully for mayor under Tammany's auspices, had been characterized by Judge Gaynor as possessing all the attributes needed by a machine candidate — "to say nothing, do nothing, and, I might almost add, know nothing."

Plunging into one of the most vituperative campaigns on record, Judge Gaynor made his nominator's speech a paragon of understatement. He broke all the rules, including his own. He had never been inside Tammany Hall itself (although he did know Delmonico's), and deferred until the middle of the campaign accepting Tammany's invitation to visit there and address the faithful. When he did arrive, it was late; as he explained, he had been obliged to telephone to find out how to reach the place. Then looking around, while the sachems seated on the platform shifted in their chairs, he said meditatively: "So this is Tammany Hall . . . But where is the Tiger? That Tiger which they say is going to swallow me up? If there happens to be any swallowing up, it is not at all unlikely that I may be on the outside of the Tiger." In the silence that ensued, the only smile in the room was a tigerish grin on the face of Gaynor.

The judge's opponents were the Republican-Fusion candidate

(the two parties had united in one), and Hearst, who had allowed himself to be nominated by an agglomeration of earnest idealists and temperamental malcontents whom he managed to coalesce under the alternative titles of the Independence League or the Civic Alliance. Hearst had entered the race in pure spite, for he had been angling to get Tammany's backing for his own freewheeling aspirations. Once in, everything that a disappointed, vindictive demagogue could do he tried, to thwart Gaynor, without harboring the least illusion that he could be elected himself. Gaynor retorted with a ferocity that made the mealy-mouthed shudder. Of the adventurer from California ("who advertises himself like a patent medicine") he said, "his face almost makes me puke," and that he was "filled up to the wesand, yes, into the goozle, with promises." Hearst's experts in Billingsgate retaliated with their best — "pseudo-paranoiac," "incapable of telling the truth," "mentally cross-eyed," and "an intellectual hypocrite." Gaynor came back with, "I believe there are more hypocrites in this city than on the whole face of the earth outside of it." The judge was said to have been the only political antagonist who ever got under Hearst's hide. From that he derived no personal satisfaction, although a host of Hearst's ill-wishers did.

How the judge could ever win a popular election surpassed the imagining of most onlookers. Snarled the *Sun*, impressed in spite of itself, "We doubt that Gaynor ever realized, until just recently, how bad a man he could be, once he let himself go." He made no effort to ingratiate, refused either to dress up or to talk down to an audience, but remained aggressively educated at all times. Hod carriers he treated to liberal doses of Epictetus and Lecky. He declined to limit his exercise of the right of free speech by anything short of the laws of libel, upon which he was an authority. If it was possible to affront, he chose the most effective time and place to do it. A meeting of Queens County voters he hailed as "Ye Long Island clam diggers!" Appearing before the convention of the New York State Federation of Women's Clubs, many of whose members were ardent suffragists, he chided: "You people of these clubs think you are the whole of womankind, but you are not. I can see that some of you want to vote. We generally aspire to the thing we are least fitted for." Speaking before the Advertising Men's League, he quoted Shakespeare relative to their occupation, "Oh, what a goodly outside falsehood hath!" Unwilling to beg a favor from anybody, he almost defied people to vote for him, and in November he was elected by a majority of 73,000, although the entire rest of the Tammany ticket was defeated. On January 1, 1910, he took office as the most unconventional, picturesque, articulate, and controversial mayor New York City ever had the good fortune to acquire.

3.

On the day of his inauguration, he told a friend: "For thirty years I have been thinking what I would do with this office. Now I am going to do it." A yearning "to do things for the people," he said, had "burned in my head like a live coal." A few observers had sensed this consuming ambition to defend the "common man" against the depredations of a political plunderbund, and to it they ascribed the strange appeal he seemed to have for the average voiceless citizen — the decent, much abused, briefly flattered and quickly forgotten average man or woman, who nevertheless had the wit to distinguish between a political charlatan and a friend.

With the vigor of ten new brooms, Mayor Gaynor started an epic housecleaning. On inaugural day, while his office was buzzing with the babble of hangers-on counting up prospective spoils, a Tammany sycophant sidled up to the mayor and inquired with a smirk, "And what can we do for Mr. Murphy?" Gaynor considered a moment, then replied sweetly, "I think we can give Mr. Murphy a few kind words." A few kind words was all Murphy and his crew received for four long, dreary, hungry years. In the annals of Tammany, Gaynor's ingratitude came to be ranked with great natural disasters — an "act of

God," unaccountable on any other grounds; an affliction which the smitten could only contemplate with stunned incomprehension and abhorrence.

The new mayor made appointments for the good of the city, choosing men whom he deemed capable of carrying out their duties and then seeing that they did. Some of these appointees came up to his expectations, others did not. He booted leeches and drones off the municipal payroll with the efficiency of a machine. His eye penetrated everywhere, or nearly everywhere; no detail escaped his scrutiny and if necessary his personal attention. For the display, trappings, and pomp of office he cared nothing. Every day he walked to work, three and one-half miles across Brooklyn Bridge from his home to City Hall, spotless and trig in frock coat and top hat. Along the way he noticed whether the streets were swept in summer, and the snow removed in winter. He observed the direction of the wind and how the weather stood in relation to farmers' crops. He abolished or curtailed to the best of his ability abuses of authority; cured the police of their tendency to "throw their weight around"; put a stop to the arresting of boys for trivial offenses. He personally ordered removed from the rogues gallery files the photograph of a guiltless man that had been there for years, labeled, "general thief." He stopped leaks in the city treasury, saw to it as best he could that contracts were negotiated honestly, and in rapid order won the admiration of most of the forces who had denounced him hardest during the campaign, Hearst excepted. Hearst never forgave Gaynor.

The mayor's almost obsessive concern with civic responsibility he had outlined clearly during the election campaign. In a revealing letter to his brother, he had recalled that years before he had noticed a long line of people, stretching for a block outside City Hall, and upon inquiring why they were standing there had been told they were waiting to pay their taxes, due that day.

"I walked along the line on the opposite side and looked at them," he related. "There they were . . . good, intelligent people, whose lives are a continuous struggle to bring up their children and make both ends meet from month to month. Their bony hands and bent bodies gave evidence of their life of toil, and most of their faces were anxious. As I looked at them, my mind became filled with the awful baseness of men, who, having got into office by the votes of these people, turn around and betray and rob them of their hard-earned money paid in as taxes. I made a covenant then and there that from that time onward . . . I should . . . work against low, base, and corrupt officials and government."

After seven months of prodigious (and for Tammany shattering) labors, Mayor Gaynor achieved a unique place in history by becoming the subject of one of the most widely published photographs ever made. This was snapped by a cameraman who chanced to be by, an instant after a dismissed jobholder stepped up behind the mayor on the deck of the liner he had just boarded to sail for Europe, and shot him in the neck.

4.

The wound was grave but not fatal; the bullet could not be extracted, and months passed before the mayor regained even comparative health; he never fully recovered. His voice was reduced to a permanent rasping whisper, and he was racked by a spasmodic cough.

How it felt to be shot from ambush he set down in a detailed letter to his sister. At first "a metallic roar" that filled his head "until I thought it would burst open," this accompanied by nausea and temporary blindness; then the gradual return of sight and a sensation of smothering. He found that by closing his mouth he could breathe, and realized that he was upright, supported by friends. "They wanted me to lie down on the deck, but I said no, I would walk to my stateroom." So, shuffling and supported, he got to his cabin, where he managed to make intelligible an order that they fetch two of the best surgeons in the city — "and be sure to tell them not to discourage me . . .

Finding my wound not immediately mortal, I had determined to make a fight of it . . ."

His character seemed changed by the injury, his eccentricity and irascibility turning at times to venom and unreasonableness, and the bright promises he had inspired at the outset of his term were imperfectly fulfilled. He was much under attack by self-constituted reformers, for whom he had no use whatsoever: to his mind, "prying" and "minding other people's business," whether done by government or by private agencies, were the capital sins against human dignity. Men and women are not perfect, he would point out, and there was no prospect that they ever would be, and he resented attempts to legislate them into purity and spotlessness.

One gadfly critic, the stridulous Dr. Parkhurst, from whose pulpit on Madison Square emanated a continuous clamor against real and supposed municipal wrongdoing, Gaynor accepted as his hairshirt, to be borne as patiently as possible. "Some people are too good for this world; the sooner they are translated the better," was his soft rejoinder. And again, "Dr. Parkhurst thinks he is pious when he is only bilious."

An idiosyncrasy to which Gaynor gave full rein was his delight in letter-writing. He made a point of answering most of the letters that came to City Hall, and they poured in from all over the country. Who the writer was, or what the subject might be, made little difference; the answer came in Gaynor's crisp style, terse, quaint, and always to the point. He handed out advice and discussed with chatty freedom public and private questions, views, tastes, facts, fads, delusions, and experiences that spread over an inexhaustible range of topics.

For example, he sided with small boys who wrote him complaining that the police broke up their games in the streets. To five such youngsters — addressing each one of them punctiliously by name — the mayor replied:

"Dear Boys — It is too bad that you cannot play ball somewhere in peace. Of course the police cannot always let you play on the streets, but now and then they can wink so hard with both eyes as not to see you when you are doing no harm to passersby and the street is not crowded . . . So, boys, do the best you can, and I will help you a little now and then if you send me word."

A letter from a man who objected to the loud striking of the great clock on the Metropolitan Life Tower overlooking Madison Square (and adjoining Dr. Parkhurst's place of weekly expostulation) received just as courteous consideration:

"You complain of the clock on the Metropolitan Building. You want me to stop it. You say it strikes 4 times on the quarter, 8 times on the half, 12 times on the three-quarters, and 16 times on the hour, making 44 times every hour, or 200 times from 8 a.m. to 12 noon every day. I am sorry for you. But really does the clock make as much noise as Dr. Parkhurst? You know we all have to bear something, and I am willing to bear my share of it."

Another correspondent who begged for relief from yowling tomcats drew this judicious response:

"I regret to say that I have so many official duties pressing upon me that I cannot just now devote any time to the tomcats, as you request by your letter. There are a few in my neighborhood, but I go to sleep and let them howl. It amuses them and doesn't hurt me. But some say that it is the pussycats that howl, and not the tomcats. How is that? We must not kill Tommy for the sins of Pussy. And, also, remember that 'the female of the species is more deadly than the male.' "

He wrote to the police force urging patrolmen to be on the lookout for cases of cruelty to horses; advised grand jurors not to feel too grand; congratulated a little girl on feeling happy ("everybody should feel happy"); and regretted that he could not undertake to find a wife for a man in Arkansas City, Arkansas. ("How could I recommend any good girl here to you? You may not be so attractive as you think you are.") He suggested that a public-spirited ratcatcher drop in and talk over his proposed bill to exempt ratcatchers from jury duty, and took issue with presumptuous judges who strike down as "unconstitutional" laws that have been enacted with the overwhelming concurrence of the "common people."

To reformers calling for extra-legal methods to combat vice and crime, he preached: "The only way to enforce the law is the way prescribed by law. That which cannot be done lawfully must not be done at all, by the police or any other public officials from the President of the United States down." His favorite precept was, "This is a government of laws, and not of men." When a taxpayer expressed a wish that he might arrest wrongdoers, the mayor counseled him:

"My dear sir, let me tell you that every citizen has full right to arrest anyone whom he sees committing any criminal offense, big or little. The law of England and of this country has been very careful to confer no more right in that respect upon policemen and constables than it confers on every citizen . . . Sail right in as hard and as fast as you want to, being careful, however, only to arrest guilty persons, for otherwise your victims will turn around and sue you for false arrest. Policemen have to take the same risk."

He lectured his own policemen that "not even a murderer can be arrested and imprisoned without evidence."

With Fusionists and all political half-breeds he had no sympathy — "mingle-mangle committee," he called their groups, and when reporters begged to know what that word might mean, advised them to "look it up in honest old Hugh Latimer; it is there; I haven't time to play dictionary with you." The reporters did look it up, found that it meant food fed to swine, and naturally the indignation of Fusionists erupted.

Gaynor would not stoop to excuses or attempts to evade responsibility for his actions or those of his subordinates. He told an investigating committee: "I do not propose to be mayor and have someone else run the city. If it is run badly, here is the man responsible; right here; just look at me."

Then going back to his office he could enjoy writing to the Reverend Basil M. Kerbawy, of Brooklyn, on the vexed subject of beards:

"Reverend and Dear Sir — Your letter informing me that as you walk about the city visiting the homes of your parishioners people apply opprobrious names to you, and throw empty cans and rubbish at you, and otherwise assault you, on account of your beard, is at hand. You ask me, 'Is it a crime in the City of New York to wear a beard?' No, it is not. I wear one myself and nobody ever takes notice of it. How is it that they take notice of your beard? Have you trimmed it in some peculiar way, contrary to the Scriptures? For you know the Scriptures say, 'Ye shall not round the corners of your beards, neither shalt thou mar the corners of thy beard.' Yes, if they assault you, and throw cans at you, you have a right to defend yourself to the last extremity; but if you find it necessary I will have a detective go around with you for a few days until we arrest some of those who are wronging you. Are you certain it is your beard which is the cause of the trouble?"

Day after day, the letters streamed out, full of pith and curious humor, on serious subjects and trivial, and each correspondent was treated with respect, and, where possible, salty sympathy. The public enjoyed it, and Gaynor enjoyed the role of omniscient counselor. He wrote about books and reading; Don Quixote was his favorite character, and in his own makeup there was something of the noble knight whose pate was addled but whose heart was as soft as a coddled egg. He expatiated upon the spirit of Christmas; on roof playgrounds; on marriage fees; on banning books from libraries; on arrests without warrant (an abomination); on making restitution; on observing Good Friday; and on converting the Jews.

"It seems to me that this work of proselytizing from other religions and sects is very often carried too far," he advised the Reverend Thomas M. Chalmers, of Brooklyn. "Do you not believe the Jews have a good religion? . . . I do not think I should give you a license to preach for the conversion of the Jews in the streets of the thickly settled Jewish neighborhoods which you designate. Would you not annoy them and do more harm than good? How many Jews have you converted so far?"

Certainly no sager counsel was ever given than Mayor Gaynor's reply to the request of a newspaper syndicate for a message which might be of interest to their readers.

"Dear Sir — You ask me to give an interview saying 'What I would say to the readers of 3,000 newspapers.' I would say to them to be very careful about believing all they see in the newspapers."

Another specimen of his home truths was his reply to a *New York Times* reader who wanted advice on the art of writing letters:

"What is the best way to write things, you ask? Often the best way is not to write them."

In constant ill-health due to the irritation set up by the bullet in his throat, which made all speech difficult, the mayor was subject to violent fits of coughing that sometimes lasted for half an hour and left him limp, with nerves jangling. Life indeed had become difficult for him, and no less difficult for New Yorkers. But never did he lose sight of his objective — to safeguard the "common people" from political footpads. Friends bore his distempers with what patience they could; enemies with furious impatience. As the *New York World* candidly put the case:

"If anybody chooses to say that Mr. Gaynor is irascible and irritable in his discussion of public affairs, we shall agree with him; but we are aware of no provision in the Constitution of the State of New York or the charter of the city which asserts that the mayor of New York must be sweet-tempered and gentle and lovable. Mr. Gaynor is difficult to get along with at times, and we are glad that we have no personal relations with him."

5.

The long drought at Tammany Hall neared an end, prospectively, when another election drew nigh. Murphy had been hard put to hold his parched and ravenous district leaders in line, and around the Wigwam there was an impression that Delmonico's was to blame for their emancipation; it was their leader's pernicious eating habits that had brought them upon the blight of Gaynor. Nevertheless, it was to a private dining room at Delmonico's that the leaders were bidden in midsummer of 1913 to decide upon their candidate for mayor this time.

Upon one point they were united: never again would they make the mistake of winning an election with the wrong man. Many cigars were reduced to ashes while the meeting congenially tore to shreds the mayor who had let them down. Only Murphy had a few kind words to say for Gaynor; the boss had a sneaking regard for any man who would not be bossed. The vote was taken, and Gaynor was consigned to a Gehenna which all trusted would be as hot as the last four years for them had been lean. The mayoral nomination was handed to a party-spear-bearer, a lawyer named Edward E. McCall.

Gaynor had wanted renomination. Despite the clangor of critics and damaging investigations, he believed that the "common people" were with him — "the people in general," who were too engrossed in their own affairs "to bother their heads very much" about the tribulations of their mayor. In a showdown vote, Gaynor was confident that he would be upheld, and he would not willingly be turned out without a fight.

A number of admirers, including many important New Yorkers and many a Delmonico regular, organized to run him independently for a second term. On September 4 he accepted this nomination in a ceremony that was held on the steps of City Hall before a large concourse of citizens. But Gaynor's appearance shocked his friends — his haggard air and, still more startling, his rumpled clothing. It was a sad decline from the days when he could castigate the mind of Hearst as "a howling wilderness."

Too feeble to speak — the bullet in his throat was a serious impediment — he had a few words he had scribbled down read for him. They were like one of his letters, addressed, this one, to the people:

"How different this vast impressive scene is to the little scene which occurred in a room at Delmonico's one night a week ago. There sat at a table eight men to decide who might run for mayor and other offices. They were all of one stripe, and of a kind to cast lots for the garments of the city. Let me read their names to you lest you have forgotten them: Charles F. Murphy, John H. McCooey, Thomas Foley, Philip Donahue, Edward E. McCall, John Fitzgerald, Arthur Murphy, John Galvin. There was no room for anyone except themselves. None of you were invited. None of you were allowed to make a suggestion. But here today all representative men have a voice . . . The people of this city are going to shovel all of these miserable little political grafters into one common dumpheap."

Two days later he boarded a ship for Europe, to get two weeks of rest and collect strength for the coming campaign. "I cannot possibly get any privacy on land, so I am going to spend two weeks on the ocean, where nobody can get at me," he told reporters. "Murphy and the chaps that sat down with him at Delmonico's the other night and guzzled and abused me until their faces were red, were ready to cut me up, I am told, and yet I never did anything to them except what tended to make them look respectable."

Shortly after the ship left port, a message came back, addressed to a newspaper: "The rentpayers and taxpayers of New York City will not throw the government of their city . . . into the control of a vulgar gang of grafters, all of one stripe, such as met at Delmonico's.

> "Give them the shovel;
> No king, no clown
> Shall rule this town;
> That day is gone forever.
> "W. J. Gaynor."

It was his last word. In mid-ocean he was found dead, slumped in a deck chair, a volume of Emerson open on his lap.

From two sources came appropriate epitaphs.

The *New York Sun*, which on the day of his election had

called him "certainly the most unfit candidate for the mayoralty in the history of the community," on the occasion of his death published its altered estimate:

"First and foremost, he was, as no other mayor ever was, the people's champion, the actual father of the city."

Thomas Foley, afterwards surrogate and memorialized in Foley Square, also paid his tribute. When asked if he wished to comment upon the late mayor, Foley said:

"I will say this about Mayor Gaynor: he did more to break up the Democratic organization than any other man ever has in this city."

Gaynor's own view of the matter, at the end of four years of struggle, was put in his familiar terse style:

"I have had a pretty hard time for four years to hold my own against all comers, and against every corrupt influence, but *I have been mayor.*"

It was a boast justifiable, and, it may be, unique in the history of American cities.

A short time after Gaynor's death, S. S. McClure, the publisher, offered to defray the cost of placing a bronze tablet in the room at Delmonico's where Mayor Gaynor had been denied a renomination, to perpetuate the memory of that historic shuffling off.

Without the need of any such visible reminder, Gaynor remained bright in New York memories for years. Humble people approved his way with the "unco guid" — "those few virtuous people," he described the class, "who think we ought to be able to make everybody as virtuous as they are, or rather as virtuous as they think and pretend they are. Now these people we forgive, of course, twice a day. We forgive them, but we desire to have nothing to do with them."

His jaunty conclusion had been summed up in fewer words:

"There is less misery in the world than some miserable people think."

CHAPTER VI

AN END OF SOBRIETY

THE NAME OF EDWARD E. McCALL does not appear on the roll of elected Mayors of New York: in 1913 the Fusionists won with John Purroy Mitchel. And that name at one bound takes us to the *götterdämmerung* of an epoch and a civilization in the fiery convulsions of the World War.

The climax did not come unheralded; it was preceded by marks of vitiation and a falling-apart of the social structure which had endured so long and had produced so much both of good and of deplorable. Society was saturated and satiated with wealth. If the favors distributed at Mrs. De Peyster's Delmonico ball in 1906 were worthy of singling out for approval as "restrained," "handsome and useful," there was a reason for this. During the Nineties extravagance had set in motion counteractions up and down the social front, and now excoriations of the "heartless rich" were emanating from more weighty sources than the lips of a maudlin nitwit engaged in shooting up Delmonico's.

At a ball given at Newport by the Oliver Belmonts in 1895, in their ornate "cottage," Belcourt, the favors had cost $7,000 — and $7,000 was a sum of money impressive enough for even a Belmont to notice. Belcourt itself typified the tasteless opulence of the period, for it was a luxurious stable for thirteen horses, with living rooms for the owners above. In the grand hall where the dancing took place, four stuffed horses with mailed knights astride their backs stood against the four walls, flanked by standing figures of knights in armor. Hundreds of tiny electric lights twinkled in masses of tropical plants banking the walls, and the favors comprised (as reported in column after column of news accounts) silver-mounted English riding whips with silver pencils in their handles: thermometers, ash trays, satin jockey caps in the Belmont racing colors — maroon and red — miniature horse blankets, cribbage boards and euchre counters, horses' heads mounted on hobbyhorse sticks, orders of nobility on neck ribbons, French walking sticks, Parisian flower fans, satin slippers filled with flowers, gilt birdcages with singing canaries, tortoise shell and silver memo tablets, silk flags of all nations, silk fans and ribbons, bouquets of rarest flowers, and other expensive knickknacks. Every favor bore the Belmont coat of arms and motto, *Sans crainte*, was stamped "Belcourt," and somewhere had a touch of the Belmont colors. "Such profusion was never before seen," reported the *Herald*'s tongue-clucking correspondent; the supply of favors was so great that many were left over.

When a limit had been reached on the amount of money that could be lavished upon such trifles, "sophisticated silliness" came to the rescue of the dreadfully bored. At a dinner given by Mr. and Mrs. W. E. D. Stokes the male guests received as favors bullfrogs in grass baskets, and these croaking comedians, escaping from their cages, produced merriment by hopping into the soup plates and wine glasses.

In 1900 occurred (at Sherry's not at Delmonico's) what was perhaps the most inane feat of sheer showing-off ever perpetrated by an American plutocrat. This was the "horseback dinner" given by a man named C. K. G. Billings (otherwise unrenowned) to thirty-six horsey friends in celebration of the opening of his $200,000 stable for thoroughbreds in what is now Fort Tryon Park. Sherry's ballroom was ruralized for the occasion by a backdrop of rustic scenery, interspersed with potted palms. Real sod overlaid the dancing floor. The guests, in white ties and boiled shirts, perched precariously on hacks hired from a livery stable and pecked at the viands placed on trays attached to the pommels of their saddles. The horses dined, too, more at ease, out of troughs filled with selected oats; while the waiters, in riding boots and hunting pink, doubled as grooms of the chamber, sweeping up the droppings from this Centaur banquet in between popping champagne corks. The egregious Billings made his splash; and his name is embalmed in time's balsam, like a beetle in amber, for the derision of centuries to come.

2.

Against this surrender to crass vulgarity Delmonico's held out. Its novelties were aimed to ingratiate rather than startle. There was considerable fanfare over its "orchid salad," which was composed of chicory grown in shades of red and green, which when opened resembled a flower. And in 1910 the restaurant was redecorated. At the autumn reopening that year (just after the summertime roof garden closed), society approved the fresh setting. "The entire atmosphere of the place seems changed, for the better, if possible, and couldn't be more cheerful," was a reporter's impression. Feminine sensibilities had been indulged: the walls of the main dining room were hung with silk, and at the windows were Louis XV curtains which harmonized with the natural wood carvings and onyx fireplace. Yellow and brown tones prevailed, and large palms and lamps with yellow shades added to the feeling of subdued richness.

An innovation that drew more favorable attention than the decorations was the tiny electric fans installed in the telephone booths, which were turned on by closing the doors. The new manager, Wilfred J. Taupier (he that year replaced Eugène Garnier upon the latter's retirement under the weight of advancing age) cooed under the plaudits of his patrons.

That autumn was gala. One specially brilliant evening was after the Yale-Harvard football game, played that year at New Haven to a scoreless tie. At "Del's" every seat was taken; many of the guests hurried there straight from the game. Women wore "jaunty hats of fur and beaver," with severely tailored costumes that set off their figures perfectly, and the tables were

bright with Yale and Harvard pennants, with flowers and blue
and crimson streamers. Everybody took in good part the strug-
gles of the Italian musicians with "Boola-boola" and "Fair Harvard." In honor of the game, "Del's" chef had invented two
ices to tempt the diners who felt they could not eat another
morsel. The first, *Grenade Lafayette*, consisted of vanilla mousse
thinly coated with raspberry ice, containing a pony of apricot
brandy. The second, *Mirabelline*, was unsweetened water ice
flavored with plum cordial, coated with orange water ice.

New Year's Eve called for turnouts all over town, and at
"Del's" the guests made merry with Parisian party hats, and
to supplement the orchestra there was a soprano soloist. And
what was Delmonico's competition on the first of January,
1911? The newspapers listed the leading hotels and restaurants
where special festivities were scheduled, and among those iden-
tifiable today were the Waldorf-Astoria, Sherry's, Hoffman
House, Hotel Imperial, Martinique, Knickerbocker, Plaza
(extremely upper-crust), Victoria, Herald Square, Latham,
Seville, Breslin, St. Regis, Ritz-Carlton, Manhattan, Savoy,
Netherland, Astor, and Belmont Hotels; the Kaiserhof (Thirty-
ninth Street and Broadway), Churchill's, Café des Beaux Arts,
Shanley's, Madrid Café, Reisenweber's, and Maxim's among the
better known cabarets. The Waldorf-Astoria catered to five
thousand revelers, most of them from out of town.

3.

The food, and much of the mood and setting, at Demonico's
remained unmarred by the restlessness of the decade; but its internal condition was not good. During 1911 there were rumors
that the business was to be sold and moved farther uptown, and
it was positive that the lease on the Forty-fourth Street location
would expire in a year. A syndicate did negotiate for a purchase
but the deal fell through; Arthur Nies told the press, with a
trace of smugness, that he was certain Miss Josephine Delmonico would not sell "to everyone who comes along"; there

would always be the matter of maintaining the Delmonico name and standards.

Then in August, 1911, the lease was renewed to run until 1927, and it was stated definitely that the restaurant would neither be sold nor transferred elsewhere. Outwardly it continued to appear prosperous; but too many factors were militating against its continuation for any length of time successfully. The factors included economic pressures, the rising value of the site, the transformation of the immediate area from residential to business uses, the decay of interest in the refinements of food, faulty management due to ingrained abuses, and absentee control. Josephine Delmonico was often out of the city, at summer or winter resorts, or abroad.

With the outbreak of war in Europe in 1914, Delmonico's became a center for relief work on behalf of England and France. Benefit dances raised funds for ambulances and service clubs in Paris and elsewhere. Strongly Francophile, the management lent every cooperation to such patriotic activity; and since German dishes had seldom appeared on its menus, the restaurant was spared the ignominy of rebaptizing sauerkraut "liberty cabbage" and the many similar mendacities to which the rathskellers of Broadway and Yorkville were reduced. The staff of the restaurant was openly pro-Allied, and no one cheered more lustily for the defeat of the Germans than John Klages, in the bar.

Although he had been born in Germany, "Old John," upon whom the years had conferred a celebrity of his own, considered himself a true-blue American. For nearly half a century he had waited on high and low, and when business was slack he liked nothing better than to reminisce about people and happenings of long ago. On Christmas Eve 1914 he did his best to cheer up the forlorn stragglers marooned in the cafe.

"I'm doing pretty well for an old man of seventy-one and still going strong," he told one customer with a chuckle, and then reeled off episodes that had occurred at Fourteenth Street, or at the Square. "That was before I was the father of nine children," he explained, and his fine white mutton-chops waggled impressively. Jim Fisk, "Ned" Stokes, Josie Mansfield — he had known them all; and Sam Ward, and General Grant, and Tammany's bosses, Croker and Murphy.

"It used to tickle me to see Sam Ward come in; then I knew there would be singing. A fine voice had Sam Ward. I've seen Boss Croker and the Republican boss sitting at the same table swapping jokes, as friendly as kittens. And speaking of Mr. Murphy, he hasn't been in recently. Guess it's because he meets too many people he knows here. Mr. Murphy makes me think of big tips." John followed this pleasant line of thought for a moment, then in response to a question: "No, I never waited on a full-blown President of the United States. But I've served many of them President-makers. You see, my experience with some men has been cut short, because I've stayed in the cafe, and the men who come around with ladies don't come in here, except for maybe one more drink at the bar that they don't want their wives to see. One of these days I'm going to graduate to the Fifth Avenue side." He laughed gingerly; it was his stock joke. "Me retire?" he replied to a question. "Not till they start eating salad by the roots! But I've got a little apple orchard in Jersey, and maybe some day I'll go there and drink cider."

As long as "Old John" remained, all seemed serene at "Old Del's." And though the racier crowds whom he remembered had largely gone elsewhere — stately Fifth Avenue being alien territory to bookies, jockeys, and gamblers — the restaurant still had raffish characters, who continued to impart éclat to the place.

One ripe specimen of rascality who dined at Forty-fourth Street was Colonel William d'Alton Mann, a pompous windbag and far-from-benign proprietor-editor of the city's best-read scandal sheet, *Town Topics*. Florid and white-bearded, a Santa Claus in appearance, the colonel had a skin of brass and a leering eye. He dealt in flowery innuendo and blackmail, and his rapacity was unlimited. Under threat of exposing their secret peccadilloes, amatory or financial, he successfully mulcted many of the city's great of largish sums; if they paid (and usually they did, by the thousands of dollars) he suppressed publication of their dallying and defalcations; if they resisted his unblushing demands, they were pilloried in what he lushly termed the "titivating tittle-tattle" of his paper.

The colonel required money for the luxuries of life; the necessities, like paying his starveling staff, he could forego. He was a punctual customer at Delmonico's, and not a bit abashed that he dined alone. Stalking from his office to Fifth Avenue and Forty-fourth Street, he would divest himself of his integuments ("overcoat and hat" seem too pallid to convey the splendor of the colonel's outer and inner raiment), and standing at the doorway of the restaurant would utter his vernacular greeting, "Woof, woof, woof!" At the same time he would smite his chest manfully. Then seating himself at a table, oblivious of the frost spreading outward, he would do himself proud, feasting upon "all the delicacies of the season," as the culinary prospectuses designated the rarities that trickled down Mann's capacious gullet. The waiters of Delmonico's found him far from pinch-penny, for as he never stinted himself in the way of food and drink, he never begrudged a fat tip tossed out with a lordly air.

4.

But custom and tradition alone cannot keep an institution alive. Even "Old John" at length faded from the bar, to be replaced by a bald-head, almost as venerable, named Battista Ravera Crispi, but known as "Jack." Delmonico's patrons themselves were being eroded by time and the times; dry rot was honeycombing the timbers of the house as it passed the three-quarters century mark and looked toward its centennial.

In November, 1917 the first crack in the structure became visible, when the Beaver Street property was sold to a shipping firm and the restaurant there was closed. Long "obituaries" appeared in the news columns upon the passing of that famous resort of businessmen, and a story told "in the old days" was resuscitated, about how Peter Delmonico enjoined Lorenzo, when making the property over to his nephew, never to let the business or the building pass out of family control. Lorenzo had lived up to the trust; the present representatives seemed incapable of it.

Josephine Delmonico had not healed the breach with her brother, Lorenzo, and in 1919, in an attempt to salvage something from his minority interest in the faltering concern, he and his heirs filed a petition in bankruptcy. Receivers were appointed, and application was made in the federal court to let the receivers operate the business until it could be sold, and trustees could be named to wind up the estate. This application came before Judge Julius M. Mayer, a crusty individualist and long-time patron of "Del's." In ruling upon the issue, he contributed an obiter dictum quite rare in judicial records. Judge Mayer reviewed the long history of the house of Delmonico, then went on:

"Throughout these many years of existence, now rapidly reaching a century, the effort of Delmonico's had been to adhere to some simple and comfortable traditions. The theory is that the relation of host and guest still exists. Some of the well known figures are gone, such as the white-haired John (quite typical), who, it is said, after three score years and ten of a life of urbanity towards the patrons and thrift for himself, now spends a vigorous and happy old age on his New Jersey farm."

The judge might have mentioned also Charles Ranhofer, who had died in 1898; and Eugène Garnier, who had succumbed in 1914. Little Philippe, too, had bowed his last bow and disappeared, whither no one now can say. But the tribute to the house rolled on:

"The guest still continues to have identity. He is respectfully but cheerfully greeted by name as he enters his favorite room and takes his favorite seat. While across the table he is discussing the affairs of the day, or closing a business transaction, or telling his tribulations to his lawyer, the waiter does not hover about, but approaches only when he is beckoned. In the quiet and dignified room in which, at the end of the day, busy men of the city were wont to dine with each other, one may hear one's self think as well as talk, without the din of the orchestra and with only the faint strains of music from the more pretentious rooms where those disposed to be more formal may gather.

"In the banquet halls, great and important addresses have been made at public gatherings by leaders of thought in their day and generation. Here, too, many young folks have gone forth into life with the good wishes of their friends and relatives. Within these walls the debutante has attended her first formal party, under circumstances different only as to time and dress from those which her mother and grandmother remember. Throughout all the years, the effort has been made to keep for the New Yorker and the visitor from elsewhere a place of dignity and quiet, and to resist those innovations, some of which have resulted in eliminating the individual, and depriving the patron of that individual attention for which some guests still crave.

"Those who know this history and those characteristics have been loath to see Delmonico's go. It is their loyalty which, in part, at least, has been responsible for the possibilities of a future; and the hope (in which this court will assist) is that the business may continue and go on, so that the institution may be kept alive, and not merely find its place on a page of some book reminiscent of New York."

The hope seemed likely to be realized when, later that year, Delmonico's was sold to a restaurateur named Edward L. C. Robins. Unluckily, the sale was consummated on the day the national prohibition law went into effect.

CHAPTER VII

JAZZ, GIN,
AND THE JITTERS

VETERANS OF NEW YORK HIGH LIFE who knew the establishment at Fifth Avenue and Forty-fourth Street after 1919 cannot claim to have known Delmonico's; they knew a shell, where ghosts of gentility strove to find a place under the garish lights, while diners dropped away in droves because dining *à la Delmonico* was no longer possible. Primarily this was due to prohibition, although there were other causes. The wine cellar was a thing of the past (the Waldorf-Astoria had converted its wine cellar into a gymnasium), and wine sales had always been a mainstay of the restaurant's prosperity. The quality of the cooking deteriorated, also because of the lack of wine.

Frank Case, host of the Algonquin Hotel, had abolished his bar two years before the dry law clampdown, having decided, as he said, that he did not want to be a "rum seller;" but he had not ventured to exclude wine from his kitchen or dining room. First, he did not feel he had the right to encroach upon the personal liberty of his guests, and second, he could see that there was some connection between good cooking and wine. He could appreciate this fact, though he was puzzled by it. Said he:

"The average good waiter in New York is probably not familiar with all the ancient and modern poetry that has been written about wine and all the pleasing classical traditions about it. But nevertheless, the same waiter when pouring wine seems a little more dignified, as if he were taking part in some rite, than when he is doing anything else his job calls for. Perhaps this ought not to be, but it is so."

Dishes that had delighted generations of gourmets no more were asked for. Terrapin could not be cooked properly without sherry or Madeira, and it all but vanished from restaurants. The game laws had stricken from restaurant menus the wild fowl and venison that had once been common, and in 1917 that classic of American gastronomy, the canvasback duck, was immolated upon the altar of Mars when Army Ordnance took over for a proving ground the canvasbacks' favorite feeding grounds in Chesapeake Bay, where the wild celery grew. The thunder of artillery and bursting shells routed ducks and hunters alike from the sedges over which George Washington had shot. Deprived of a ready supply of their accustomed food, the canvasbacks took to eating like other ducks and lost their distinctive flavor. This downfall of "one of the noblest institutions of the republic" was lamented wherever good feeders gathered; nowhere more keenly than by a San Francisco weekly of Delmonican tastes, *The Argonaut*, which was entitled to boast that it was "read around the world."

"It seems too, too terrible," mourned the *Argonaut's* editors. "An afflicted world must bear with such fortitude as it may a truly grievous calamity."

The effect upon Delmonico's customers was devastating. Crispi, captain of waiters in the cafe, glumly remarked that his best patrons ceased to come there: "Sometimes they come for lunch," he said, "but for dinner they stay at home." The reason was plain to see: at home they had laid down a stock of what could no more be bought or sold legally or with the least reliance upon the veracity of the label.

Delmonico's vintage wines and fine liquors had been disposed of as the evil day drew near, mainly to customers. During the last weeks before the blow fell, the public had been invited to buy; a small and discreet advertisement appearing in the newspapers announced the dispersal. Already Louis Sherry had taken the easy way out by turning over his cellar to favored customers, and shutting up shop altogether. Some time later he would reopen as a candy store, thus reverting to his start in business.

2.

Robins, the inheritor of Delmonico's, struggled to maintain old standards. Many of the staff remained to assist in this laudable attempt, but the best intentions were helpless against the fever of war times and the hysteria of the postwar years. Dining had become passé; boozing took its place. A disillusioned generation succumbed to the master illusion that it had no illusions at all, and jigged along on jazz and gin.

Now and then belated sparks of prewar lightheartedness flickered up but they were ephemeral. On the day before Christmas in 1919, the *New York Times* recounted on its front page the exploits of two "tabasco bandits" — two Spaniards who tried to rob a jewelry salesman in a room of the Hotel Knickerbocker at Times Square. They were driven off, and climbed out a window and down the wall like human flies, chased by six policemen. From time to time they paused to squirt tabasco sauce in their pursuers' faces, and while running through the restaurant on the ground floor reloaded their squirt guns from the sauce bottles on the tables. They were finally collared in the basement and soundly clouted by the weeping policemen. Ambulances carried away antagonists and protagonists — the bandits with smarting skulls, their captors with poultices on their streaming eyes.

This midnight disturbance (which had drawn throngs of spectators, although Caruso, who lived in the hotel, slept through it all) moved the *Times* to ponder, in a Christmas editorial, whether the robbers had resorted to tabasco sauce as a defensive and offensive weapon because they were Spaniards and naturally fiery, or because they had highly imaginative and original minds. The incident also raised the question: "Would it be worse to be shot with a bullet — elsewhere than in a vital spot, of course — or to have the most fiery of all pepper juices thrown in one's eyes?" There appeared to be little likelihood of settling this issue, because only persons who had suffered both fates could judge, and the *Times* ventured to suspect that that qualification was very rare.

The outlook grew grimmer as restaurant after restaurant fell foul of the prohibition laws. Famous names appeared with monotonous regularity in the lists of places raided by enforcement agents. Hotels like Claridge, Ansonia, McAlpin, Astor, and Ambassador; the Knickerbocker Grill, Shanley's, Dinty Moore's, Mouquin, Reisenweber's, Jack's, and Churchill's were invaded by remorseless "snoops." Captain John Churchill decided, "This is a good time to go out of the restaurant business," and closing his cabaret, turned to real estate. Other landmarks toppled. Along Broadway's night-life belt hotels were transformed into office buildings, and dining rooms known by name all over the nation were shuttered. Delmonico's could not hope to remain immune, and in April, 1921, the low estate to which the city's premier eating-house had been brought was proclaimed in a headline which blazoned: "DRY AGENTS SEIZE 2 AT DELMONICO'S."

To all who could recall the glory that once emanated from "Del's," the story of the raid read like profanation. Two prohibition agents named Carroll and Taylor had gone to the second floor at Forty-fourth Street and Fifth Avenue, where a "tea dansant" was in progress. Accompanied by another man and "a fashionably dressed woman," they had waited in line almost an hour to get a table. When finally seated and the waiter asked their order, Carroll had replied, "We'll have a round of Scotch and gin."

(At this point oldtimers teetered on the verge of apoplexy. "A round of Scotch and gin" at Delmonico's! Where connoisseurs had pored through the many-paged wine list, lovingly selecting precisely the right bottle!)

According to the agents, the "round" was brought and the waiter collected $1.75 for each drink, plus $1 "couvert" charge

— another foundling left in the wake of war. Agent Taylor then ordered a second round, which was allegedly served in the same manner. Whereupon the raiders revealed their identity and arrested the waiter and floor manager. Taylor, who had been furnished with a diagram of the room, "walked behind an expensive Japanese screen which concealed a carved mahogany sideboard [to quote the *New York Times*]. The polished top of the sideboard was covered with expensive glassware, bearing the monogram of the Delmonico family. Further investigation, said Carroll, revealed a secret compartment in the sideboard, in which, under several crumpled linen napkins, he found a bottle of gin and a bottle of Scotch whisky."

(The awed — or class-conscious — rewrite man at the *Times* appeared to lean somewhat obtrusively upon the upper-class adjectives in "*expensive* screen," "*carved* mahogany," "*polished* sideboard," "*secret* compartment," "*linen* napkins." But when *Delmonico's* was being brought down to the level of a cellar speakeasy, the enormity may have been unnerving.)

It was "mene, mene, tekel, upharsin" scrawled upon the restaurant's wall, and ten months later a second raid repeated the ill-omened prophecy. For another year Robins kept up the struggle. Then he was sued for nonpayment of rent, and judgment for $18,750 was obtained against him. He countercharged that he had been prevented from remodeling the ground floor of the building into shops, that could be rented profitably, but lost his appeal. In rapid succession a second and a third judgment were entered, for arrears of rent, taxes, and incidental expenses totaling more than $180,000. Thereupon Robins threw in the sponge and announced that on May 21, 1923, Delmonico's would close its doors.

3.

The farewell evening proved to be no festive occasion. A number of old patrons who had received personal invitations showed up in the dining room, where at one table Josephine

Delmonico was entertaining friends. The atmosphere was in
no way comparable to that which had prevailed on the night
in 1899 when Delmonico's at Madison Square had served its
last dinner. This time there was no refuge elsewhere. And nobody seemed much to care. There was no "one last glass," no
pushing of tables together, no greetings called across the room;
and at the end no old New Yorker stumping out, sick at heart.
Mineral water was a poor enlivener. Many of the diners were
going on to the theater or night clubs, and left early; and when,
at nine o'clock, the doors were shut and the orchestra struck
up "Auld Lang Syne," there were only about thirty persons in
the dining room. They clapped a little, but that was all.

The bald, polite Crispi, as he bowed reporters out, said that
he personally was "well fixed" after thirty-nine years with
"Del's," and he was going to take a vacation. John McCue, the
doorman, felt that he, too, could afford to take a rest; in fourteen years of opening carriage and automobile doors, he had
saved $15,000 from tips, and by investments had increased this
to $35,000. Employees who could not retire had been found
other jobs by the Society of Restaurateurs. Only the restaurant was unprovided for: the building was to be torn down to
make way for a thirty-story office skyscraper.

At eleven o'clock the last guest departed. George McLean,
the watchman, switched off the lights and locked the doors.
Four years less than one century after the first Delmonico door
was opened in New York, the institution died.

4.

Of course, there was widespread and rather pointless discussion of the reasons for Delmonico's demise, but the *Times* laid
its finger upon the main reason: New York simply had outgrown
Delmonico's. Prohibition, the deterioration of dining habits,
upward spiraling costs, a hurried, oblivious generation, the
breakup of social distinctions, the disintegration of society as
it had once flourished — all these, aggravated by internal decay,

had contributed to the ending. But principally, the enormous expansion of the city and changing customs had outmoded Delmonico's. There was random talk of reopening, but the time had gone by when that could be done: Delmonico's had disappeared, and that was the end of it, and the *Times*, like all contemporary commentators, could only do its memory the justice to state that "to the end, Delmonico's maintained its high culinary standards unchanged." At least by intention.

The fittings and furnishings, from cellar to garret, were sold at auction. Three days were required to run through the long list. Private buyers were few. The blue-and-gold English dinner service, bearing the three-feathers crest of the Prince of Wales, which had been used at the New York reception to the future Edward VII, catered by Delmonico in 1860, went to a collector for $600. Robert Treat, of Newark, bought the stemware remaining from that occasion for $100. A rug dealer paid $320 for a large Agra carpet. The baby grand piano from the ballroom brought $400, the ballroom's crystal chandelier, $125. The last item sold was the Delmonico motor truck, parked at the entrance; it went for $350. The total receipts came to a disappointing $49,600. Then the wreckers moved in.

There was a memorial salute, two years after the orchestra had played "Auld Lang Syne" — a reunion in the ruins, on August 19, 1925 — Delmonico's centennial year, counting from John Delmonico's first little wine shop. All that remained of the building was the walls of what had been the main dining room; these had been roughly covered with American flags. Some fifty persons sat down to luncheon while a few feet away bricks and mortar hurtled down the loading chutes to waiting trucks. "Oscar" of the Waldorf was there, and "Big Bill" Edwards, who had been a member of Mayor Gaynor's cabinet. The three sons of Lorenzo Crist Delmonico — Charles C. Delmonico II, Lorenzo C. Delmonico II, and Gardiner C. Delmonico — were guests, although none of them had been connected with the restaurant. The menu and service were in the Delmonico tradition, for the caterers — a Brooklyn firm — had been trained at the old "Del's" on Madison Square. The table decorations were flowers made of crystallized sugar; the fruit was served in dishes of ice with ferns frozen in them; the soup and chicken and ice cream and coffee were up to Ranhofer standards. Amid the dust and rubble, all ate heartily; but it was not a celebration, it was a wake.

At the end, Arthur Nies, who had started as a boy in the Delmonico's on lower Broadway, read some verses he had written. They exuded an epitaph flavor:

> No more the grape with fire divine
>   Shall light the torch of pleasure gay,
> And where the gourmand paused to dine,
>   Hot dog and fudge shops have their day.

Still, was not that less bitter than the fate which awaited Diana the Huntress? Deposed from her tower when Madison Square Garden was torn down in 1925 — banished to Brooklyn, and for two decades buried in a warehouse, shrouded in burlap — rejected and forgotten by her own Manhattan — to be at last brought to light and granted a sanctuary — *in Philadelphia!*

Though Delmonico's disappeared, its name and spirit survived. In New York today two establishments endeavor to uphold the tradition — the Delmonico Hotel, uptown on Park Avenue, and Delmonico's Restaurant, downtown, in the building at Beaver and South William Streets. Neither of these has any connection with the Delmonico family or the original business. The hotel was erected in 1929, well after the last real Delmonico's had vanished, while the restaurant, formerly known as "Oscar's Delmonico's," has as its only link with the founders of the historic institution the Pompeiian pillars in its portico, that were brought from Italy by John and Peter more than a century ago.

There is also a Delmonico's restaurant of luxury standards

on the Avenue de l'Opéra in Paris, but it, too, merely perpetuates the name and has no kinship with the original.

Delmonico descendants attempted to prevent the unauthorized use of the family name commercially; but the court decided that once the Delmonicos themselves abandoned the use of their name in business, it might be employed by others. "Delmonico," the court ruled in effect, had become so synonymous with excellence in food and service that for practical purposes it had passed into general currency and had been absorbed into the language.

A proper name can attain no higher apotheosis than to be transmuted by popular usage into a common noun.

KITCHEN NOTES

A DINER USUALLY is best served if the apparatus employed in preparing the meal is kept out of sight, in its proper place, the kitchen. For that reason no saucepan battery of footnotes and source references has been allowed to clutter this historical repast.

However, for cooks, amateur and professional, and for the recipe-minded, there is always interest in the ingredients of a dish — their provenance, selection, proportions, and treatment — and for any who may be curious under this heading the following details are provided.

The perceptive diner-reader will have realized long before now that this book is more a potpie than a *pièce montée*, and in its preparation a number of cooks have had a hand; let us hope that the multiplicity for once has disproved the adage and not spoiled the broth. Be that as it may, the responsibility for final success or failure is solely the chef's; he signs the menu.

The principal source of information about Delmonico's throughout its career is the newspaper press. Delmonico doings were of constant interest to New Yorkers, and in the daily newspapers they were reported in a lively and contemporaneous manner which formal literature could not achieve: the trivial mingled with the important in chatty news columns.

Another invaluable source exists in the memoirs left by contemporaries who frequented the restaurants. Wherever possible, preference has been given to one of these contemporaneous accounts, as against a retrospective view; the feeling of a period is usually best conveyed by those who took part in its activities and shared its tastes. Gratitude is therefore owing to the men and women, some of them anonymous, who took the pains to write about the Delmonico's they knew, and thus preserved a record that has survived the institution itself. But for these on-the-spot testimonials, we should grope in a fog of dates and ledger entries, uncertain of our subject, of our direction, and of our impressions. With their help we can to some extent savor again what was savored with such relish by the vanished generations of another age.

In this connection, the finding of the Delmonico restaurant menu of 1838, which is reproduced on the opening pages of this book, supplied information that has not been available heretofore. Search for such a menu card had been carried on for several years, without success. Libraries, museums, and private collections had been ransacked; dealers in rare manuscripts had been consulted, to no avail; every approach had drawn a blank.

What was sought was a specimen of the menu an ordinary customer dropping into the restaurant would have picked up, dating from the earlier years. After all, Delmonico's had made its reputation upon the fare served day by day, not on the exceptional occasions, like banquets or specially ordered private dinners, when exceptional efforts would have been made. Banquet menus were found, preserved as souvenirs of outstanding events, but these could not be considered typical of the restaurant's regular bill of fare. This left a gap in the documentation of the story, and hope of remedying the defect had about been given up.

Then, unexpectedly, in the Print Room of the New-York Historical Society, a menu card of the sort so long hunted was discovered. Unfortunately, this was incomplete in several particulars: the cover was missing, there was no date on it, and there were no prices indicated. From internal factors it could be dated around 1840, and there was no doubt that it represented the run-of-the-mill fare offered to Delmonico customers at an early stage in the restaurant's development. The discovery, incomplete though it was, opened the door to many conjectures.

Then the unpredictable coincidence, which makes real life so much less logical than fiction, occurred: a complete specimen of the same menu card was turned up in the Museum of the City of New York, across Central Park from the Historical Society. This at a glance was seen to be a major contribution to the documenting of American social history; a whole chapter of authoritative conclusions could now safely be drawn, and the Delmonico story itself took on a larger dimension. The Museum's specimen proved, beyond question, that all that Delmonico's devotees had claimed for the restaurant was impressively true; and the luster of the institution was increased and confirmed.

The Print Rooms of both the Museum and the Historical Society are therefore to be congratulated upon their persistence, and both the readers and the author of this book are under an obligation to them which can be acknowledged, though hardly repaid.

It may be noted that protracted search for business records kept by the Delmonicos proved futile. Theirs was not a literary family, and the preservation of either family or business records for any length of time probably would have seemed to them useless and even undesirable. Whatever documents relating to the internal operations of the restaurants might have survived apparently were destroyed inadvertently several years ago, although this is not certain. In any event, primary sources of information regarding the restaurants' business affairs, which might prove of historical value, seem to have disappeared permanently.

Fortunately an exact record of the cooking at Delmonico's in its prime does exist in Charles Ranhofer's monumental book, *The Epicurean*. Recipes, menus, methods of preparation, and details down to the composition of the coffee that Delmonico's served (coffee from three regions, each kind roasted differently, and blended in correct proportions) — all this is packed into its eleven hundred pages; and from this treasury, which is still a classic among professional cooks, Delmonican cooking could be recreated, were we able to resurrect the gourmets who could cope with its amplitude.

Among personal well-wishers of this project who have contributed generously to the research should be named, first of all, two great-great-granddaughters of Peter Delmonico — Mrs. Edward Kirchner, of Stamford, Connecticut, and Mrs. Henry A. Campbell, of Princeton, New Jersey. These two charming representatives of a famous line opened for study family papers, the family Bible with its vital statistics, John Delmonico's fragmentary receipt book of the 1830's, and other memorabilia down to the silver coffin plates of Delmonicos interred at old St. Patrick's. They also recounted family traditions of the sort which sometimes throw a revealing light upon events otherwise impenetrable.

Genealogical researches into the Del-Monico family in Switzerland were carried out with the assistance of the Ticino cantonal authorities in Bellinzona and the Mairengo district.

A special obligation is owed to the management of the then still extant and now unhappily defunct *New York World-Telegram and Sun*, and to Miss Lillian Primack, its librarian, for having made available the sole existing copy of the *Index* of the *New York Herald*. During much of the Nineteenth Century the *New York Herald* was New York's best written and on the whole best informed newspaper, particularly lively and authoritative in regard to social life and sports. Miss Primack's efficient and cheerful assistance, together with that of her staff, rendered easier weeks of tedious research, and brought to light not a few nuggets that had lain forgotten in the files for fifty years.

The staffs of the New York Public Library, The New York Genealogical Society, and the Henry E. Huntingdon Library, at San Marino, California, have been uniformly helpful.

Once more the generosity of the Aldrich family, at "Rokeby" on the Hudson, should be recorded, in providing access to Sam Ward's manuscript notes for his intended (but never written) history of Delmonico's. These provided unique glimpses of the early days of the restaurant especially.

Mrs. Lawrence Grant White is thanked again for making available the unpublished proof of Sam Ward's *Memoirs*, left uncompleted at his death in 1884. These reminiscences contain numerous allusions to Delmonico's.

For her counsel and sustaining interest, a wealth of appreciation is due to M. F. K. Fisher, distinguished and ever-enjoyable writer on gastronomy. Were this book by her, it would have a more expert touch.

The readers are also under obligation to another writer of wit and charm, Andy Logan, for bringing to light several delightful details.

Leonard Louis Levinson — himself versed in the history of Delmonico's and equipped by temperament and practice to enter into its spirit — was helpful beyond the limits of mere friendly interest. The use made of his numerous suggestions is the best expression of the author's gratitude.

Not least among those who have lent their good taste, broad experience and keen insight to the project is Craig Wylie, long-suffering critic of the work in its first form. As everyone knows, authors are the bane of editors, and certainly vice versa; but in this instance the difficult modulations were carried through without producing discords, and the book gained thereby.

Finally, to the constant support of Robert Lescher the book owes much of whatever merit it can claim. Appeals to his educated judgment of words, foods, and wines in more than one moment of indecision have saved the dish from burning and the kettle from boiling dry.

BIBLIOGRAPHY

To mention the publications in which Delmonico's appears by name would double or triple the following generalized reading list. Only those publications and sources that have been actually consulted, and from which at least one fact, or figure, has been knowingly gleaned, are set down. Many of the books, in particular, are background sources, giving less data on Delmonico's itself than on the atmosphere and feeling of the decades that Delmonico's spanned.

NEWSPAPERS

New York Times
New York Herald
New York World
New York Evening World
New York Evening Post
New York Tribune
New York Weekly Journal
Recorder (New York)
New York Courier
Town Topics (New York)
Philadelphia Public Ledger

Philadelphia Evening Times
Boston Transcript
Hartford Courant
The Times (London)
The Standard (London)
St. James Gazette
Westminster Gazette
Pall Mall Gazette
Chronicle (London)
Field (London)
Glasgow Herald

PERIODICALS

Albion
Harper's

Contemporary Review
Galaxy

Harper's Weekly   *Putnam's*
Leslie's Illustrated   *Spirit of the Times*
  Weekly Newspaper   *Scribner's*
Scientific American   *Century*
New Yorker   *Argonaut*
American Heritage   *Police Gazette*
    Saturday Review of Literature

MANUSCRIPT SOURCES

Unpublished "Memoirs" by Samuel Ward.
Unpublished Notes for a History of Delmonico's by Samuel
    Ward.
S. L. M. Barlow Papers, Henry E. Huntingdon Library.

BOOKS AND ARTICLES

ALLEN, FREDERICK LEWIS, *The Great Pierpont Morgan.*
    New York: Harper, 1949.
American Heritage Cookbook and Illustrated History of Ameri-
    can Eating and Drinking. New York: American Heritage
    Publishing Company, 1964.
AMORY, CLEVELAND, *The Last Resorts.* New York:
    Harper, 1948.
————, *Who Killed Society?* New York: Harper, 1960.
AMORY, CLEVELAND and FREDERIC BRADLEE, *Van-*
    ity Fair. New York: The Viking Press, 1960.
ARESTY, ESTHER B., *The Delectable Past.* New York:
    Simon & Schuster, 1964.
ARMSTRONG, HAMILTON FISH, *Those Days.* New
    York: Harper & Row, 1963.
ARMSTRONG, HAMILTON FISH, edit., *The Poetry of*
    New York. New York: Putnam, 1917.
ASBURY, HERBERT, *The Gangs of New York.* New York:
    Knopf, 1927.
————, *Sucker's Progress.* New York: Dodd Mead, 1938.

BALES, WILLIAM ALAN, *Tiger in the Streets*. New York: Dodd Mead, 1962.

BARRETT, WALTER, *The Old Merchants of New York*. 5 vols. New York: Knox, 1885.

BAYLES, W. HARRISON, *Old Taverns of New York*. New York: Frank Allagen Genealogical Company, 1915.

BEATON, CECIL, *Cecil Beaton's New York*. London: Blatchford, 1938.

BEER, THOMAS, *The Mauve Decade*. New York: Knopf, 1926.

BERGER, MAX, *The British Traveller in America 1836-1860*. New York: Columbia University Press, 1943.

BELMONT, PERRY, *An American Democrat*. New York: Columbia University Press, 1940.

BERSTL, JULIUS, *Kean*. New York: Orion Press, 1962.

BLAY, JOHN S., *After the Civil War*. New York: Crowell, 1960.

BOWEN, CROSWELL, *The Elegant Oakey*. New York: Oxford University Press, 1956.

BRILLAT-SAVARIN, JEAN ANTHELME, *The Physiology of Taste*, translated with notes by M. F. K. Fisher. New York: The Heritage Press, 1949.

BROOKS, WALTER R., New York, *An Intimate Guide*. New York: Knopf, 1931.

BROUN, HEYWOOD and MARGARET LEECH, *Anthony Comstock, Roundsman of the Lord*. New York: Albert and Charles Boni, 1927.

BROWN, HENRY COLLINS, *The Book of New York*. Privately printed, New York, 1922.

———, *Brownstone Fronts and Saratoga Trunks*. New York: Dutton, 1935.

———, *Delmonico's — A Story of Old New York*. New York: Valentine's Manual, Inc., 1928.

———, *Fifth Avenue Old and New*. New York: The Fifth Avenue Association, 1924.

BROWN, HENRY COLLINS, *From Alley Pond to Rocke-feller Center*. New York: Dutton, 1936.

——, edit., *Valentine's Manual of Old New York, Second Series*. Hastings-on-Hudson: Valentine's Manual, Inc., 1916-1928.

BROWN, JUNIUS HENRI, *The Great Metropolis: The Mirror of New York*. New York, 1869.

BURFORD, ROBERT, *A Description of the City of New York*. London, 1834.

BUTTERFIELD, ROGER, *The American Past*. New York: Simon & Schuster, 1947.

CARLSON, OLIVER, *The Man Who Made News — James Gordon Bennett*. New York: Duell Sloan & Pearce, 1942.

CARSON, GERALD, *The Social History of Bourbon*. New York: Dodd Mead, 1963.

CASE, FRANK, *Tales of a Wayward Inn*. New York: Stokes, 1938.

The Century, 1847-1946. New York: The Century Association, 1947.

CHAFETZ, HENRY, *Play the Devil*. New York: Potter, 1960.

CHANLER, JULIE, *From Gaslight to Dawn*. Privately printed, New York, 1956.

CHAPELL, GEORGE S., *Restaurants of New York*. New York, 1925.

CHURCHILL, ALLEN, *Park Row*. New York: Rinehart, 1958.

CLEWS, HENRY, *Fifty Years in Wall Street*. New York, 1908.

COLLINS, FREDERICK L., *Money Town*. New York: Putnam, 1946.

COMBE, GEORGE, *Notes on the United States of America*. Edinburgh: Maclachlan, Stewart & Company, 1841.

CRAM, ALLAN G., *Fifth Avenue*. New York: Dodd Mead, 1918.

CRAWFORD, F. MARION, *Katherine Lauderdale*. New York: Macmillan, 1894.

———, *The Ralstons*. New York: Macmillan, 1893.

CROCKETT, ALBERT STEVENS, *Peacocks on Parade*. New York: Sears Publishing Company, 1931.

CROLY, MRS. J. C. (JENNIE JUNE), *The History of the Women's Club Movement in America*. New York: Henry G. Allen Company, 1898.

———, *Sorosis: Its Origin and History*. New York: Little, 1896.

CROWNINSHIELD, FRANK, *The Unofficial Palace of New York — A Tribute to the Waldorf-Astoria*. Privately printed, New York, 1939.

DALY, MARIA LYDIG, *Diary of a Union Lady*, edited by Earl Hammond. New York: Funk & Wagnalls, 1962.

DANA, NATALIE, *Young in New York*. New York: Doubleday, 1963.

DAVIS, ELMER, *History of the New York Times 1851-1921*. New York: New York Times, 1921.

DAVIS, RICHARD HARDING, *Adventures and Letters of Richard Harding Davis*. Edited by Charles Belmont Davis, New York: Scribner's, 1918.

DENNETT, TYLER, *John Hay: From Poetry to Politics*. New York: Dodd Mead, 1934.

DERBY, J. C., *Fifty Years Among Authors, Artists and Publishers*. New York: Carlton, 1884.

DE VOE, THOMAS F., *The Market Book — Historical Account of the Public Markets in the Cities of New York, Boston, Philadelphia and Brooklyn*. Privately printed, New York, 1862.

DICKENS, CHARLES, *American Notes*. New York: Dutton, 1934.

———, *The Life and Adventures of Martin Chuzzlewit*. New York: Macmillan, 1899.

DUNNE, PETER FINLEY, *Mr. Dooley in the Hearts of His*

Countrymen. Boston: Small, Maynard & Company, 1899.

DUNRAVEN, EARL of, *Past Times and Pastimes.* 2 vols. London: Hodder and Stoughton, 1922.

ELLIOTT, MAUD HOWE, *Uncle Sam Ward and His Circle.* New York: Macmillan, 1938.

ELLIS, EDWARD ROBB, *The Epic of New York City.* New York: Coward-McCann, 1966.

EVANS, MERYL R., "Knickerbocker Hotels and Restaurants 1800-1850." *New-York Historical Society Quarterly*, October, 1952.

FAY, THEODORE, *Views in New York.* New York: Peabody & Company, 1831.

FELHEIM, MARVIN, *The Theater of Augustin Daly.* Cambridge: Harvard University Press, 1956.

FILIPPINI, ALESSANDRO, *The Table.* New York: Webster, 1889.

FINLEY, RUTH E., *The Lady of Godey's.* Philadelphia: Lippincott, 1938.

FISHER, M. F. K., *The Art of Eating.* New York: World, 1954.

———, *Here Let Us Feast, A Book of Banquets.* New York: Viking Press, 1946.

FISKE, STEPHEN, *Off-Hand Portraits of Prominent New Yorkers.* New York: Lockwood, 1884.

FLOWER, MILTON E., *James Parton, The Father of Modern Biography.* Durham: Duke University Press, 1951.

FORNEY, J. W., *Anecdotes of Public Men.* New York: Harper, 1873.

FORSTER, JOHN, *The Life of Charles Dickens.* 2 vols. Philadelphia: Lippincott, 1873-74.

FOSTER, GEORGE C., *Celio: Or New York Above-Ground and Under-Ground.* New York: Robert M. De Witt, 1850.

———, *New York in Slices.* New York: Dick & Fitzgerald, 1848.

FOWLER, GENE, *Skyline.* New York: Viking Press, 1961.

FRANCIS, JOHN W., *Old New York*. New York: Middleton, 1866.

FREWEN, MORETON, *Melton Mowbray and Other Memories*. London: Jenkins, 1924.

FULLER, ROBERT H., *Jubilee Jim, the Life of Colonel James Fisk, Jr.* New York: Macmillan, 1928.

FURNAS, J. C., *The Life and Times of the Late Demon Rum*. New York: Putnam, 1965.

GARDINER, ALEXANDER, *Canfield, the True Story of the Greatest Gambler*. New York: Doubleday Doran, 1930.

GAYNOR, WILLIAM J., *Mayor Gaynor's Letters and Speeches*. New York: Greaves Publishing Company, 1913.

GERARD, JAMES W., *My First Eighty-three Years in America*. New York: Doubleday, 1951.

GOLDBERG, ISAAC, *Tin Pan Alley*. New York: F. Ungar Publishing Company, 1961.

GOUVERNEUR, MARIAN (Mrs. M. C.), *As I Remember*. New York: Appleton, 1911.

GOWER, LORD RONALD, *My Reminiscences*. 2 vols. London: Kegan, Paul & Trench, 1883.

GRAND, PASCAL, "A Chef and His Development." *Munsey's Magazine*, February, 1902.

GRATTAN, THOMAS, *Civilized America*. London: Bradbury & Evans, 1859.

GRAVES, CHARLES, *Leather Armchairs*. London: Cassell, 1963.

GRISCOM, LLOYD C., *Diplomatically Speaking*. New York: Literary Guild, 1940.

HARRIS, CHARLES T., *Memories of Manhattan of the Sixties and Seventies*. New York: Derrydale Press, 1928.

HARRISON, MRS. BURTON, "The Myth of the 400." *Cosmopolitan Magazine*, July, 1895.

———, *Recollections Grave and Gay*. New York: Scribner, 1911.

HASWELL, CHARLES, *Reminiscences of an Octogenarian of the City of New York (1816-1860)*. New York: Harper, 1896.

HEMSTREET, CHARLES, *Nooks and Corners of Old New York*. New York: Scribner, 1899.

————, *When Old New York Was Young*. New York: Scribner, 1902.

HENDERSON, HELEN W., *A Loiterer in New York*. New York: Doran, 1917.

HERBODEAU, EUGÈNE and PAUL THALAMAS, *Georges Auguste Escoffier*. London: Practical Press, Ltd., 1955.

HEWITT, EDWARD R., *Those Were the Days*. New York: Duell, Sloan & Pearce, 1943.

HILL, THOMAS E., *Hill's Manual of Social and Business Forms: A Guide to Correct Writing*. Chicago: Hill's Standard Book Company, 1883.

A History of the St. George's Society of New York from 1770 to 1913. New York: St. George's Society, 1913.

HOLBROOK, STEWART H., *The Golden Age of Quackery*. New York: Macmillan, 1959.

HOLT, HENRY, *Garrulities of an Octogenarian*. Boston: Houghton Mifflin, 1923.

HUBBARD, N. I., *Autobiography, With Personal Reminiscences of New York City, 1798 to 1875*. New York: Trow & Sons, 1875.

HUGHES, RUPERT, *The Real New York*. New York: Smart Set Publishing Company, 1904.

HUNGERFORD, EDWARD, *The Story of Louis Sherry*. New York: William Edwin Rudge, 1929.

————, *The Story of the Waldorf-Astoria*. New York: Putnam, 1925.

HUNT, GAILLARD, *Life in America One Hundred Years Ago*. New York: Harper, 1914.

IRWIN, WILL, with EARL CHAPIN MAY and JOSEPH

HOTCHKISS, *A History of the Union League Club of New York City*. New York: Dodd Mead, 1952.

JEFFERSON, JOSEPH, *"Rip Van Winkle," An Autobiography*. New York: Appleton-Century-Crofts, 1949.

KAHN, E. J., Jr., *The Merry Partners — The Age and Stage of Harrigan and Hart*. New York: Random House, 1955.

KERFOOT, J. B., *Broadway*. Boston: Houghton Mifflin, 1911.

KEYES, ERASMUS DARWIN, *Fifty Years Observation of Men and Events*. New York: Scribner, 1884.

King's Handbook of New York City. Boston: Moses King, 1893.

King's Photographic Views of New York. Boston: Moses King, n.d.

KOFOED, JACK, *Brandy for Heroes, A Biography of the Honorable John Morrissey*. New York: Dutton, 1938.

KOUWENHOVEN, JOHN A., *Adventures of America 1857-1900*. New York: Harper, 1938.

——, *The Columbia Historical Portrait of New York*. New York: Doubleday, 1953.

KRAUS, RENÉ, *Young Lady Randolph*. New York: Putnam, 1943.

LABANDE, LÉON-HONORÉ, *Histoire de la Principauté de Monaco*. Monaco: Archives du Palais, 1934.

LAMB, MRS. MARTHA J. and MRS. BURTON HARRISON, *History of the City of New York*. 3 vols. New York: Barnes, 1877-1896.

LANGTRY, LILY, *The Days I Knew*. New York: Doran, 1925.

LANIER, HENRY, *A Century of Banking in New York*. New York: Doran, 1926.

LENT, HENRY B., *The Waldorf-Astoria*. Privately printed, New York, 1934.

LESLIE, ANITA, *The Remarkable Mr. Jerome*. New York: Holt, 1954.

LESLIE, SEYMOUR, *The Jerome Connection*. London: Murray, 1964.

LESLIE, SHANE, *Studies in Sublime Failure*. London: Ernest Benn, 1932.

LEVINSON, LEONARD LOUIS, "Cosmopolitan Tastes," *The American Heritage Cookbook*. New York: American Heritage Publishing Company, 1964.

———, "Delmonico's," *The American Heritage Cookbook*. New York: American Heritage Publishing Company, 1964.

———, *Wall Street: A Pictorial History*. New York: Ziff-Davis, 1961.

LEWIS, LLOYD and HENRY JUSTIN SMITH, *Oscar Wilde Discovers America*. New York: Harcourt Brace, 1936.

LOGAN, ANDY, *The Man Who Robbed the Robber Barons*. New York: Norton, 1965.

———, "The Palace of Delight." *The New Yorker*, February 27, 1965.

LOOMIS, ALFRED F., "Ah, Your Majesty, There is No Second." *American Heritage*, August, 1958.

LYNCH, DENNIS TILDEN, *"Boss" Tweed*. New York: Boni & Liveright, 1927.

———, *The Wild Seventies*. New York: Appleton-Century, 1941.

McALLISTER, WARD, *Society As I Have Found It*. New York: Cassell, 1890.

McCABE, JAMES D., Jr., *Great Fortunes and How They Were Made*. Cincinnati and Chicago: Hannaford, 1971.

McCARTHY, JAMES REMINGTON, *Peacock Alley*. New York: Harper, 1931.

McCLELLAN, GEORGE B., Jr., *The Gentleman and the Tiger, Autobiography*. Edited by Harold C. Syrett. Philadelphia: Lippincott, 1956.

MAISEL, ALBERT Q., "The Swiss Among Us." *Readers Digest*, June, 1956.

MANDELBAUM, SEYMOUR J., *Boss Tweed's New York*. New York: Wiley, 1965.

"Manna-hatin", The Story of New York. New York: The Manhattan Company, 1929.

MARIO, THOMAS, *The Face in the Aspic*. New York: Simon & Schuster, 1944.

MARRYAT, FREDERICK, *A Diary in America*. London: Longman, Orme, Green, Brown & Longmans, 1839.

MARTIN, EDWARD SANDFORD, *The Life of Joseph Hodges Choate*. New York: Scribner, 1920.

MATTHEWS, BRANDER and LAURENCE HUTTON, *The Life and Art of Edwin Booth and His Contemporaries*. Boston: L. C. Page, 1886.

MAYER, GRACE M., *Once Upon a City*. New York: Macmillan, 1958.

MAURICE, ARTHUR BARTLETT, *New York in Fiction*. New York: Dodd Mead, 1899-1901.

MEEHAN, REV. THOMAS F., S.J., "Long Links to Italy." *America*, August 28, 1937.

MINNEGERODE, MEADE, *The Fabulous Forties: 1840-1850*. New York: Putnam, 1924.

MITCHELL, EDWIN VALENTINE, *The Horse and Buggy Age in New England*. New York: Coward-McCann, 1937.

MOODY, RICHARD, *Edwin Forrest*. New York: Knopf, 1960.

MORRIS, LLOYD L., *Incredible New York*. New York: Random House, 1951.

NEVINS, ALLAN, *American Social History as Recorded by British Travellers*. New York: Holt, 1928.

————, *History of the Bank of New York & Trust Company*. Privately printed, 1934.

New York City Directories, 1825-1925.

New York City Guide. Federal Writers Project. New York: Random House, 1939.

NICHOLS, THOMAS, *Forty Years of American Life.* New York: Stackpole, 1937.

NOEL, MARY, *Villains Galore, The Heyday of the Popular Story Weekly.* New York: Macmillan, 1954.

NOYES, ALEXANDER D., *Forty Years of American Finance.* New York: Putnam, 1941.

O'CONNOR, RICHARD, *Courtroom Warrior — The Combative Career of William Travers Jerome.* Boston: Little, Brown, 1963.

——, *Gould's Millions.* New York: Doubleday, 1962.

PELLETREAU, WILLIAM S., *The Beaver Street Plot — A Reminiscence of Old New York.* (Unpublished ms.) n.d.

PERIERA, JONATHAN, *A Treatise on Food and Drink.* New York: Fowler & Wells, 1843.

PLAYFAIR, GILES, *Kean.* London: Reinhardt & Evans, 1950.

PLEASANTS, SAMUEL AUGUSTUS, *Fernando Wood of New York.* New York: Columbia University Press, 1948.

POPE-HENNESSEY, JAMES, *Monckton Milnes.* 2 vols. New York: Farrar, Straus & Cudahy, 1955.

POST, MARIE CAROLINE, *The Life and Memoirs of Comte Régis de Trobriand.* New York: Dutton, 1910.

"Procuration for Guardianship of the Three Christ Children." (ms.) Paris, July, 1870.

Prominent Americans of Swiss Origin. A Compilation by the Swiss-American Historical Society. New York: James T. White & Company, 1932.

PRYOR, MRS. ROGER A., *Reminiscences of Peace and War.* New York: Macmillan, 1924.

RACOWITZA, PRINCESS HELENE von, *An Autobiography.* New York: Macmillan, 1924.

RANHOFER, CHARLES, "Delmonico's Seen From the Kitchen." *Metropolitan Magazine*, December, 1894.

——, *The Epicurean.* New York: R. Ranhofer, 1893.

RANNEY, DAVE, *Thirty Years on the Bowery*. New York: American Tract Society, 1910.

RAY, GORDON N., edit., *Letters and Private Papers of William Makepeace Thackeray*. Cambridge: Harvard University Press, 1945-1946.

———, *Thackeray: The Age of Wisdom*. New York: McGraw-Hill, 1958.

RECTOR, GEORGE, *The Girl from Rector's*. New York: Doubleday, Page, 1927.

REID, T. WEMYSS, *The Life, Letters and Friendships of Richard Monckton Milnes, First Lord Houghton*. London: Cassell, 1890.

Report to the New York Board of Aldermen on Alternative Proposals for Laying Out a Large City Park, Either Central, or on the East Side. New York, January 2, 1852.

RIDER, FREMONT, *Rider's New York City*. New York: Macmillan, 1924.

RIMMER, LEOPOLD, *History of Old New York and the House of Delmonico's*. Privately Printed, New York, 1898.

RIORDON, WILLIAM L., *Plunkitt of Tammany Hall*. New York: Knopf, 1948.

ROSS, ISHBEL, *Crusades and Crinolines*. New York: Harper, 1963.

———, *Silhouette in Diamonds, the Life of Mrs. Potter Palmer*. New York: Harper, 1960.

ROTHSCHILD, SALOMON de, *A Casual View of America — The Home Letters of Salomon de Rothschild*. Translated and edited by Sigmund Diamond. Stanford: Stanford University Press, 1961.

ROVERE, RICHARD H., *The Magnificent Shysters*. New York: Grosset & Dunlap, 1947.

RUGGLES, ELEANOR, *Prince of Players*. New York: Norton, 1953.

SACHS, EMANIE, *"The Terrible Siren," Victoria Woodhull*. New York: Harper, 1928.

SALA, GEORGE AUGUSTUS, *America Revisited*. London: Vizetelly, 1882.

——, *The Life and Adventures of George Augustus Sala*. 2 vols. New York: Scribner, 1895.

——, *My Diary in America in the Midst of War*. London: Tinsley, 1865.

SALTUS, EDGAR, *Vanity Square*. Philadelphia: Lippincott, 1906.

SCHLIEMANN, HEINRICH, *First Visit to America*. Cambridge: Harvard University Press, 1942.

SCHRIFTGIESSER, KARL, *Oscar of the Waldorf*. New York: Dutton, 1943.

SCHURZ, CARL, *Reminiscences*. 3 vols. New York: Scribner, 1906-1908.

SEITZ, DON C., *The Dreadful Decade*. Indianapolis: Bobbs-Merrill, 1926.

——, *The James Gordon Bennetts*. Indianapolis: Bobbs-Merrill, 1928.

SHACKELTON, ROBERT, *The Book of New York*. Philadelphia: Penn Publishing Company, 1920.

SHAPLEN, ROBERT, "Delmonico." *The New Yorker*, November 10 and 17, 1956.

——, *Free Love and Heavenly Sinners*. New York: Knopf, 1954.

SHERMAN, W. T., *Memoirs*. New York: Webster, 1891.

SICHEL, PIERRE, *The Jersey Lily*. New York: Prentice-Hall, 1958.

SIMPSON, WILLIAM R., and FLORENCE K. SIMPSON, with CHARLES SAMUELS, *Hockshop*. New York: Random House, 1954.

Sketches of Men of Progress. New York and Hartford Publishing Company, 1870.

SMITH, MATTHEW HALE (Burleigh), *Sunshine and Shadow in New York*. Hartford: Burr, 1868.

SMITH, MORTIMER, *William Jay Gaynor*. Chicago: Regnery, 1951.

STEPHENSON, BYRON C., "Delmonico's." *The Illustrated American*, May 16, 1891.

STERN, MADELEINE B., *Purple Passage, The Life of Mrs. Frank Leslie*. Norman: University of Oklahoma Press, 1953.

STEVENSON, LIONEL, *The Showman of Vanity Fair*. New York: Scribner, 1947.

STILL, BAYARD, *Mirror for Gotham*. New York: New York University Press, 1956.

STODDARD, HENRY LUTHER, *Horace Greely: Printer, Editor, Crusader*. New York: Putnam, 1946.

STOKES, I. N. PHELPS. *The Iconography of Manhattan Island 1498-1909*. 3 vols. New York: Robert H. Dodd, 1928.

STRONG, GEORGE TEMPLETON, *The Diary of George Templeton Strong*. Edited by Allan Nevins and William Hansley Thomas. 4 vols. New York: Macmillan, 1952.

SWANBERG, W. A., *Citizen Hearst*. New York: Scribner, 1964.

———, *Jim Fisk*. New York: Scribner, 1959.

———, *Sickles the Incredible*. New York: Scribner, 1956.

THOMAS, LATELY, *Sam Ward: "King of the Lobby."* Boston: Houghton Mifflin, 1965.

TOWNE, CHARLES HANSON, *This New York of Mine*. New York: Cosmopolitan Book Corporation, 1931.

TOWNSEND, REGINALD T., *Mother of Clubs, The History of the First Hundred Years of the Union Club of the City of New York 1835-1935*. Privately printed, New York, 1936.

TROLLOPE, ANTHONY, *North America*. London: Chapman & Hall, 1862.

TROLLOPE, FRANCES, *The Domestic Manners of the Americans*. New York: Knopf, 1949.

TRUAX, CAROL, *Father Was a Gourmet*. New York: Doubleday, 1965.

VAIL, R. W. G., *Knickerbocker Birthday — A Sesqui-Centennial History of the New-York Historical Society*. New York: New-York Historical Society, 1954.

VAN DUSEN, C. C., *Thurlow Weed: Wizard of the Lobby*. Boston: Little Brown, 1947.

VAN DYKE, JOHN C., *The New New York*. New York: Macmillan, 1909.

VAN EVERY, EDWARD, *The Sins of New York*. New York: Stokes, 1930.

VAN RENSSALAER, MRS. JOHN KING, *The Social Ladder*. New York: Holt, 1924.

VAN WYCK, FREDERICK, *Recollections of an Old New New Yorker*. New York: Liveright, 1932.

VANDERBILT, CORNELIUS, Jr., *Queen of the Golden Age*. New York: McGraw-Hill, 1956.

The Volcano Under the City. By a Special Volunteer. New York: Fords, Howard & Hurlbert, 1887.

WALKER, STANLEY, *Mrs. Astor's Horse*. New York: Stokes, 1935.

WALL, E. BERRY, *Neither Pest Nor Puritan*. New York: Dial, 1940.

WARD, SAMUEL, *Lyrical Recreations*. London: Macmillan, 1883.

WARSHOW, ROBERT IRVING, *The Story of Wall Street*. New York: Greenberg, 1929.

WATERS, EDWARD N., *Victor Herbert, A Life in Music*. New York: Macmillan, 1955.

WATTS, STEPHEN, *The Ritz of Paris*. New York: Norton, 1964.

WECTER, DIXON, *The Saga of American Society*. New York: Scribner, 1937.

WEED, THURLOW, *The Life of Thurlow Weed: Autobiography and Memoir*, by Thurlow Weed Barnes. Boston: Houghton Mifflin, 1883.

WEEKS, LYMAN H., edit., *Prominent Families of New York*. New York: The Historical Company, 1897.

WELLES, GIDEON, *Diary of Gideon Welles*, edited by Howard K. Beale. New York: Norton, 1960.

WERNER, M. R., *It Happened in New York*. New York: Coward-McCann, 1957.

———, *Tammany Hall*. New York: Doubleday Doran, 1928.

WHARTON, EDITH, *The Age of Innocence*. New York: Appleton, 1920.

———, *The House of Mirth*. New York: Scribner, 1905.

———, *Old New York — The 'Forties, The 'Fifties, The 'Sixties, The 'Seventies*. 4 vols. New York: Appleton, 1924.

WHITE, BOUCK, *The Book of Daniel Drew*. New York: Doubleday-Page, 1910.

WILKINS, THURMAN, *Clarence King*. New York: Macmillan, 1958.

WILKINS, WILLIAM GLYDE, *Charles Dickens in America*. New York: Scribner, 1911.

WILLIAMSON, JEFFERSON, *The American Hotel*. New York: Knopf, 1930.

WILSON, FRANCIS, *Francis Wilson's Life of Himself*. Boston: Houghton Mifflin, 1924.

WILSON, JAMES GRANT, edit., *The Memorial History of the City of New York*. 3 vols. New York History Company, 1892.

———, *Thackeray in the United States*. 2 vols. New York: Dodd Mead, 1906.

WILSON, RUFUS ROCKWELL and OTILIE ERICKSON WILSON, *New York in Literature*. Privately printed, Elmira, New York, 1947.

YATES, NORRIS W., *William T. Porter and the Spirit of the Times*. Baton Rouge: Louisiana State University Press, 1957.

INDEX